Digital Cura
A How-To-Do-It Manual®

Ross Harvey

HOW-TO-DO-IT MANUALS®

NUMBER 170

Neal-Schuman Publishers, Inc.

New York   **London**

Don't miss the companion website for this book!
Download checklists and templates for developing
digital curation plans and procedures at:
www.neal-schuman.com/curation

Published by Neal-Schuman Publishers, Inc.
100 William St., Suite 2004
New York, NY 10038

Library of Congress Cataloging-in-Publication Data

Harvey, D. R. (Douglas Ross), 1951-
    Digital curation : a how-to-do-it manual / Ross Harvey.
        p. cm. — (How-to-do-it manuals ; no. 170)
    Includes bibliographical references and index.
    ISBN 978-1-55570-694-4 (alk. paper)
    1. Digital libraries. 2. Digital preservation. 3. Digital libraries—Management. I. Title.

ZA4080.H37 2010
025.00285—dc22

2010020400

Contents

Contents

Contents

List of Figures

List of Abbreviations

ACE	Audit Control Environment
AHDS	Arts and Humanities Data Service
AIFF	Audio Interchange File Format
AIP	Archival Information Package
ALA	American Library Association
AONS	Automatic Obsolescence Notification System
API	Application Programming Interface
APSR	Australian Partnership for Sustainable Repositories
ARCHER	Australian Research Enabling Environment
BADC	British Atmospheric Data Centre
BAT	BnF Arc Tools
BBSRC	Biotechnology and Biological Sciences Research Council
BMP	Bitmap
CAD	Computer-Aided Design
CAIRO	Complex Archive Ingest for Repository Objects
CASPAR	Cultural, Artistic and Scientific Knowledge for Preservation, Access and Retrieval
CHIN	Canadian Heritage Information Network
CIC	Committee on Institutional Cooperation
CLADDIER	Citation, Location, and Deposition in Discipline and Institutional Repositories
CRC	Cyclic Redundancy Checks
CRiB	Conversion and Recommendation of Digital Object Formats
Data-PASS	Data Preservation Alliance for the Social Sciences
DCC	Digital Curation Centre
DDI XML	Data Documentation Initiative XML
DIFFUSE	Dissemination of Informal and Formal Useful Specifications and Experiences
DigCCurr	Digital Curation Curriculum
DIP	Dissemination Information Package

DISC-UK	Data Information Specialists Committee—United Kingdom
DOI	Digital Object Identifier
DPC	Digital Preservation Coalition
DPE	DigitalPreservationEurope
DRAMBORA	Digital Repository Audit Method Based on Risk Assessment
DROID	Digital Record Object Identification
DTD	Document Type Definition
EAD	Encoded Archival Description
ECDL	European Conference on Digital Libraries
EML	Ecological Markup Language
EROS	Earth Resources Observation and Science
ERPANET	Electronic Resource Preservation and Access Network
ESDS	Economic and Social Data Services
ESRC	Economic and Social Research Council
EU	European Union
Exif	Exchangeable Image File Format
FAT	File Allocation Table
Fedora	Flexible Extensible Digital Object and Repository Architecture
FITS	File Information Tool Set
FLAC	Free Lossless Audio Codec
GIF	Graphics Interchange Format
GIS	Geographic Information System
GPS	Global Positioning System
GRATE	Global Remote Access to Electronic Services
HATII	Humanities Advanced Technology and Information Institute
HOPPLA	Home and Office Painless Persistent Long-Term Archiving
HTML	Hypertext Markup Language
IB	Integrative Biology
ICADL	International Conference on Asian Digital Libraries
IIPC	International Internet Preservation Consortium
InSPECT	Investigating the Significant Properties of Electronic Content over Time
InterPARES	International Research on Permanent Authentic Records in Electronic Systems
IP	Internet Protocol
iPres	International Conference on Preservation of Digital Objects

ISMS	Information Security Management System
ISO	International Organization for Standardization
JCDL	Joint Conference on Digital Libraries
JHOVE	JSTOR/Harvard Object Validation Environment
JISC	Joint Information Systems Committee
JPEG	Joint Photographic Experts Group
KEEP	Keeping Emulation Environments Portable
koLibRI	kopal Library for Retrieval and Ingest
LIFE	Lifecycle Information for E-literature
LOCKSS	Lots of Copies Keep Stuff Safe
MADS	Metadata Authority Description Schema
MARC	MAchine Readable Cataloging
METS	Metadata Encoding and Transmission Standard
MODS	Metadata Object Description Schema
MPEG	Moving Picture Experts Group
NDIIPP	National Digital Information Infrastructure and Preservation Program
NERC	National Environment Research Council
NIH	National Institutes of Health
NISO	National Information Standards Organization
NISPOM	National Industrial Security Program Operating Manual
NLNZ	National Library of New Zealand
NOST	NASA/Science Office of Standards and Technology
NSF	National Science Foundation
NTFS	New Technology File System
OAIS	Open Archive Information System
ODF	Open Document Format
PADI	Preserving Access to Digital Information
PARADIGM	Personal Archives Accessible in Digital Media
PARSE	Permanent Access to the Records of Science in Europe
PDF	Portable Document Format
PDF-A	Portable Document Format—Archival
PDI	Preservation Description Information
PeDALS	Persistent Digital Archives and Library System
PGP	Pretty Good Privacy
PLANETS	Preservation and Long-Term Access through Networked Services
PLATTER	Planning Tool for Trusted Electronic Repositories
PLN	Private LOCKSS Network

PNG	Portable Network Graphics
PoWR	Preservation of Web Resources
PREMIS	Preservation Metadata: Implementation Strategies
PURL	Persistent Uniform Resource Locator
RIN	Research Information Network
RODA	Repositório de Objectos Digitais Autênticos
RTF	Rich Text Format
SAA	Society of American Archivists
SAS	Statistical Analysis System
SHAMAN	Sustaining Heritage Access through Multivalent ArchiviNg
SHERPA	Securing a Hybrid Environment for Research Preservation and Access
SIP	Submission Information Package
SPSS	Statistical Package for the Social Sciences
TDR	Trusted Digital Repository
TIFF	Tagged Image File Format
TRAC	Trusted Repositories Audit and Certification
URL	Uniform Resource Locator
URN	Uniform Resource Name
UVC	Universal Virtual Computer
WAV	Waveform Audio File Format
Xena	XML Electronic Normalizing for Archives
XML	eXtensible Markup Language

Preface

We live in an environment where data (information in binary digital form) surrounds us and is essential for most activities in which we participate. Librarians and archivists act as data creators, data users and reusers, and/or data curators in increasingly digitally oriented environments. Despite this, professional practice has not caught up with digital practice in many respects. Caring for data, ensuring its usability and reuse in the future, and ensuring its accessibility and understandability over time require new strategies, practices, and tools. Traditional library and archival practices developed in a predigital and largely paper-oriented environment do not automatically transfer to the current digitally oriented environments. Although the past decade has seen the rapid development of new strategies, practices, and tools, these are not yet sufficiently mature. Consider these facts:

- Immense quantities of information in binary digital form are being generated in all walks of life.
- The quantities are increasing at a rapid rate.
- The scientific, scholarly, and research communities increasingly rely on networked computing, as trends such as the move from *in vitro* to *in silico* science and the development of large digital libraries in the humanities become dominant.
- Computer technology (hardware, software, and communications networks) quickly becomes obsolete.

All of these place data at risk from factors such as technology obsolescence, digital object fragility, a lack of understanding about what constitutes good practice, insufficient resources, and inappropriate organizational infrastructure.

Although the body of practice known as *digital preservation* is developing to address the factors that place data at risk, it is starting to be commonly accepted that its outcomes provide only part of the answer. For example, it is relatively straightforward to maintain a bit stream over time: there are more than 40 years of practice to call on in this respect. However, there is no guarantee that the data represented in this bit stream have the characteristics that allow them to be used and understood in the future, and to remain unchanged. How can these characteristics be retained in the data that is maintained for use in the future?

To answer this question effectively, more than simply a focus on maintaining the data (i.e., digital preservation) is required. What must also be considered is what comes before preservation and what comes after—that is, how the data are created and how they are used before they get to an archive or library and how they will be used, and by whom, in the future. This requires a focus on data that differs from that applied to physical artifacts such as books, manuscripts, and photographic prints in a predigital environment.

Digital curation is a developing set of techniques that address these issues, emphasizing the maintenance of data and adding value to these data for current and future use. Because it is still developing, digital curation is not yet described in detail in the literature. *Digital Curation: A How-To-Do-It Manual* therefore makes a significant contribution by describing in detail, in one place, the basics and current practices of digital curation.

Various models of the lifecycle of data are available. These typically begin with the creation of data and move through its various stages, ending with data use. The *Curation Lifecycle Model* developed by the Digital Curation Centre (DCC) (DCC, 2008; Higgins, 2008) is one of these. It was developed by the DCC to describe the processes involved in digital curation. The DCC Curation Lifecycle Model encompasses data from their conceptualization and creation through all aspects of their selection, archiving, maintenance, and use, to their reuse in the future. The DCC Curation Lifecycle Model provides an action-oriented structure for this book.

Digital Curation: A How-To-Do-It Manual is intended for anyone who creates data, anyone who uses and reuses data, and anyone who curates data. In essence, this means everyone who uses computers. More specifically, this book is intended to be read by librarians and archivists and by students of these professions. It should also have wider appeal, for example, to scientists and scholars who plan research and collect and use data. Whoever its readers, it will assist them to incorporate curation procedures, where relevant, into their own practice, figure out where to start when developing and implementing digital curation processes, and explore digital curation issues by providing a context for digital curation.

Digital Curation: A How-To-Do-It Manual is designed to be read in several ways. Its chapters can be read consecutively as an overview of digital curation, or they can be dipped into for general background and for advice on specific actions. The book's accompanying website (www.neal-schuman.com/curation) provides checklists that can be used separately as guidance and reminders about the tasks that comprise digital curation actions and templates that can be downloaded and used as the basis for developing digital curation plans and procedures for specific libraries, archives, and other organizations, as well as providing guidance for informing individual practice.

This book is based on the author's extensive international experience as a researcher, author, and presenter in the field of digital preservation and digital curation. It draws in particular on his experience with digital curation in Australia (which is widely acknowledged as representing international best practice) and in the European Union context (including a period based at the Humanities Advanced Technology and Information Institute [HATII] at the University of Glasgow), and his current work at Simmons College in Boston. The book's content was developed through observing digital curation practice, attendance at relevant international conferences, developing material for the DCC, and investigating the real-life experiences of digital curators, especially in the United States. It is also informed by a series of in-depth interviews with digital preservation professionals, which the author carried out as part of the preparation of his book *Preserving Digital Materials* (Harvey, 2005).

Examples of digital curation practice from the United Kingdom and Europe are well represented, as are examples from the United States and from other countries. It may on the surface seem surprising to the American reader that there are not more examples from the United States. There are three main reasons for this. The first is that digital curation is highly international and collaborative to an extent that is perhaps unprecedented in library science and archival practice (as noted in more detail in Chapter 8). This means that developments and practice in the field in one country are keenly observed and adopted, with modifications to suit local requirements, in other countries. The second is that, as Jordan and his colleagues note, "U.S. funding dedicated to digital preservation has traditionally lagged behind that available in the European and British contexts in particular" (Jordan et al., 2008). This means that the large majority of documented examples of digital curation developments and practice have to date come from outside the United States. This is likely to change in the next two to three years as funding such as the National Science Foundation's DataNet program comes on stream. The third is that the more centralized U.K. and European environments have required freely available documentation of any digital curation activities funded by public money. This point applies in particular to the material available on the DCC's website, which represents the only public documentation of a prolonged effort to identify and describe digital curation and to investigate practice in the field. This book therefore makes heavy use, with the permission of the DCC, of the materials accessible through the Centre's website.

Organization

Digital Curation: A How-To-Do-It Manual is organized in three parts. "Part I. Digital Curation: Scope and Incentives" provides a broad context for digital curation by introducing the main concepts and providing an overview. Chapter 1 indicates the reasons why digital curation is necessary, identifies what digital curation encompasses, suggests why one should be interested in digital curation, notes the main incentives for digital curation, and examines who does digital curation and what tasks they carry out. Chapter 2 notes the changing landscape in which librarians, archivists, researchers, and scholars work, its requirements for different ways of working and new kinds of infrastructure, and the different skill sets for data curation. Chapter 3 examines an important conceptual model for digital curation, the DCC Curation Lifecycle Model, on which this book is based, and a key standard, the OAIS Reference Model. Chapter 4 investigates in more detail what is meant by the term *data* and other related terms. This is important to think about because it allows us to address better an important question—What exactly is it that we want to curate?

"Part II. Key Requirements for Digital Curation" examines the DCC Curation Lifecycle's Full Lifecycle Actions—the essential basic requirements for all aspects of digital curation, which apply to all of the Sequential Actions noted in Part III of this book. Chapter 5 covers *Curate and Preserve*, one of four Full Lifecycle Actions, noting how digital preservation and digital curation differ, examining the aims of digital curation, and describing how these aims are achieved. Chapter 6 examines another Full Lifecycle Action, *Description and Representation Information*, the metadata and other information required for effective data curation. Chapter 7 notes the essential nature of planning and policy in data curation by describing a third Full Lifecycle Action, *Preservation Planning*. Chapter 8 completes the examination of Full Lifecycle Actions by describing *Community Watch and Participation* and noting the high value placed in digital curation on sharing knowledge and on collaboration.

"Part III. The Digital Curation Lifecycle in Action" is based on the DCC Curation Lifecycle's Sequential Actions and also notes its Occasional Actions. Chapter 9 notes the Sequential Action "Conceptualise," stressing the need to think about curation at the very first stages of planning research or creating digital objects. Chapter 10 examines the second Sequential Action, *Create or Receive*, noting the requirements for curation-ready digital objects. Chapter 11 describes *Appraise and Select*, the third Sequential Action, noting the importance of selection of the digital objects to be curated. This chapter also notes the Occasional Actions *Reappraise and Dispose*. The fourth Sequential Action, *Ingest*— the actions required when digital objects are taken into an archiving system—is the topic of Chapter 12. Chapter 13 discusses the preservation strategies and actions associated with *Preservation Action*, the fifth Sequential Action. Also included in this chapter is the Occasional Action *Migrate*. Chapter 14 focuses on the sixth Sequential Action, *Store*, which is concerned with what is required to provide acceptable data storage in the archiving system. Chapter 15 notes the seventh Sequential Action, *Access, Use, and Reuse*, examining the requirements for successful sharing and reuse of data in the future. It also notes the eighth Sequential Action, *Transform*, thus completing the data Curation Lifecycle Model.

A decade ago, little was known about how to assess and preserve the immense body of digitized material that can double in size in a matter of a few short years. Today, we have a body of international experience and expertise to draw on. *Digital Curation: A How-To-Do-It Manual* and its companion website (www.neal-schuman.com/curation) are designed as a comprehensive resource for best practices in this area. Preserving knowledge is a sacred trust; this resource will enable practitioners in all areas of human experience to better succeed at this crucial task.

References

Digital Curation Centre. 2008. "The DCC Curation Lifecycle Model." Edinburgh: Digital Curation Centre. Available: www.dcc.ac.uk/docs/publications/DCCLifecycle.pdf (accessed April 26, 2010).

Harvey, Ross. 2005. *Preserving Digital Materials.* Munich: K. G. Saur.

Higgins, S. 2008. "The DCC Curation Lifecycle Model." *International Journal of Digital Curation* 3, no. 1: 134–140. Available: www.ijdc.net/index.php/ijdc/article/viewFile/69/48 (accessed April 26, 2010).

Jordan, Christopher, Ardys Kozbial, David Minor, and Robert H. McDonald. 2008. "Encouraging Cyberinfrastructure Collaboration for Digital Preservation." Paper presented at iPres 2008, British Library, London, September 30, 2008. Available: www.bl.uk/ipres2008/presentations_day2/39_Jordan.pdf (accessed April 26, 2010).

Acknowledgments

No book of this nature can be written without considerable input and assistance from a host of people. If I have inadvertently omitted anyone from my acknowledgments, I apologize in advance.

I owe Rachel Salmond more than I can express for ongoing assistance over nearly three decades and especially for her patience with me as the preparation of this book took over normal schedules.

My ideas about digital curation have been formed over many years and by many people. Most recently these have included students who have enrolled in my courses on digital preservation at the Department of Library and Information Science, Yonsei University, Seoul, in 2008, and students enrolled in LIS444 at the Graduate School of Library and Information Science, Simmons College, Boston, in 2008 and 2009. Advice about content came from many people in several countries, in particular Kevin Bradley, Simon Coles, Joy Davidson, David Giaretta, Sarah Higgins, Meredith A. Lane, Cal Lee, Andrew McHugh, Bob Mann, Graham Pryor, Seamus Ross, Chris Rusbridge, Kellie Snow, and participants and presenters in the Digital Curation Centre (DCC) Digital Curation 101 Workshop held in London, March 10–12, 2009.

The genesis of this book lies in a period in 2007 when I had the privilege to be a Visiting Professor in the Humanities Advanced Technology & Information Institute (HATII) at the University of Glasgow and Research Fellow in the DCC, which is led by the University of Edinburgh. The structure of the book, in particular, is developed from research undertaken there. I gladly acknowledge that this book is based on research carried out to produce material for the DCC during that period. I am very grateful for the hospitality of HATII and also that of the School of Library, Archival and Information Studies at the University of British Columbia and the Graduate School of Library and Information Science, Simmons College, Boston.

I acknowledge with thanks the support of the Emily Hollowell Research Fund, Graduate School of Library and Information Science, Simmons College, which allowed me to employ Leah Nickell to identify and further develop documentation about digital curation procedures. Leah's work was essential in furthering my understanding of workplace practices in digital curation. I also thank Anne Sauer, Director and

University Archivist, Digital Collections and Archives at Tufts University for permission to access internal documentation.

Finally, I gratefully acknowledge the individuals and organizations who have given permission to reproduce their materials in this book. I am particularly indebted to Chris Rusbridge of the DCC for permission to quote many of his perceptive comments. The Curation Lifecycle Model was designed by Sarah Higgins on behalf of the DCC and is reproduced with the permission of the DCC. In Chapter 14, the excerpt from the Core Requirements for Digital Archives is used courtesy of the Center for Research Libraries, and the excerpt from "Fedora and the Preservation of University Records" (2006) is quoted courtesy of Digital Collections and Archives, Tufts University and Manuscripts & Archives, Yale University. The excerpts from publications of the UK Data Archive are used with the permission of the UK Data Archive, University of Essex.

Digital Curation: Scope and Incentives

The four chapters in "Part I. Digital Curation: Scope and Incentives" provide a broad context for digital curation by introducing the main concepts and giving an overview of the field.

Chapter 1 indicates the reasons why digital curation is necessary, identifies what digital curation encompasses, suggests why you should be interested in digital curation, notes the main incentives for digital curation, and examines who does digital curation and what tasks they carry out.

Chapter 2 notes the changing landscape in which librarians, archivists, researchers, and scholars work; its requirements for different ways of working and new kinds of infrastructure; and the different skill sets for data curation.

Chapter 3 describes the application of lifecycle models to digital curation and looks in more detail at a key conceptual model and a key standard for digital curation. The first, the Digital Curation Centre (DCC) Curation Lifecycle Model, outlines the actions that comprise digital curation and presents these actions in graphic form. This Lifecycle Model is used as the structural basis of Parts II and III of this book. The second lifecycle model, the Open Archive Information System (OAIS) Reference Model, is widely used as the basis for the design and implementation of digital archival systems.

Chapter 4 notes in more detail the meaning of the term *data* and of other related terms. Investigating the meaning of the term *data* is particularly important if a key question is to be answered satisfactorily: What exactly is it that we want to curate?

Introduction

Chapter 1 sets the scene for digital curation and argues that it is central to professional practice in all digital environments. It begins by indicating why digital curation is necessary, then identifies what it encompasses, briefly defines terms such as *data*, *digital object*, and *database* in this context, suggests why an interest in digital curation is important, notes the main incentives for digital curation, and examines the tasks that comprise digital curation and who carries them out.

Some definitions set the scene. First is a short working definition of digital curation. Digital curation is defined briefly by the Digital Curation Centre (DCC) as

> maintaining and adding value to a trusted body of digital research data for current and future use; it encompasses the active management throughout the research lifecycle. (Digital Curation Centre, accessed 2010)

Definitions of the terms *data*, *digital object*, and *database* used in this book come from the DCC Curation Lifecycle Model, the model upon which the structure of this book is based (Digital Curation Centre, 2008). *Data* is "any information in binary digital form." This definition is intentionally very broad and extends beyond the narrow connection of the word with the outputs of scientific research. It includes *digital objects* and *databases*. *Digital objects* can be simple or complex. "*Simple digital objects* are discrete digital items; such as textual files, images or sound files, along with their related identifiers and metadata. *Complex digital objects* are discrete digital objects, made by combining a number of other digital objects, such as Web sites." *Databases* are "structured collections of records or data stored in a computer system." These definitions of the terms *data*, *digital object*, and *database* and their implications are expanded on in Chapter 4.

Why There Is a Need for Digital Curation

The increasingly digital world that we all inhabit is changing the ways we work and play. It is a truism that this results in the generation of massive quantities of data in all areas of our lives. Furthermore, these quantities are increasing at significant rates. (This point is easy to illustrate. Consider the amount of personal data—word-processed documents, digital photographs, video files, and so on—you thought you needed to store ten, even only five, years ago, and compare that with the quantity you now think you need to store.) Data, whether personal or of any other kind, has certain characteristics that require it to be actively managed. It is at risk from many factors, including:

- technology obsolescence—computers and software are updated frequently, often resulting in inability to access data;

- technology fragility—digital objects can become inaccessible if only a small part of them is changed or corrupted;

- lack of understanding about what constitutes good practice—digital curation is a new and still-developing field of practice, and much about what is needed to make it work is still unknown;

- inadequate resources—libraries, archives, and museums are usually not resourced to carry out all they want to do; digital curation is not always given a high priority, and understanding what skill sets are required to make digital curation work is not fully known; and

- uncertainties about the best organizational infrastructures to achieve effective digital curation.

Digital curation is also necessary for many other reasons. Many of the current developments in the field—its practices, tools, storage facilities, and theoretical bases—are coming from the scientific, scholarly, and research communities. These communities have been rapidly accommodating new ways of working that rely increasingly on networked computing to link researchers and scholars around the world and to generate and share large—in some cases extremely large—data sets. Historians, for example, "ignore the future of digital data at their own peril" if they do not "ensure the future of their own scholarship" which involves new prospects such as "linking directly from footnotes to electronic texts" (Rosenzweig, 2003: paragraph 64). A researcher in the future will work differently:

> Not only will there be text, with hyperlinks to related literature or citations within the article, there will be links to the data reported within the article, through graphs, tables, illustrations, that will link to related datasets. (ARL Workshop on New Collaborative Relationships, 2006: 141)

This will only be possible if stable digital curation is achieved.

These trends are often described in the context of science as the move from *in vitro* to *in silico* science—broadly speaking, from laboratory-based science to science based on data and performed using computers. These new contexts are collectively termed in the United States as *cyberscholarship* and in other countries as *e-science* or *e-scholarship*. Chapter 2 describes these trends in more detail.

Cyberscholarship generates large quantities of data. This data is often unique and cannot be reproduced without major cost, if at all. An example is environmental data. The data may be generated in an extremely expensive experiment, and the cost alone means that the experiment cannot be reproduced: an example, perhaps extreme, is the massive amounts of data generated from runs of the world's largest and highest energy particle accelerator, the Large Hadron Collider.

Cyberscholarship also requires that data be available for use and for reuse in the future. There are many reasons. Large data sets can be the basis of analysis by scholars around the world, so they must be available for access. Good research and scholarship are based on data that can be verified and built on to lead to new knowledge. Data may be records that have legal requirements: for example, financial records of business transactions may be required to be kept for periods of time specified in legislation. Some funding agencies require that data created during the course of activities they fund be made available for public use and reuse. The long-acknowledged roles of libraries and archives in preserving social memory should also be noted as a significant reason for ensuring data are available for use and reuse in the future, as social memory is increasingly held in digital form.

One articulation of cyberscholarship is the U.K. Research Information Network's *Stewardship of Digital Research Data: A Framework of Principles and Guidelines* (Research Information Network, 2008: 3). The Framework's five principles are based on sharing and reusing research data. The principles indicate the need for international standards to be developed and applied to the creation and collection of data, the importance of making this data able to be located and easy to use, and the need to protect rights of data creators and owners—all with an emphasis on efficiency and cost-effectiveness. The last of these principles is: "Digital research data of long term value arising from current and future research should be preserved and remain accessible for current and future generations."

For all of these reasons, actively managing data over their lifecycle is essential. Digital curation is a set of techniques that address the issues of data protection and risk management to ensure that the data are available and usable now and in the future.

What Digital Curation Is

The brief working definition of digital curation noted at the beginning of this chapter comes from the DCC, the principal organization in the United Kingdom for developing and promoting digital curation concepts and practices. Another definition, this one from the United States, is provided by the Digital Curation Curriculum (DigCCurr) project based at the University of North Carolina at Chapel Hill in a description of its interests. It expands on the DCC's brief definition:

> Our cultural heritage, modern scientific knowledge, and everyday commerce and government depend upon the preservation of

reliable and authentic electronic records and digital objects. While digital data holds the promise of ubiquitous access, the inherent fragility and evanescence of media and files, the rapid obsolescence of software and hardware, the need for well-constructed file systems and metadata, and the intricacies of intellectual property rights place all of these materials at risk and offer little hope of longevity for information that is not intentionally preserved. A decade of work in digital preservation and access has resulted in an emerging and complex life-cycle constellation of strategies, technological approaches, and activities now termed "digital curation." (DigCCurr, accessed 2010)

Being aware of where these definitions originated helps us to better understand the concerns of digital curation and its current emphases. There were two drivers to the establishment of the DCC in the United Kingdom: e-science, the "data deluge" and continuing access to the data sets generated; and digital preservation, particularly the realization that digital preservation activities were by themselves insufficient to address many of the issues associated with maintaining data over time. In the United Kingdom this resulted in the development by the Joint Information Systems Committee (JISC) of a "Continuing Access and Digital Preservation Strategy" (Joint Information Systems Committee, 2002) and Lord and Macdonald's (2003) report about data curation for e-science, one outcome of which was the release of funding in 2003 to establish a digital curation center. The DCC was established in 2004. Because of its basis in e-science, much of the data curation literature and activities in the United Kingdom were initially focused heavily on scientific data, although in recent years this scope has broadened. In general, the same can be said for the United States, where initial interest in the need for data curation came from the National Science Foundation. But the scope has recently been broadened considerably through the interest of groups such as the Research Libraries Group (now merged with OCLC), the Association of Research Libraries, and the National Endowment for the Humanities to include humanities and social science data. In both countries significant interest has also been expressed in the curation of personal data.

It is important to reinforce the last point: that significant interest has been shown in the curation of personal data. While it is true that most of the recent understandings and practices of digital curation have been developed for and by the scientific communities, much of it is highly applicable, often without modification, to all information in digital form, whether personal data or data preserved by libraries and archives. The reader is urged to keep this in mind when reading and applying the points noted to his or her own context or area of interest.

Just which of the "emerging and complex life-cycle constellation of strategies, technological approaches, and activities" (DigCCurr, accessed 2010) make up digital curation? This is understood differently by different groups. Some of the activities that make up digital curation are reported by Brophy and Frey (2006: 38):

- Maintaining the links between digital information and associated annotations or published materials, including citations

- Ensuring the long-term accessibility and reusability of digital information
- Performing archiving activities on digital information such as selection, appraisal, and retention
- Ensuring the authenticity, integrity, and provenance of digital information are maintained over time
- Performing preservation activities on digital information such as migration or emulation
- Maintaining hardware components to enable digital information to be accessed and understood over time
- Managing digital information from its point of creation
- Managing risks to digital information
- Ensuring the destruction of digital information

These are all aspects of digital curation, but this list does not present the whole picture. So we are still left with the question: what is digital curation? We can state what digital curation is *not*:

1. It is not *digital archiving*—one definition of digital archiving is "the process of backup and ongoing maintenance as opposed to strategies for long-term digital preservation" (Digital Preservation Coalition, 2008: 24).

2. It is not *digital preservation*—defined as "all of the actions required to maintain access to digital materials beyond the limits of media failure or technological change" (Digital Preservation Coalition, 2008: 24) and as "policies, strategies and actions that ensure access to digital content over time" (ALCTS Preservation and Reformatting Section, 2007).

Although digital archiving and digital preservation are important aspects of digital curation, they are not the whole story. Lavoie and Dempsey (2004) describe the position:

> Our understanding of the totality of the challenges associated with maintaining digital materials over the long-term is coming more sharply into focus. New questions are emerging, having less to do with digital preservation as a technical issue *per se*, and more to do with how preserving digital materials fits into the broader theme of *digital stewardship*. These questions surface from the view that digital preservation is not an isolated process, but instead, one component of a broad aggregation of interconnected services, policies, and stakeholders which together constitute a digital information environment.

Digital curation is a more inclusive concept than either digital *archiving* or digital *preservation*. It addresses the whole range of processes applied to digital objects *over their lifecycle*. Digital curation begins before digital objects are created by setting standards for planning data collection that results in "curation-ready" digital objects that are in the best possible condition to ensure they can be maintained and used in the future. Digital curation emphasizes *adding value* to data sets and digital objects, through things such as additional metadata or annotations, so that they can be reused. Digital curation involves a *wide range of stakeholders* cutting across disciplinary boundaries: as well as cultural heritage organizations such as libraries, archives, and museums, it also involves funding agencies, government bodies, national data centers, institutional repositories, and learned societies. (In fact, digital curation is the concern of all who create and use data.) Digital curation is also concerned with *risk management*: it "is about converting uncertainties into measurable and manageable risks" (DRAMBORA, 2007). It is also about *good data management* practices.

Digital curation is concerned with and applicable to a wide range of digital objects. It is as equally applicable to complex digital objects that are *linked* to other resources in a range of formats, large science data sets, or data sets that are changing every second, as it is to relatively simple digital objects such as the static documents usually handled by libraries and archives. However, most data archiving and digital preservation practices were developed for static documents; they do not transfer successfully to more complex data. Although professional attention has been paid to digital collections in libraries and archives for many years (digital library activities are a case in point), it has typically focused on only part of the lifecycle, usually digitizing and providing access to the digitized information. Such actions cannot be considered as sufficient for digital curation, which is concerned with the whole lifecycle and emphasizes maintaining digital information over time and ensuring its availability and usability in the future. In this new era of data-driven scholarship and research, new strategies and processes are needed to handle the wide range of data created and maintained by many different kinds of user communities.

Taking all of this into account, an expanded definition of digital curation might read: Digital curation is concerned with actively managing data for as long as it continues to be of scholarly, scientific, research, administrative, and/or personal interest, with the aims of supporting reproducibility, reuse of, and adding value to that data, managing it from its point of creation until it is determined not to be useful, and ensuring its long-term accessibility, preservation, authenticity, and integrity.

Why We Should Be Interested in Digital Curation

That digital curation is necessary and a matter of urgency is generally understood by anyone who uses computers. Seamus Ross (2007: 2), a prominent researcher in several areas of digital curation, describes the reasons why digital objects and data become unusable:

> They are bound to varying degrees to the specific application packages (or hardware) that were used to create or manage them. They are prone to corruption. They are easily misidentified. They are generally poorly described or annotated. . . . Where they do have sufficient ancillary data, these data are frequently time constrained.

Figure 1.1 lists the threats to digital continuity—that is, to the continuing accessibility and usability of data. The figure clearly indicates the most significant reasons why digital curation is an urgent imperative.

Obsolescence is probably the most commonly recognized of these threats. Our abilities to maintain digital objects and to use them over time are challenged by the wide range of formats, of both software and hardware, and by their rapid rates of change. Examples abound, among them the fact that personal computers are no longer supplied with a drive to read and write three-and-a-half inch diskettes, which were only a few years ago the standard data storage medium for personal use. Some of the wide range of storage media and computer formats are displayed in online exhibits. Two of these are:

1. *Timeline: Digital Preservation and Technology* and *Chamber of Horrors: Obsolete and Endangered Media*—accessed through the introduction to the Cornell University Library's online tutorial *Digital Preservation Management* (Cornell University Library, 2003–2007)

Figure 1.1. Threats to Digital Continuity

The carriers used to store . . . digital materials are usually unstable and deteriorate within a few years or decades at most
Use of digital materials depends on means of access that work in particular ways: often complex combinations of tools including hardware and software, which typically become obsolete within a few years and are replaced with new tools that work differently
Materials may be lost in the event of disasters such as fire, flood, equipment failure, or virus or direct attack that disables stored data and operating systems
Access barriers such as password protection, encryption, security devices, or hardcoded access paths may prevent ongoing access beyond the very limited circumstances for which they were designed
The value of the material may not be recognised before it is lost or changed
No one may take responsibility for the material even though its value is recognised
Those taking responsibility may not have adequate knowledge or facilities
There may be insufficient resources available to sustain preservation action over the required period
It may not be possible to negotiate legal permissions needed for preservation
There may not be the time or skills available to respond quickly enough to a sudden and large change in technology
The digital materials may be well protected but so poorly identified and described that potential users cannot find them
So much contextual information may be lost that the materials themselves are unintelligible or not trusted even when they can be accessed
Critical aspects of functionality, such as formatting of documents or the rules by which databases operate, may not be recognised and may be discarded or damaged in preservation processing

Source: Guidelines for the Preservation of Digital Heritage, March 2003. © UNESCO 2003. Used by permission of UNESCO.

2. The Computer History Museum's virtual exhibit *Timeline of Computer History* (Computer History Museum, 2006)

The increasing quantities of data produced in digital form and their increasingly dynamic nature (exemplified by large online databases that are continually being added to by contributors around the world) pose another major threat to digital continuity, challenging our ability to capture, store, and access these data. The increasing quantities also demand that decisions are made about which data to curate, as not all data are created equal. This raises challenging questions such as: How do we decide what is likely to be useful in the future? Useful to whom? How long should we plan to keep them? Do we want them to be usable (functional), and to what extent, in the future?

Responses to threats to digital continuity that are based on traditional preservation approaches do not work. Simply capturing data on stable storage media and copying them onto new storage media when obsolescence threatens are in themselves not sufficient to ensure digital continuity. Digital data must be managed from the point that they are created (or, ideally, before they are created) if their survival is to be ensured. Active management of data over the whole of their life is necessary, requiring "constant maintenance and elaborate 'life-support' systems" (Hedstrom, 2002). Social and institutional issues must also be addressed: where, for example, does the continuing funding come from to maintain data in a research environment that is project oriented? This book identifies responses to these challenges.

An analysis of the curation of research data in Canada in 2008 provides a snapshot of the current situation and indicates clearly that there is cause for alarm (Research Data Strategy Working Group, 2008). Using a four-part data lifecycle framework (data production, data dissemination, long-term data management, data discovery and repurposing) and ten indicators (policies, funding, roles and responsibilities, standards, data repositories, skills and training, accessibility, and preservation), this analysis assessed Canada's current state against an "ideal state" based on existing international best practice. The conclusion was that major barriers exist to accessing and preserving research data in Canada, with significant implications for the future of Canadian research and innovation. For example, large amounts of data are currently being lost because Canada does not have enough trusted data repositories. The following main issues in the curation of research data in Canada were identified:

- Data Production
  - Priority is on immediate use, rather than potential for long-term exploitation.
  - Limited funding mechanisms to prepare data appropriately for later use.
  - Few research institutions require data management plans.
  - No national organization that can advise and assist with application of data standards.
- Data Dissemination
  - Lack of policies governing the standards applied to ensure data dissemination.

- ○ Researchers unwilling to share data, because of lack of time and expertise required.
- ○ Some policies require certain types of data be destroyed after a research project is over.
- Long-Term Management of Data
  - ○ Lack of coverage and capacity of data repositories.
  - ○ Preservation activities in repositories are not comprehensive.
  - ○ Limited funding for data repositories in Canada.
  - ○ Few incentives for researchers to deposit data into archives.
- Discovery and Repurposing
  - ○ Most data rests on the hard drives of researchers and is inaccessible by others.
  - ○ Per [i.e., pay] per view and licensed access mechanisms are common where data are available.
  - ○ Many researchers are reluctant to enable access to their data because they feel it is their intellectual property. (Research Data Strategy Working Group, 2008: 16)

Canada is by no means alone in facing significant barriers in curation of research data. The Canadian report notes similar issues in the United States, the United Kingdom, Australia, and elsewhere.

Another cause for alarm is expressed in a 2008 survey of the preparedness for digital preservation of local governments in the United Kingdom. Over 80 percent of the respondents already held digital records. Although nearly half had a digital preservation policy, had undertaken some planning, and gave high priority to preserving digital records, awareness of the issues was low. Barriers to digital preservation were identified as cultural ("organisation, political, awareness, external partnerships/relations and motivation"), resource ("time, costs, funding, storage"), and skills gap ("Training, competencies, IT") (Boyle, Eveleigh, and Needham, 2008). If digital curation practice in this sector is not addressed as a matter of some urgency, there will be crucial losses of data.

The situation is not, however, as uniformly bleak as some commentators would lead us to believe. The issues were initially described and promoted in alarmist terms, to the extent that the term "digital dark age" has entered the collective consciousness through a Wikipedia entry (Wikipedia, 2009; Harvey [2008] provides other examples of alarmist terms and their consequences). But, as Lavoie and Dempsey (2004) remind us, "accumulating experience in managing digital materials has tempered this view."

Incentives for Digital Curation

To date, much of the money for digital preservation and digital curation has been short-term project-based funding. This project-based funding model does not support good digital curation practice. Because of the finite time span of projects, employees focus on their next job application or on getting funding for the next project. In this context a high priority is not usually placed on getting the data in good shape for curation beyond the life of the project. For example, there is often a lack of metadata to describe the data so that they are understandable. Data curation tasks are "that extra burden, the one just beyond what is currently possible, in the queue behind meeting the conference deadline and writing the grant application" (Rusbridge, 2007: 4). In these contexts it is important to be clear about how data curation is of benefit so that continuing interest in and application of digital curation are encouraged and maintained.

In an environment of competing priorities and multiple demands on our time, why should we be interested in the curation of data? The answer is clear: curation has immediate and short-term benefits for all who create, use, and manage data, in four main ways:

1. **Improving access.** Digital curation procedures allow continuing access to data and improve the speed of access to reliable data and the range of data that can be accessed.

2. **Improving data quality.** Digital curation procedures assist in improving data quality, improving the trustworthiness of data, and ensuring that data are valid as a formal record (such as use as legal evidence).

3. **Encouraging data sharing and reuse.** Digital curation procedures encourage and assist data sharing and use by applying common standards and by allowing data to be fully exploited through time (thus maximizing investment) by providing information about the context and provenance of the data.

4. **Protecting data.** Digital curation procedures preserve data and protect them against loss and obsolescence.

Digital curation does all of this by providing tools and services to migrate digital objects plus their associated metadata into new formats that stay meaningful to users and by providing a management infrastructure for preserving them over time.

The benefits of participating in digital curation can be considered in three categories: direct benefits to data creators, "public good" obligations (such as the increasing interest in open access), and compliance reasons.

Direct Benefits to Data Creators

Good digital curation practices benefit data creators in many ways: improved quality of data, improved access to data, increased visibility of the research, and improved visibility and citation rates of the creator. Good digital curation practices also result in improved risk management, meaning that digital objects are more likely to remain usable over time. Examples of risks related to data, as noted earlier, include failure of storage media, hardware, or network services; obsolescence of media, hardware, and software; economic failure resulting in insufficient funding to maintain data over the long term; and organizational failure, where the parent organization no longer sees itself in the digital archiving business and wishes to dispose of its data. Risk management methodologies assist with developing lists of potential risks, assessing the likelihood of them occurring, and identifying their potential impact. These form the basis of policies and procedures to minimize the likelihood of risky events occurring and to manage risks.

"Public Good" Obligations

Some incentives for digital curation relate to public good. Pressure is increasingly being brought to bear to make data more broadly available for public scrutiny by community groups, for example, taxpayers' groups.

The Open Access movement is an example of the acknowledgment of "public good" obligations. The aim of open access is the free and unrestricted online availability of research results—a typical definition of it is "free, immediate, permanent online access to the full text of research articles for anyone, webwide" ("Open Access," accessed 2010). Participation in open access initiatives can assist data creators such as researchers and scholars to maximize their research impact. (A bibliography on the Open Citation Project [accessed 2010] website lists studies about the effects of open access on citation impact.) The return on public investment in research can also be maximized by reporting and citing that research more widely so that it forms the basis of further research; here, open access initiatives can assist. Research funding bodies are increasingly expecting open access to the research they fund. The Wellcome Trust, a major U.K.-based funder of medical research, has called for "Open and unrestricted access to the outputs of published research" (Wellcome Trust, accessed 2010).

Open access initiatives are gaining strength. A 2007 petition to the European Commission ("Petition for Guaranteed Public Access to Publicly-Funded Research Results," 2007) urges the adoption, as a matter of urgency, of a recommendation to guarantee public access to publicly funded research results shortly after publication. Open access journals are firmly established; for example, the Public Library of Science (PLoS, accessed 2010) is a library of open access journals and other scientific literature: "Everything we publish is freely available online for you to read, download, copy, distribute, and use (with attribution) any way you wish." The strength of the Open Access movement can be seen in the Directory of Open Access Journals (DOAJ, accessed 2010).

Compliance Reasons

Digital curation can also be compliance driven. Commonly encountered examples are compliance with the requirements of funding bodies and of publishers and the need to comply with specific legal requirements.

Research funding bodies now commonly require that grant applications include provision for digital curation. A data management plan, or a plan for the deposit of data into a publicly accessible data repository, is a common example. The National Institutes of Health (NIH) in the United States illustrates this point. "Data sharing is essential for expedited translation of research results into knowledge, products and procedures to improve human health," begins the NIH's data-sharing policy

(National Institutes of Health, 2007). The NIH criteria for peer reviewing of grant applications include an expectation that data will be shared. Their statement "Access to Research Data" (National Institutes of Health, 2003) defines research data and outlines the process of seeking access. The NIH provides a *Data Sharing Workbook* (National Institutes of Health, 2004a). Testimonials on the NIH website (National Institutes of Health, 2004b) indicate the benefits of data sharing, such as more rapid availability of data and higher take-up and reuse rates. In the United Kingdom, deposition of data in existing databases or repositories, which are sometimes prescribed, is mandated. For example, the U.K. Economic and Social Research Council (ESRC) specifies the Economic and Social Data Service (2003–2009) repository, and the U.K. National Environment Research Council (NERC) specifies the NORA repository (NERC Open Research Archive, 2009).

Compliance with legislation may necessitate good digital curation practice. Many countries have data protection acts and freedom of information acts. Discipline-specific compliance requirements may also determine practice. In the United Kingdom, the Freedom of Information Act (2000), the Data Protection Act (1998), and the Environmental Information Regulations (2004) mandate requirements for data that require careful curation. Natural environment research in the United Kingdom, for example, may have to comply with the Antarctic Treaty; data sets may contain "environmental information" that falls within the definition of the Environmental Information Regulations 1992; a contract or Memorandum of Understanding with another body may specify what can and cannot be done with the data. Details of these examples can be found in the *NERC Data Policy Handbook* (Natural Environment Research Council, 2002, Section 3.5).

In some disciplines publishers now insist that potential authors demonstrate aspects of digital curation. The publisher may require specific conditions to be met before publication of research results, such as registering clinical trials in a publicly accessible database as a precondition of publication—this is the case for major medical journals, such as the *British Medical Journal*, the *Journal of the American Medical Association*, the *New England Journal of Medicine*, and *The Lancet*.

Digital Curators

The creators, users, and curators of data all play roles in the digital curation process. The roles range from those of curators of large data sets in scientific, library, and archive contexts, right down to those played by individuals who create and use digital information for personal use and who wish to keep some of it over time.

Creators of data include scholars, researchers, and librarians and archivists who manage digitization programs. The best time to ensure that digital objects are usable is when they are created. For these objects to be usable and reusable, they must be of high quality, well structured, and adequately documented. Data creators, therefore, should ensure that the digital objects they create are structured and documented to ensure their longevity and reusability. Data reusers ensure that any annotations they produce are captured and documented to a level that ensures their annotations are understandable to other users of those data.

Curators of digital information—people who have a primary role of managing or "looking after" data—have job titles that include archivist, librarian, data librarian, and annotator, as well as data curator. Their roles vary according to the context in which they work. For example, in a bioscience context the data curator's tasks include ongoing data management, intensive data description, ensuring data quality, collaborative information infrastructure work, and metadata standards work.

The DCC's website provides case studies that describe what curation actually involves in practice (www.dcc.ac.uk/resources/case-studies). Among the full range of tasks and responsibilities encompassed by digital curation are these:

- Developing and implementing policies and services
- Analyzing digital content to determine what services can be provided from it
- Providing advice to data creators and users/reusers
- Ensuring submission of data to a repository
- Negotiating agreements
- Ensuring data quality
- Ensuring that data are structured in the best way to provide access, rendering, storage, and maintenance
- Enabling the use and reuse of data
- Enabling data discovery and retrieval
- Preservation planning and implementation (e.g., ensuring appropriate storage and backup routines, obsolescence monitoring)
- Ensuring that policies and services are in place to make sure that data is viable, able to be rendered, understandable, and authentic
- Promoting interoperability

Summary: Main Characteristics of Digital Curation

Digital curation is characterized by:

- the range of processes applied to digital objects *over their whole lifecycle*, from creation to ultimate disposal (e.g., it places strong emphasis on the importance of designing for curation at the point that digital objects are created);
- a concern with reproducibility of data as the basis of validation of scholarly output, accountability, and recordkeeping;

- adding value to digital objects so that they can be reused or repurposed (e.g., by adding metadata that assists in their discovery, management, and retrieval);
- involving a wide range of stakeholders cutting across disciplinary boundaries: these include heritage organizations (libraries, archives, museums, art galleries), e-science and e-research groups, researchers and scholars, and government bodies who fund e-science, higher education, and other activities;
- a strong interest in open source solutions; and
- strong links between research and practice.

Our understanding of digital curation is evolving. This becomes clear when we attempt to apply current digital curation practices to the e-science context. Much current digital curation practice has been developed in cultural heritage contexts, libraries and archives in particular, and is most effective for static data. This does not transfer readily to the new scholarship based on collaborative computing. This new scholarship is evolving very rapidly, lacks standards, and deals with very large data sets. There is a huge potential for reuse of data, but the infrastructure components to allow this reuse are currently very primitive or—more likely—do not yet exist. The next chapter examines the new ways of working, their requirements for digital curation, and the need to develop new kinds of skills.

References

ALCTS Preservation and Reformatting Section. 2007. "Definitions of Digital Preservation." Chicago: Association for Library Collections & Technical Services (June 24, 2007). Available: www.ala.org/ala/mgrps/divs/alcts/resources/preserv/defdigpres0408.pdf (accessed April 26, 2010).

ARL Workshop on New Collaborative Relationships. 2006. "To Stand the Test of Time: Long-term Stewardship of Digital Data Sets in Science and Engineering: A Report to the National Science Foundation from the ARL Workshop on New Collaborative Relationships: The Role of Academic Libraries in the Digital Data Universe, September 26–27, 2006, Arlington, VA." Washington, DC: Association of Research Libraries. Available: www.arl.org/bm~doc/digdatarpt.pdf (accessed April 26, 2010).

Boyle, Frances, Alexandra Eveleigh, and Heather Needham. 2008. "Report on the Survey Regarding Digital Preservation in Local Authority Archive Services." York: Digital Preservation Coalition (November 3, 2008). Available: www.dpconline.org/docs/reports/digpressurvey08.pdf (accessed April 26, 2010).

Brophy, Peter, and Jeremy Frey. 2006. "Digital Curation Centre Externally-Moderated Reflective Self-Evaluation: Report." Edinburgh: Digital Curation Centre. Available: ie-repository.jisc.ac.uk/198/1/dcc_evaluation_report_final.pdf (accessed April 26, 2010). Used by permission of Peter Brophy.

Computer History Museum. 2006. *Timeline of Computer History*. Mountain View, CA: Computer History Museum. Available: www.computerhistory.org/timeline (accessed April 26, 2010).

Cornell University Library. 2003–2007. *Digital Preservation Management: Implementing Short-Term Strategies for Long-term Problems*. Ithaca, NY:

Cornell University Library. Available: www.icpsr.umich.edu/dpm/dpm-eng/eng_index.html (accessed April 26, 2010).

DigCCurr. Available: ils.unc.edu/digccurr/aboutI.html (accessed April 26, 2010).

Digital Curation Centre. "DCC Charter and Statement of Principles." Edinburgh: Digital Curation Centre. Available: www.dcc.ac.uk/about-us/dcc-charter (accessed April 26, 2010).

———. 2008. *The DCC Curation Lifecycle Model*. Edinburgh: Digital Curation Centre. Available: www.dcc.ac.uk/docs/publications/DCCLifecycle.pdf (accessed April 26, 2010).

Digital Preservation Coalition. 2008. *Preservation Management of Digital Materials: The Handbook*. York: Digital Preservation Coalition. Available: www.dpconline.org/docs/advice/digital-preservation-handbook.html (accessed April 26, 2010).

DOAJ: Directory of Open Access Journals. Lund: DOAJ. Available: www.doaj .org (accessed April 26, 2010).

DRAMBORA: Digital Repository Audit Method Based on Risk Assessment. 2007. Edinburgh: DRAMBORA. Available: www.repositoryaudit.eu/img/drambora_flyer.pdf (accessed April 26, 2010).

Economic and Social Data Service. 2003—2009. Colchester: UK Data Archive. Available: www.esds.ac.uk (accessed April 26, 2010).

Harvey, Ross. 2008. "So Where's the Black Hole in Our Collective Memory? A Provocative Position Paper." Glasgow, Scotland: DigitalPreservationEurope. Available: www.digitalpreservationeurope.eu/publications/position/Ross _Harvey_black_hole_PPP.pdf (accessed April 26, 2010).

Hedstrom, Margaret. 2002. "Research Challenges in Digital Archiving and Long-term Preservation." Address to the Workshop on Research Challenges in Digital Archiving and Long-Term Preservation, Washington, DC, April 12–13, 2002. Available: www.sis.pitt.edu/~dlwkshop/paper_hedstrom.doc (accessed April 26, 2010).

Joint Information Systems Committee. 2002. "Continuing Access and Digital Preservation Strategy for JISC." Bristol: JISC (October 1, 2002). Available: www.jisc.ac.uk/publications/publications/pub_access_pres_strategy.aspx (accessed April 26, 2010).

Lavoie, Brian, and Lorcan Dempsey. 2004. "Thirteen Ways of Looking at . . . Digital Preservation." *D-Lib Magazine* 10, no.7/8 (July/August). Available: www.dlib.org/dlib/july04/lavoie/07lavoie.html (accessed April 26, 2010).

Lord, Philip, and Alison Macdonald. 2003. "e-Science Curation Report: Data Curation for e-Science in the UK: An Audit to Establish Requirements for Future Curation and Provision." Twickenham: Digital Archiving Consultancy. Available: www.jisc.ac.uk/uploaded_documents/e-ScienceReportFinal.pdf (accessed April 26, 2010).

National Institutes of Health. 2003. "Access to Research Data." In *NIH Grants Policy Statement*. Bethesda, MD: National Institutes of Health. Available: grants.nih.gov/grants/policy/nihgps_2003/NIHGPS_Part5.htm#_Access_ to_Research (accessed April 26, 2010).

———. 2004a. *Data Sharing Workbook*. Bethesda, MD: National Institutes of Health. Available: grants1.nih.gov/grants/policy/data_sharing/data_sharing _workbook.pdf (accessed April 26, 2010).

———. 2004b. "Testimonials." Available: grants1.nih.gov/grants/policy/data _sharing/testimonials.doc (accessed April 26, 2010).

———. 2007. *NIH Data Sharing Policy*. Bethesda, MD: National Institutes of Health. Available: grants1.nih.gov/grants/policy/data_sharing/index.htm (accessed April 26, 2010).

Natural Environment Research Council. 2002. *NERC Data Policy Handbook, Version 2.2.* Swindon: NERC. Available: badc.nerc.ac.uk/data/NERC_Handbookv2.2.pdf (accessed April 26, 2010).

NERC Open Research Archive (NORA). 2009. Swindon: Natural Environment Research Council. Available: www.nerc.ac.uk/about/access/repository.asp (accessed April 26, 2010).

"Open Access." eprints. Available: www.eprints.org/openaccess (accessed April 26, 2010).

Open Citation Project. "The Effect of Open Access and Downloads ('Hits') on Citation Impact: A Bibliography of Studies." Available: opcit.eprints.org/oacitation-biblio.html (accessed April 26, 2010).

"Petition for Guaranteed Public Access to Publicly-Funded Research Results." 2007. Available: www.ec-petition.eu/index.php?p=index (accessed April 26, 2010).

PLoS: Public Library of Science. San Francisco, CA: Public Library of Science. Available: www.plos.org (accessed April 26, 2010).

Research Data Strategy Working Group. 2008. *Stewardship of Research Data in Canada: A Gap Analysis.* Ottawa: National Research Council Canada. Available: data-donnees.gc.ca/docs/GapAnalysis.pdf (accessed April 26, 2010). Used by permission of the Research Data Strategy Working Group.

Research Information Network. 2008. *Stewardship of Digital Research Data: A Framework of Principles and Guidelines: Responsibilities of Research Institutions and Funders, Data Managers, Learned Societies and Publishers.* London: RIN. Available: www.rin.ac.uk/system/files/Stewardship-data-guidelines.pdf (accessed April 26, 2010).

Rosenzweig, Roy. 2003. "Scarcity or Abundance? Preserving the Past in a Digital Era." *American Historical Review* 108, no. 3 (June): 735–762. Available: www.historycooperative.org/journals/ahr/108.3/rosenzweig.html (accessed April 26, 2010).

Ross, Seamus. 2007. "Digital Preservation, Archival Science and Methodological Foundations for Digital Libraries." Keynote address to the 11th European Conference on Research and Advanced Technology for Digital Libraries, Budapest, September 16–21, 2007. Available: www.ecdl2007.org/Keynote_ECDL2007_SROSS.pdf (accessed April 26, 2010).

Rusbridge, Chris. 2007. "Create, Curate, Re-Use: The Expanding Life Course of Digital Research." Paper presented at EDUCAUSE Australasia 2007. Available: hdl.handle.net/1842/1731 (accessed April 26, 2010). Used by permission of Chris Rusbridge, Digital Curation Centre.

UNESCO. 2003. *Guidelines for the Preservation of Digital Heritage.* Paris: Information Society Division, United Nations Educational, Scientific and Cultural Organization. Available: unesdoc.unesco.org/images/0013/001300/130071e.pdf (accessed April 26, 2010).

Wellcome Trust. "Open and Unrestricted Access to the Outputs of Published Research." London: Wellcome Trust. Available: www.wellcome.ac.uk/About-us/Policy/Spotlight-issues/Open-access/index.htm (accessed April 26, 2010).

Wikipedia. 2009. "Digital Dark Age." Wikipedia (March 5, 2010). Available: en.wikipedia.org/wiki/Digital_Dark_Age (accessed April 26, 2010).

The Changing Landscape

As noted in Chapter 1, one of the factors that make digital curation necessary is the embedding of new ways of working in many scientific, scholarly, and research communities. These new ways of working are characterized by their reliance on networked computing and on the creation, management, use, and reuse of large data sets. Scholarship is already substantially data driven, and this will rapidly expand. The new ways of working are in turn influencing the management of digital information in libraries and archives.

The new data driven scholarship has various terms associated with it, including cyberscholarship, e-science, e-research, derivative science, and cyberinfrastructure. The term *cyberscholarship* is more prevalent in the United States, whereas in other countries the terms *e-science* and *e-scholarship* are more commonly used. In this book *cyberscholarship* is the term used to refer to the ways in which networked computing, data, and scholars work together. The term *e-science* is used here to refer more specifically to research in scientific fields, and *cyberinfrastructure* is used to refer to what needs to be in place for the new ways of working.

This chapter examines in more detail the characteristics of the changing landscape, its requirements for digital curation, and the need for new kinds of skills to curate data. These topics are discussed in greater depth by Christine Borgman (2007) in *Scholarship in the Digital Age*.

Cyberscholarship: New Ways of Working

What, more precisely, are these new ways of working? What characterizes them?

Cyberscholarship is based on the availability of scholarly materials in digital form through computer networks. These scholarly materials range from large scientific data sets to digitized versions of the analog resources held in the collections of libraries and archives. (The nature of these scholarly materials is examined in more detail in Chapter 4.) New forms of research and scholarship are developing based on the availability of these digital materials and on computing techniques to analyze and present them; they differ significantly from traditional practices—Larsen (2008) notes "the transformative potential of digital scholarship." The new forms of research and scholarship include working in larger groups whose members may be based at different (perhaps many) geographic locations. The outcome is that research is collaborative, based on large digital data sets developed, shared, and used by international communities of scholars, although this is not yet widespread (Larsen, 2008).

Cyberscholarship is characterized not only by new collaborative structures but also by the enhanced ability to compute large quantities of data. New discoveries are made through these computations: more detailed analyses can be carried out and data can be visualized and simulated more readily. In the humanities, for example, new opportunities created by the conjunctions of data, networked computing, and scholars are encouraging new ways of carrying out scholarship. Examples from a 2008 symposium describe an art historian who reconstructs an ancient site in digital form, a professor of Romance languages who creates an interactive map illustrating how Spanish language and culture spread over time, and a linguist applying social network tools. The symposium's report notes that "Students and researchers alike are using simulation and interactive model-based learning. Mass digitization makes it possible to query large corpora of heterogeneous source materials, synthesize information across disciplines, and perform new types of analysis" (Smith, 2008: 1). Another example is the development of electronic cultural atlases. As well as including all of the features of their paper versions, such atlases also allow different research questions to be posed and new relationships to be identified by offering innovative ways of grouping, analyzing, and visualizing the data within them. They allow, for example, visualization through animated maps, enhanced search capabilities, and the engagement of a much wider community in providing the data. The Electronic Cultural Atlas Initiative (ecai.org) illustrates the possibilities.

Another characteristic of cyberscholarship is that it generates large quantities of data. This has major implications for how data are stored, managed, preserved over time, and used. To take one example: scholars can read and analyze only a small number of documents compared with the millions they can analyze using a high-speed computer. Computing of large data sets enables new kinds of results: "Profound research is possible by simple analysis of huge amounts of information. Computer programs can identify latent patterns of information or relationships that will never be found by human searching and browsing" (Arms, 2008).

Cyberscholarship places heavy emphasis on sharing and reusing data. Data sets may be unique and able to be reproduced only at great cost and sometimes not at all. Many consider that these data sets should be available for reuse by scholars other than those who developed and collected them. This implies the widespread adoption of standards for creating and collecting data to ensure they can be discovered, located, and preserved over time. A further implication is that ways of protecting the rights of data creators and owners are required.

A further characteristic of cyberscholarship is its reliance on the increasing availability of all kinds of materials in digital form, from digital versions of material created on paper and in other analog forms to the reports, drafts, data sets, images, video, and other materials that are increasingly created in digital form and exist *only* in digital form. This demands and drives the availability of these digital materials. It also suggests both that the roles of established institutions such as libraries and archives need to be redefined and that new kinds of institutions need to be developed to support scholarship.

Cyberscholarship in Practice

More examples of cyberscholarship in practice illustrate these characteristics. The National Virtual Observatory (us-vo.org) provides the means for researchers to group together data from astronomical data sets that are widely dispersed, allowing analysis of combined data sets to derive previously unattainable results. To provide this, the National Virtual Observatory has developed software such as an application programming interface (API), standards such as an XML encoding scheme for astronomical data, and applications that work with the API (Arms, 2008).

An informative collection of cyberscholarship examples in the humanities, social sciences, and scientific/technical/medical subject areas in the United States is available in a 2008 study carried out for the Association of Research Libraries (Maron and Kirby Smith, 2008). Some of these are "quite novel, making use of the space, speed, and interactivity that the Internet allows" (Maron and Kirby Smith, 2008: 9). One example noted is eBird (ebird.org/content/ebird), "harnessing the power of users" to develop a large central database of bird sightings submitted by amateur bird-watchers. The database is used by professional ornithologists and environmentalists (Maron and Kirby Smith, 2008: 27).

Visualization possibilities are demonstrated in the "Comparing Victorian & Second Life Immersive Environments" project (sydenham crystalpalace.wordpress.com). This presents in Second Life a virtual three-dimensional model of the Pompeii Court of the Sydenham Crystal Palace, which opened as a museum in South London in 1854.

Data-intensive websites that provide access to data sets and to the tools to extract data from them, analyze the data, and visualize them are increasingly common. An example is Data.gov, which aims to "increase public access to high value, machine readable datasets generated by the Executive Branch of the Federal Government" in the United States by providing easy access to these data sets and tools.

E-science

Much of the literature about digital curation comes from the e-science context. E-science is the term used in the United Kingdom to denote "the systematic development of research methods that exploit advanced computational thinking," enabling "new research by giving researchers access to resources held on widely-dispersed computers as though they were on their own desktops. The resources can include data collections, very large-scale computing resources, scientific instruments and high performance visualization" (www.rcuk.ac.uk/escience/default.htm). E-science activities in the United Kingdom are funded by Research Councils UK. Its characteristics are noted by British computer scientist David de Roure (Rusbridge, 2008a).

One characteristic is the increasing scale and diversity of participation; more people, both amateurs and professionals, can potentially participate. (This characteristic is capitalized on in collaborative sites such as eBird, noted earlier.) Another characteristic relates to the data, which, like participation, are also increasing in scale and diversity. New data collection tools and methods allow massive quantities of data that are increasingly more complex to be collected. Data are being shared more frequently through new online mechanisms, such as social tools (wikis, blogs, Twitter). Data, research, and journals are becoming readily available through the Open Access movement. Also being shared are scientific tools, such as workflows (noted in Chapter 4), which contribute to research becoming more easily repeatable, reproducible, and reusable. Arguably the most significant characteristic of e-science noted by de Roure is that it "is now enabling researchers to do some completely new stuff! As the pieces become easy to use, researchers can bring them together in new ways and ask new questions" (cited in Rusbridge, 2008a).

Cyberscholarship's Requirements and Challenges

To implement fully the new opportunities that cyberscholarship's new ways of working allow, different kinds of systems and facilities, that is, *cyberinfrastructure*, are needed. These include computer networks, libraries and archives, online repositories, and much more. New skill sets are also required. The requirements and challenges of cyberscholarship can be considered using William Arms's useful categorization of them into content, tools and services, and expertise (Arms, 2008; Nelson, 2009).

Content

Cyberscholarship requires that data are available for use and reuse in the future. Access to data is required as the foundation of high-quality scholarship, that is, scholarship that is based on verifiable data and that builds on them to lead to new knowledge. Access to data sets is required for analysis and querying by scholars who may be located anywhere in the world. But the data are often widely scattered, never made available, poorly archived, or even destroyed. Even if locatable and available, their use may be restricted by intellectual property rights or privacy legislation.

Changing processes of scholarly communication are also a major factor that is altering scholarship and curation practice. Scholarly communication has been based on the self-contained nature of books, journals, and conference proceedings as the key outputs of scholarship and on publishing structures and reward systems that acknowledge this self-contained nature. The data sets on which the publications are based have low priority in this process and, Nelson (2009) tells us, "are treated as second-class artifacts." The processes to capture, store, and manage data sets over time are not supported well—to quote Nelson again: "While the scientific process is becoming more data-driven, the scholarly communication process, even though largely automated, continues much as it has for hundreds of years."

In addition, the nature and quantities of data and the methods of their collection are changing. Take just one example—social networking sites. The issues of whether and how to preserve blogs are the subject of attention that is resulting in the development of workable solutions (e.g., Maureen Pennock's presentation at the 2009 iPres conference; Pennock, 2009). Facebook, Flickr, YouTube, and Twitter are also becoming mechanisms for the collection and sharing of data that are likely to be of interest to scholars in the future, but at present we lack viable ways of preserving them. The rapid developments in social networking sites also create problems for their curation.

Tools and Services

Effective and easy-to-use tools and services for locating, managing, analyzing, visualizing, and storing data are required for cyberscholarship, but sufficient of them are not yet available. Cyberscholarship demands data that need to be curated, and curation tasks, such as refreshing, migrating to new formats, tracking changes to data and verifying their provenance, must be much more effectively handled on a large scale. Automation of services is the key. (Automation of procedures and tools are noted in Chapter 13.) In the humanities, the shortage of such tools is acknowledged as a challenge. Better tools to make scholarly resources interoperable so that they can be used in other work were noted in a 2008 symposium (Smith, 2008). Specifically identified were federated searching services, better tools for ontology development, further development of standards, such as Open GIS (www.opengeospatial.org/standards), and better tools to track contributions to collaborative works. Also noted was the need for new models for teaching humanities scholars about how to collaborate.

Expertise

Nelson (2009) poses this question: "Who will capture this data, and where will it live?" Not only are the nature and quantities of data changing in cyberscholarship, but the ways they are acquired and stored are also changing (Nelson, 2009). The expertise required to acquire and store large quantities of data is in very short supply and, as Arms (2008)

The Internet Archive, founded in 1996, is a nonprofit organization that aims to preserve born-digital materials. It initially collected and archived webpages but has expanded to include moving images, texts, audio, and software. The Internet Archive collaborates with major libraries, archives, and museums around the world to preserve a record for generations to come. It places particular emphasis on open and free access to information and makes its collections readily available. The Wayback Machine (available at www.archive.org) is a search tool that provides access to websites archived by the Internet Archive.

notes, is concentrated in the Internet Archive (www.archive.org) and in commercial organizations such as Google, Amazon, and Microsoft. The skills required for curation are noted later in this chapter.

The existing infrastructure, based as it is on print-focused scholarly communication processes and on libraries and archives developed in response to these processes, is not proving to be adequate to accommodate the new demands of cyberscholarship. What is needed is a new form of infrastructure to address the challenges. The shape of what is needed, the *cyberinfrastructure*, is being developed and implemented, albeit slowly, and the role of libraries and archives within it is being vigorously debated. A 2009 OCLC report (Palmer, Teffeau, and Pirrman, 2009) suggests that the most important role for cyberinfrastructure is "providing the collections and tools needed for producing new scholarship." It notes that scholars are increasingly conducting their activities online, so the services that research libraries provide will need to be integrated into this digital work environment and that "good service will be defined by scholars' ability to find and use the digital information they need for all stages of research." The report concludes that the question for libraries and other institutions that provide information services is "not what services need to be offered digitally, but rather how do we proceed in the long term to move all services to an e-research platform" (Palmer, Teffeau, and Pirrman, 2009: 34).

In a traditional library, the user personally selects information by searching catalogs and browsing collections to locate and examine specific items. In new digital ways of working, large digital collections are searched and examined by computer programs directed by the user. For this to happen, digital content must be organized so computers can analyze it. This requires standardized data formats and software, as well as the ability to access data without legal barriers (Larsen, 2008). Curation and preservation of digital materials pose additional challenges, investigated in the chapters that follow.

The current laissez-faire approach to developing cyberinfrastructure is widely considered to be inadequate. A workshop jointly sponsored by the United States' National Science Foundation (NSF) and the United Kingdom's JISC proposed as a goal that, by 2015, "all publicly-funded research products and primary resources will be readily available, accessible, and usable via common infrastructure and tools through space, time, and across disciplines, stages of research, and modes of human expression" (Larsen, 2008).

PARSE.Insight (www.parse-insight.eu) is a research project funded by the European Union. (PARSE stands for Permanent Access to the Records of Science in Europe.) It has developed a roadmap to guide the development of a cyberinfrastructure for scientific data in Europe. This roadmap specifies "Organisational and Social Infrastructure concepts and components" that include policies to mandate the deposit of research data; robust and reliable places to deposit those data; and making publication of data "as valued and as referencable as is a publication of a paper in a journal" (PARSE.Insight, 2009: 12). The roadmap also notes "Technical Science Data Concepts and Components" that need to be addressed: create and maintain representation information; sharing of information about hardware and software; authenticity of a digital object; digital rights; persistent identifiers; transfer of custody and brokering services; and certified repositories.

New structures not yet envisaged will also develop. We could probably not have foreseen a few years ago the widespread implementation of cloud computing. It is now viewed as offering new possibilities: Chris Rusbridge (2008b: 217) conjectures "Can we combine the institution and the discipline to achieve network effects with institution components?", for example, the cloud's "mass appeal [and] highly scalable centralized services" with libraries?

Digital Curation: A New Profession, New Requirements

New skill sets are required for effective digital curation, and considerable research has been undertaken to identify and map these skill sets. Although this research has been carried out in different contexts, the results are similar.

One of the more comprehensive listings of skills is an outcome of the SHERPA (Securing a Hybrid Environment for Research Preservation and Access) Project (www.sherpa.ac.uk/index.html). The SHERPA Project is set in the context of institutional repositories and encompasses most aspects of curation as indicated in the Digital Curation Centre's Curation Lifecycle Model, although with different emphases (e.g., less importance is placed on use and reuse of data). The *Institutional Repositories: Staff and Skills Set* (Robinson, 2009) breaks down the knowledge and skills required by repository managers and administrators into nine categories: management; software; metadata; storage and preservation; content; advocacy, training, and support; liaison (internal); liaison (external); and current awareness and professional development. These categories are further developed; for example, the software category notes "familiarity with standard web-based software systems including (but not limited to) Unix, Linux, SQL Server, MySQL, SGML, XML, PHP, JAVA, PERL, Apache [and] at least one major repository software including (but not limited to) EPrints, DSpace, Fedora, OPUS." The specifics will change over time; what is more important and more useful is the identification of the areas where skills are required. These nine skills categories, identified in the institutional repository context, map well to other contexts.

In the archives context, Adrian Cunningham (2008: 541–542) proposes the "skills and capabilities required for digital archiving." In addition to a range of generic personal attributes, such as flexibility and research ability, the skills and capabilities he identifies for the archives domain can be mapped easily to SHERPA's areas. For example, Cunningham's "Auditing and compliance, QA, Preparing business cases, Modeling and analytical ability, [and] System design and implementation" fit comfortably in the management category identified by SHERPA. Both place strong emphasis on the areas of (to use SHERPA's terminology) Advocacy, Training and Support, and Liaison. Cunningham's phrase "out of the basement and into the boardroom" summarizes neatly one of the requirements, and his "Communication, influence, change management" and "Consultation and negotiation" terms also map closely.

In the e-science context, Pryor and Donnelly (2009) identify core skills for research data management. A model developed for the Research Data Management Forum (see Figure 2.1) indicates that different skills are needed by different players in research data management: data managers; data creators; data librarians; and data scientists ("RDMF2: Core Skills Diagram," 2008). Their list of key skills acknowledges data analysis and reuse ("Data Analysis and Manipulation"; "Extracting Information from

Figure 2.1. Core Skills for Data Management

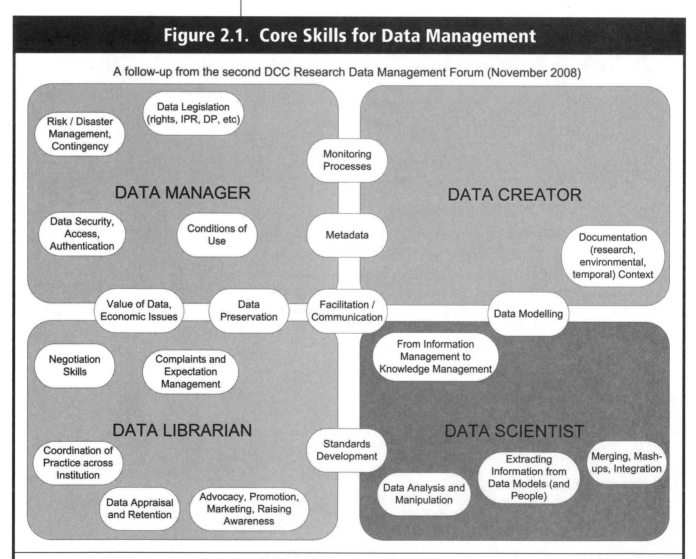

A follow-up from the second DCC Research Data Management Forum (November 2008)

Source: data-forum.blogspot.com/2008/12/rdmf2-core-skills-diagram.html. © Chris Rusbridge/Martin Donnelly/Research Data Management Forum. Developed for a meeting of the Research Data Management Forum in November 2008, and reproduced by permission of Martin Donnelly, Chris Rusbridge, and the Research Data Management Forum.

Data Models [and People]"; "Merging, Mashups, Integration") in a way that is not evident in the SHERPA list, but in other areas, for instance, "Facilitation/Communication" and "Negotiation Skills," it is in general accord with the SHERPA list.

Fyffe, Ludwig, and Warner's (2005: 4) *Sample Digital Preservation Curriculum Framework* is specifically focused on universities. Its five broad areas are General Awareness; Information Life Cycle Management (ILM); Information Storage Management and System Maintenance; Best Practices and Standards; and Legal Issues and University Policies. This list is also in broad agreement with the previous lists in that it does not focus exclusively, or even heavily, on the technical system and preservation aspects but emphasizes the context in which curation happens and the need for strong advocacy.

The most comprehensive listing of the knowledge and competencies is that developed by the DigCCurr Project based at the School of Information and Library Science, University of North Carolina at Chapel Hill. This project has among its outcomes two comprehensive listings, of "High-Level Categories of Digital Curation Functions" (Lee, 2008) and a "Matrix of Digital Curation Knowledge and Competencies" (Lee, 2009).

The DigCCurr Project's high-level categories can be mapped closely to the SHERPA Project's skills, as the partial comparison in Figure 2.2 indicates. The DigCCurr and SHERPA listings diverge when the use and reuse aspects of curation are considered. As already indicated these aspects

Figure 2.2. Comparison of Skills Required for Digital Curation

SHERPA Project	DigCCurr Project
Management	Management Administration Preservation Planning and Implementation Purchasing and Managing Licenses to Resources Analysis and Documentation of Curation Functions Evaluation and Audit of Curation Functions
Metadata	Description, Organization, and Intellectual Control
Storage and Preservation	Archival Storage Preservation Planning and Implementation Data Management
Content	Selection, Appraisal, and Disposition Destruction and Removal Analysis and Characterization of Digital Objects/Packages Validation and Quality Control of Digital Objects/Packages
Advocacy, Training, and Support	Advocacy and Outreach Education and Sharing of Expertise or Guidance on Curation Functions
Liaison (External)	Collaboration, Coordination, and Contracting with External Actors

are not emphasized by the SHERPA listing, which was developed in the context of institutional repositories. DigCCurr lists, for example, "Use, Reuse and Adding Value to Accessed Information" and "Reference and User Support Services."

Educating and Training Digital Curators

The recognition that new skills are required for digital curation has led to the development of courses through which students can learn curation skills. New courses of formal study are now emerging. These range from single subjects to full postgraduate programs at the master's level. Pryor and Donnelly (2009: 161–163) list some of the opportunities for acquiring the new skills required for digital curation. They point to the range of skills that are required, from "the basic toolkit that will equip researchers with the ability to plan for the longevity of their data to the more sophisticated suite of tools required by a data management professional that may need to be assimilated" (Pryor and Donnelly, 2009: 159).

Among the full academic programs at the postgraduate certificate or master's level is the MA in Digital Asset Management at King's College London. Its focus is on "curatorial and technical standards that arise throughout the 'digital resource life-cycle', from creation through management, access and dissemination to long-term preservation" (www.kcl.ac.uk/schools/humanities/depts/cch/pg/madam). Another program is the MSc in Information Management and Preservation offered by the Humanities Advanced Technology & Information Institute at the University of Glasgow (www.gla.ac.uk/departments/hatii), which aims to equip its graduates to work as archivists, records managers, and digital curators through developing their skills in digital curation and preservation issues as well as in the competencies required by these professions.

Other programs are specializations or concentrations within an established master's program, particularly within Master in Library and Information Science programs in the United States. An example of this is the Specialization in Data Curation within the Master of Science at the Graduate School of Library and Information Science (GSLIS) at the University of Illinois at Urbana-Champaign. This focuses on "data collection and management, knowledge representation, digital preservation and archiving, data standards, and policy" in the research context (www.lis.illinois.edu/programs/ms/data_curation.html). Flexible delivery of some programs is also developing. The University of Arizona's fully online Graduate Certificate in Digital Information Management (digin.arizona.edu) combines "intensive, hands-on technology learning" with theoretical principles to develop the skills needed to manage large digital collections, including digital curation skills.

The importance of developing skills and knowledge in digital curation is acknowledged by scholarship and fellowship programs, such as those funded by the Institute of Museum and Library Services in the United

States. These include scholarships for students enrolled in the University of Arizona's Graduate Certificate in Digital Information Management and in the Carolina Digital Curation Doctoral Fellowship Program associated with the DigCCurr Project at the University of North Carolina at Chapel Hill.

Digital curation is a field where up-to-date skills and knowledge have typically been acquired on the job, supplemented by attendance at workshops and short courses. A wide range of workshops and courses are offered on an ongoing basis. One listing of these is available at the DCC's website (www.dcc.ac.uk). Summer schools and professional institutes are also available, such as DigCCurr's Curation Practices for the Digital Object Lifecycle (www.ils.unc.edu/digccurr/institute.html). Symposia in the field are well established, most notably the International Digital Curation Conference, iPres (rdd.sub.uni-goettingen.de/conferences/ipres/ipres-en.html) and the DigCCurr conference.

Training of researchers in digital curation awareness and skills is also receiving attention in many countries. In the Australian context, for example, where cyberinfrastructure is developing rapidly, work is taking place to determine the skills required. These need to be available through a range of venues and modes. While technical skills are often closely linked to specific disciplines, it is generally agreed that nontechnical skills are equally important. Generic skills such as project management, negotiation, team building, and problem solving were identified as important nontechnical skills. In addition, researchers need a general understanding of the e-research environment and how it can assist their research (Henty, 2008).

Summary: Meeting the New Demands

The rapid evolution of new kinds of scholarship based on the use and reuse of data is changing how many disciplines operate. The nature of participation in scholarship is also rapidly changing so that individuals can and do contribute through "citizen science" projects and online social networking mechanisms. To meet the challenges posed by this rapid evolution, changes in the kinds of infrastructure that support scholarship are essential and new skills are required. These will develop over coming years.

The next chapter introduces the DCC Curation Lifecycle Model, which provides a structure for the rest of this book. It also describes the OAIS (Open Archival Information System) Reference Model, a key conceptual model for digital curation.

References

Arms, William Y. 2008. "Cyberscholarship: High Performance Computing Meets Digital Libraries." *Journal of Electronic Publishing* 11, no. 1. Available: dx.doi.org/10.3998/3336451.0011.103 (accessed April 26, 2010).

Borgman, Christine L. 2007. *Scholarship in the Digital Age.* Cambridge, MA: MIT Press.

Cunningham, Adrian. 2008. "Digital Curation/Digital Archiving: A View from the National Archives of Australia." *American Archivist* 71 (Fall/Winter): 530–543.

Fyffe, Richard, Deborah Ludwig, and Beth Forrest Warner. 2005. "Digital Preservation in Action: Toward a Campus-Wide Program." *EDUCAUSE Center for Applied Research Research Bulletin* 19 (September). Available: www.educause.edu/ECAR/DigitalPreservationinActionTow/157552 (accessed April 26, 2010).

Henty, Margaret. 2008. "Developing the Capability and Skills to Support eResearch." *Ariadne* 55 (April). Available: www.ariadne.ac.uk/issue55/henty (accessed April 26, 2010).

Larsen, Ronald L. 2008. "On the Threshold of Cyberscholarship." *Journal of Electronic Publishing* 11, no. 1. Available: dx.doi.org/10.3998/3336451 .0011.102 (accessed April 26, 2010).

Lee, Christopher A. 2008. "High-level Categories of Digital Curation Functions. Draft, Version 14." Chapel Hill, NC: DigCCurr (September 8, 2008). Available ils.unc.edu/digccurr/digccurr-funct-categories.pdf (accessed April 26, 2010).

———. 2009. "Matrix of Digital Curation Knowledge and Competencies (Overview). Draft, Version 13." Chapel Hill, NC: DigCCurr (June 17, 2009). Available: ils.unc.edu/digccurr/digccurr-matrix.html (accessed April 26, 2010).

Maron, Nancy L., and K. Kirby Smith. 2008. *Current Models of Digital Scholarly Communication: Results of an Investigation Conducted by Ithaka for the Association of Research Libraries.* Washington, DC: Association of Research Libraries. Available: www.arl.org/bm~doc/current-models-report.pdf (accessed April 26, 2010).

Nelson, Michael L. 2009. "Data-driven Science: A New Paradigm?" *Educause Review* 44, no. 4 (July/August): 6–7. Available: www.educause.edu/EDU CAUSE+Review/EDUCAUSEReviewMagazineVolume44/DataDriven ScienceANewParadigm/174196 (accessed April 26, 2010).

Palmer, Carole L., Lauren C. Teffeau, and Carrie C. Pirrman. 2009. *Scholarly Information Practices in the Online Environment: Themes from the Literature and Implications for Library Service Development.* Dublin, OH: OCLC. Available: www.oclc.org/programs/publications/reports/2009-02.pdf (accessed April 26, 2010).

PARSE.Insight. 2009. *Draft Road Map.* Didcot. Available: www.parse-insight .eu/publications.php#d2-1 (accessed April 26, 2010).

Pennock, Maureen. 2009. "ArchivePress: A Really Simple Solution to Archiving Blog Content." Paper presented at iPres (October 6, 2009). Available: www.cdlib.org/iPres/presentations/Pennockm.pdf (accessed April 26, 2010).

Pryor, Graham, and Martin Donnelly. 2009. "Skilling Up to Do Data: Whose Role, Whose Responsibility, Whose Career?" *International Journal of Digital Curation* 4, no. 2: 158–170. Available: www.ijdc.net/index.php/ijdc/article/ viewFile/126/133 (accessed April 26, 2010).

"RDMF2: Core Skills Diagram." The RDMF Blog, comment posted December 17, 2008. Available: data-forum.blogspot.com/2008/12/rdmf2-core-skills-diagram.html (accessed April 26, 2010).

Robinson, Mary. 2009. *Institutional Repositories: Staff and Skills Set.* Nottingham: SHERPA. Available: www.sherpa.ac.uk/documents/Staff_and_Skills_Set_ 2009.pdf (accessed April 26, 2010).

Rusbridge, Chris. 2008a. "David de Roure on 'the new e-Science.'" Digital Curation Blog, comment posted September 15, 2008. Available: digitalcuration.blogspot.com/2008/09/david-de-roure-on-new-e-science.html (accessed April 26, 2010). Used by permission of Chris Rusbridge, Digital Curation Centre.

———. 2008b. "Tomorrow, Tomorrow, and Tomorrow: Poor Players on the Digital Curation Stage." In *Digital Convergence: Libraries of the Future* (pp. 207–217), edited by Rae Earnshaw and John Vince. London: Springer. Used by permission of Chris Rusbridge, Digital Curation Centre.

Smith, Kathlin. 2008. "Symposium Examines Research Topics at Nexus of Digital Humanities and Computing." *CLIR Issues* 65 (September/October). Available: www.clir.org/pubs/issues/issues65.html (accessed April 26, 2010).

Conceptual Models

This chapter describes and investigates the application of two key conceptual models for digital curation. The first, the Digital Curation Centre (DCC) Curation Lifecycle Model, outlines the actions that comprise digital curation and presents these actions in graphic form. This Curation Lifecycle Model is used as the structural basis of Parts II and III of this book. The second conceptual model, the Open Archival Information System (OAIS) Reference Model, is an International Organization for Standardization (ISO) standard that is widely used as the basis for the design and implementation of digital archival systems. Several other models of the lifecycle of data are also noted in this chapter.

An important difference between these two models must be noted. The OAIS Reference Model does not take account of activities outside the digital archival system: in particular, it does not offer guidance on the creation of data or on the use and reuse of data. The DCC Curation Lifecycle Model explicitly includes the activities that take place outside the archival system—that is, it describes *curation* rather than archiving or preservation alone.

Standards and models are significant in any context in which information is managed. This point is readily demonstrated. The National Information Standards Organization (NISO; www.niso.org/standards) publishes a considerable number of standards for library and information science, and there are many standards for archives management and preservation, for example, in the areas of archival description, preservation, and storage. A concise and informative summary of the use of standards in the library and information community, their importance, and their uses is provided by the National Library of Australia (2004).

For digital curation, standards and models are especially important. Although standards such as the OAIS Reference Model are applied widely, others need to be developed or be more widely adopted if digital curation challenges are to be more fully met. The need for standards is noted further in Chapter 8, and specific standards are referred to in following chapters.

The DCC Curation Lifecycle Model

The DCC Curation Lifecycle Model is the structural basis of Chapters 5 to 15 in this book (Digital Curation Centre, 2008b). The DCC Curation Lifecycle is represented graphically on the back cover of this book. A draft version of the Model was published in 2007, and after a period of public consultation it was finalized in 2008. One example of its application is as the entry point to the listing of standards relating to digital curation and preservation (the DIFFUSE Standards Framework) on the DCC's website (Digital Curation Centre, 2008a).

A lifecycle model is particularly apposite to visualizing what happens when digital materials are curated. Actions applied (or not applied) at each stage of the information lifecycle directly influence how effectively that information can be managed and preserved in following stages of the lifecycle. For example, the addition of metadata during early stages of the lifecycle assists significantly in the long-term management of the data to which they are applied. Additionally, representing digital curation in a lifecycle model provides a checklist that can be used to ensure, when developing and implementing a curation plan, that all of the necessary stages are identified in the most appropriate order.

The DCC Curation Lifecycle Model offers a high-level overview of the activities that comprise digital curation. It is intended for organizations to use to model their digital curation activities, identifying the specific actions, technologies, standards, and skills required at each stage and adding to it or deleting from it where required. The Model was not designed for any specific digital curation operation or for application to any particular discipline. It can be applied in a wide range of digital curation contexts, including institutional repositories, digital archives, and electronic records management.

The DCC Curation Lifecycle Model notes three sets of actions: Full Lifecycle Actions, Sequential Actions, and Occasional Actions. The *Full Lifecycle Actions* are represented in the Model by four concentric inner rings: "Description and Representation Information," "Preservation Planning," "Community Watch and Participation," and "Curate and Preserve." These apply to every stage in the lifecycle. The innermost point (the bull's eye of the diagram) is "Data," indicating their centrality to the Model and emphasizing that it is data that are being curated.

The *Sequential Actions* in the outer ring represent the key actions needed to curate data as they move through their lifecycle, from their creation to their ultimate use and reuse. The sequence is not carried out once only; rather, it is repeated for as long as the data are being curated. This is indicated in the Model by the "Transform" action: data, through the process of being reused, can be transformed so that they form a new data set, which in turn needs to be created or received by an archive and so feeds back into the start of the lifecycle.

Occasional Actions may occur when specific conditions are met, but they do not apply to all data. For example, data may need to reappraised

---

CURATION LIFECYCLE MODEL

Full Lifecycle Actions
Description and Representation
    Information
Preservation Planning
Community Watch and
    Participation
Curate and Preserve

Sequential Actions
Conceptualise
Create or Receive
Appraise and Select
Ingest
Preservation Action
Store
Access, Use, and Reuse
Transform

Occasional Actions
Dispose
Reappraise

(hence the "Reappraise" action), or they may be disposed of as an outcome of the appraisal process (hence "Dispose").

The Full Lifecycle Actions are essential for the success of the curation process. They apply to most of the Sequential Actions. For example, "Preservation Planning" activities are ongoing activities that must be taken into account as data move through the Sequential Actions, and they are especially relevant to "Conceptualise," "Preservation Action," and "Access, Use, and Reuse." "Description and Representation Information" applies to all of the Sequential Actions—metadata (description information), for instance, is essential to all aspects of curation.

The DCC's website provides useful information about the DCC Curation Lifecycle Model (Digital Curation Centre, 2008c). It describes the Lifecycle's importance for data creators, data archivists, and data reusers. *Data creators* will find the Model relevant because the design of data has a crucial effect on their effective curation. Much of the information necessary for long-term curation and reuse needs to be captured when data are collected—for example, metadata that describes the data. The relevance of the Model to *data archivists* is that it identifies and describes what is required for effective data curation, assisting data archivists to ensure that the procedures and systems they develop are complete. *Reusers of other people's data* will find the Model relevant because access to data depends on how well they have been curated.

The DCC's website also indicates how the Curation Lifecycle Model can be applied in practice. It helps data curators ensure that their activities are appropriate by comparing these activities with the Lifecycle actions and developing actions that are missing or strengthening those that need it. The benefits of the Model are represented as enabling better mapping of activities against the Lifecycle; identifying weaknesses in practice; assisting in identifying collaborators (e.g., data creators) in the data curation process; supporting the documentation of policies and processes; encouraging the development of standards and technologies; and assisting with identifying tools and services for data curation. An extended digital curation lifecycle model based on the DCC's Model has been developed (Constantopoulos et al., 2009).

The Digital Curation Centre

The DCC is the organization that developed the DCC Curation Lifecycle Model, and it is also responsible for developing and promoting digital curation concepts and practices. It is a consortium of four major partners in the United Kingdom—the University of Edinburgh, the University of Glasgow, UKOLN (at the University of Bath), and the Science and Technology Facilities Council. It aims to support and promote continuing improvement in the quality of digital curation and digital preservation, particularly for the management of all research outputs in digital format. The DCC is a center of excellence in digital curation and preservation, providing authoritative expert advice and guidance on digital curation. Its website hosts a wide range of resources, software, tools, and support services. Although the DCC is based in the United Kingdom and has a primary audience in that country, its activities are highly significant for anyone working in the field of digital curation, no matter where they are based. In particular, the wide range of documentation about its activities and research it disseminates makes the DCC website an invaluable resource for anyone interested in digital curation.

Other Lifecycle Models

The DCC Curation Lifecycle Model is only one of many models that presents what happens in digital curation. Three other models are noted here.

A simple four-step model is presented in a 2008 report on the stewardship of research data in Canada (Research Data Strategy Working Group, 2008). The four steps are Production, Dissemination, Long-Term Management, and Discovery and Repurposing. This model was developed for the specific purpose of assisting with the identification of gaps in the research data stewardship processes currently in place. It does not attempt to be comprehensive.

Humphrey provides a model of the lifecycle of research knowledge creation (see Figure 3.1). He notes that "Life cycle models are shaping the way we study digital information processes" (Humphrey, 2006: 1). They assist us to understand better the complex relationships that exist among the stages and activities in research. This improved understanding is essential for the development of useful data curation processes and practices that reflect actual practice and, therefore, stand a better chance of being widely adopted. As Humphrey (2006: 1) notes, "The life cycle approach makes us more aware of possible information losses in the gaps

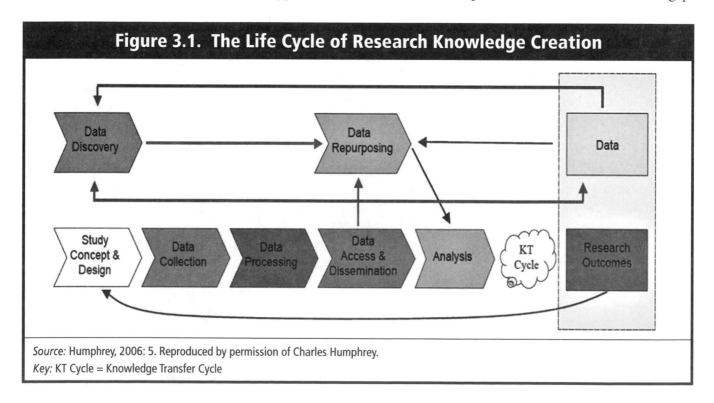

Figure 3.1. The Life Cycle of Research Knowledge Creation

Source: Humphrey, 2006: 5. Reproduced by permission of Charles Humphrey.
Key: KT Cycle = Knowledge Transfer Cycle

between stages." Note the strong emphasis on data in this model: data-driven research (e-science) focuses on the data, rather than the results, with reuse of data as a key component.

A more complex model comes from the Paradigm (Personal Archives Accessible in Digital Media) Project *Workbook on Private Digital Papers* (Paradigm Project, 2005–2007b). This model (see Figure 3.2) describes the long-term preservation of digital archives.

Many other lifecycle models are also relevant to digital curation, such as SHERPA's *A Lifecycle Model for an E-print in the Institutional Repository* (Knight, 2006). These have been developed for specific categories of material, whereas the DCC Curation Lifecycle Model is intended to be generic. They are not noted further in this book.

Higgins (2007) notes more lifecycle models. The significance of these lifecycle models, and of the DCC Curation Lifecycle Model and the OAIS Reference Model in particular, is that by mapping out the steps

Figure 3.2. Digital Archives and the Records Cycle

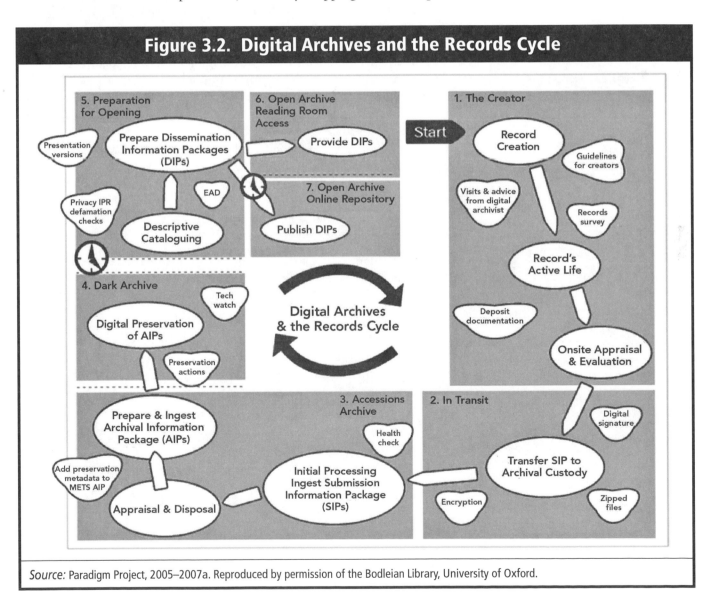

Source: Paradigm Project, 2005–2007a. Reproduced by permission of the Bodleian Library, University of Oxford.

and actions needed for each specific context they describe, they allow comprehensive strategies and actions for effective digital curation to be planned and developed.

The OAIS Reference Model

The OAIS Reference Model is a widely adopted key standard for managing digital materials in a digital archiving system. It provides a generic framework for building a digital archive and is applicable to most actions in the curation lifecycle. The OAIS Reference Model has three primary aims. First, it provides a vocabulary of concepts related to preservation that is understood and adopted by people from a wide range of backgrounds (librarians, archivists, cultural heritage professionals, information technology [IT] personnel, scientists, scholars). Next, it defines an information model. Third, it defines a functional model: that is, it describes the key functions needed in a digital archive, and it provides information about the kinds of activities undertaken by each function.

The OAIS Reference Model was originally developed for the space data community in the 1990s. Input was sought from other interested communities to ensure that its concepts and terminology were commonly understood across different domains. It was widely adopted as a de facto standard (Consultative Committee for Space Data Systems, 2002) and formally adopted as ISO standard 14721:2003 (International Organization for Standardization, 2003). In 2009 it was being reviewed as part of the ISO's normal five-year review process.

The OAIS Reference Model is used as the basis for planning digital archives that are sustainable. Characteristics that contribute to its value as a planning tool include:

- clear identification of the responsibilities and interactions of data creators, users, and data archivists;
- definition of the processes required for effective long-term preservation and access to digital objects;
- the common language it establishes: this facilitates communication among archivists, librarians, data creators, and data users (who potentially come from a wide range of disciplines), each of whom has a different terminology to describe curation actions;
- unambiguous articulation of a framework for a digital archive, which significantly assists in planning and successful implementation; and
- detailed models of the functions of a digital archive. (Based on Higgins, 2006)

OAIS Functions

The OAIS Reference Model defines an Open Archival Information System that provides long-term information preservation and access. This

---

OAIS REFERENCE MODEL: KEY FUNCTIONS

Ingest
Archival Storage
Data Management
Administration
Access
Preservation Planning
Common Services

system is "An archive, consisting of an organization of people and systems, that has accepted the responsibility to preserve information and make it available for a Designated Community." An OAIS archive is different from other kinds of archives by virtue of its meeting "a set of responsibilities, as defined in [the OAIS Reference Model]" (Consultative Committee for Space Data Systems, 2002: 1-1). The "Open" in OAIS refers to the development of the Model in open forums, not to the notion that access to the archive developed according to its criteria is unrestricted. The key functions of an OAIS, as defined in the Model, are summarized here:

- The **Ingest** function—the process of accepting information provided by Producers. Ingest is "responsible for receiving information from producers and preparing it for storage and management within the archive."

- The **Archival** storage function ensures that archival context remains secure and is stored appropriately—it "handles the storage, maintenance and retrieval of the AIPs [Archival Information Packages] held by the archive."

- The **Data Management** function supports access and updates information—it "coordinates the Descriptive Information pertaining to the archive's AIPs, in addition to system information used in support of the archive's function."

- The **Administration** function manages day-to-day operations and coordinates other functions.

- The **Access** function is the interface with the Designated Community—it "helps consumers to identify and obtain descriptions of relevant information in the archive, and delivers information from the archive to consumers."

- The **Preservation Planning** function develops preservation strategies, undertakes technology watch, etc. (Lavoie, 2000)

This is represented diagrammatically in Figure 3.3. A seventh function, **Common Services** (not noted in Figure 3.3), refers to the services that any IT system needs to function.

Actors and Objects

OAIS is based on the concept of actors and objects. *Actors* (who can be humans or computer systems) can perform in the roles of Producers, Managers, or Consumers. *Producers* are individuals, organizations, or computer systems that transfer digital information to the OAIS for preservation. *Managers* develop policy, define scope, and perform other management functions. *Consumers* are the individuals, organizations, or systems that are expected to use the information preserved by the OAIS.

An important concept in the OAIS Reference Model is the OAIS *Designated Community*. The Designated Community is a category of Consumer. It is the primary user group of the OAIS, to whom the OAIS must supply information that is understandable by this group. This means that the OAIS must have an understanding of the Designated

Figure 3.3. OAIS Functional Entities

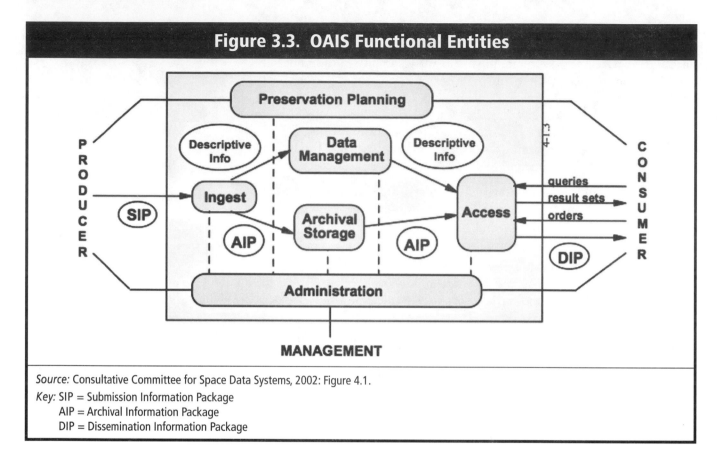

Source: Consultative Committee for Space Data Systems, 2002: Figure 4.1.

Key: SIP = Submission Information Package
    AIP = Archival Information Package
    DIP = Dissemination Information Package

Community's knowledge base. Defining the knowledge base of the Designated Community requires data creators to think about who the users in the future might be and about the knowledge and understanding that future users can be assumed to have. Understanding potential future requirements allows data curators to better identify the data they need to preserve. *Objects* in OAIS are of three kinds: the Submission Information Package (SIP), the Archival Information Package (AIP), and the Dissemination Information Package (DIP).

OAIS Information Packages

OAIS is based on the concept of *information package*. An information package has three parts:

1. The digital object(s) to be preserved
2. The metadata required at that point in the system
3. Packaging information

The information package concept recognizes that a digital object consists of more than simply the digital content, in the form of a bit stream, which we want to preserve. An information package also includes information that we need in order to preserve the digital object, such as information about its attributes, or about what actions have been applied to it, and so on.

The OAIS Reference Model specifies three kinds of information packages. The *Submission Information Package* (SIP) is what arrives at the repository. It consists of the digital object, plus any descriptive and technical metadata accompanying the digital object and/or any other information the content provider considers relevant. SIPs may also be supplied to an OAIS from another digital repository.

The *Archival Information Package* (AIP) is produced by taking the SIP and adding to it, if required, further information about the digital object. The added information is either *Preservation Description Information* or *Representation Information*. Preservation Description Information is needed to manage the preservation of the digital objects submitted to the OAIS (referred to by the OAIS Reference Model as a *Content Data Object*). It has four components:

1. **Reference Information**: a unique and persistent identifier that assists in identifying and locating the Content Data Object

2. **Provenance Information**: the history of the archived Content Data Object

3. **Context Information**: information about the relationship of the Content Data Object to other objects; for example, the hierarchical structure of a digital archive

4. **Fixity Information**: a demonstration of authenticity, such as a hash value or checksum.

Representation Information is required to make the Content Data Object intelligible to its Designated Community. Representation Information is the technical metadata required to make the bit stream retrievable as a meaningful digital object. For example, a webpage that includes graphics needs descriptions of the web environment (browser, etc.), the text (ASCII standard), and the image files to make it understandable. (Representation Information is noted in more detail in Chapter 6.)

All of this (the Content Data Object, Preservation Description Information, and Representation Information) is parceled together as an AIP. The AIP is the basic element of the digital repository.

The DIP is produced when a user requests access to an object in the OAIS. The DIP consists of a copy of the Content Data Object plus any metadata and support systems necessary to retrieve and use the Content Data Object. The accompanying metadata and Representation Information will be a subset of all the metadata relating to that object. The nature of the metadata and Representation Information supplied is determined by the assumed knowledge of the Designated Community.

OAIS and the DCC Curation Lifecycle Model

The DCC's Curation Lifecycle Model follows the OAIS Reference Model closely. In particular, the sequential actions of the Lifecycle emulate what happens in OAIS. Figure 3.4 indicates the correlation (which, it should be noted, is not exact).

Figure 3.4. Correlations between the DCC Curation Lifecycle Model and the OAIS Reference Model

Curation Lifecycle Model	OAIS Reference Model	Typical Actions (RLG-OCLC, 2002)
Description and Representation Information	Relevant to all OAIS activities	
Conceptualise Create or Receive Appraise and Select Reappraise Dispose	Submission and "pre-ingest" activities (not part of the OAIS Reference Model)	• Check any existing deposit schedules to ensure everything expected has been received • Assign the digital object's unique identifier(s), if not already available, and provide labels for the physical artifact • Check for viruses and validate the integrity of the digital object and its physical carrier • Assess in detail the significant properties of the digital object, such as its look and feel, or functionality • Validate or improve the documentation • Where appropriate, reformat the digital object according to repository policies • Ensure that all necessary metadata for long-term maintenance and continuing access accompanies the object (Note: Some of these actions are also applied in later stages of the lifecycle)
Ingest	Ingest	• Assign and/or validate unique identifier • Select and validate the agreed underlying technology or underlying abstract form based on the object's significant properties • Transform the object as it was submitted, along with its associated metadata, into a byte stream that can be stored on suitable hardware in the repository • Establish necessary Representation Information • Verify all Preservation Description Information
Store Migrate	Archival Storage	• Move Archival Information Packages from Ingest into permanent storage • Manage the storage hierarchy • Refresh the storage media • Provide all necessary information to allow objects to be disseminated from the repository
Preservation Action	Data Management	• Develop pricing information (if applicable) and access controls • Develop customer profiles • Track user requests • Manage security information, including any usernames, passwords, digital certificates—anything used to authenticate users of the repository • Generate statistical information to improve operation
Preservation Planning Community Watch and Participation	Preservation Planning	• Monitor the designated community • Monitor technology • Monitor the significant properties of the repository's contents • Develop preservation strategies and standards for continuing access • Develop packaging designs and migration or routine transfer plans

(Continued)

Figure 3.4. Correlations between the DCC Curation Lifecycle Model and the OAIS Reference Model *(Continued)*

Curation Lifecycle Model	OAIS Reference Model	Typical Actions (RLG-OCLC, 2002)
Store	Administration	• Negotiate submissions agreements with content producers and providers • Review procedures • Maintain systems configurations for hardware and software • Develop and maintain repository policies and standards
Access, Use, and Reuse Transform	Access	• Prepare the Dissemination Information Package (DIP) • Verify the integrity of the information in the DIP • Ensure that users have permission for access to the material

Source: Consultative Committee for Space Data Systems, 2002; Digital Curation Centre, 2008b; RLG-OCLC, 2002.

Summary: The Importance of Models

Effective digital curation is based on the use of conceptual models. One model in particular, the OAIS Reference Model, is widely used as the basis for planning digital archives. It specifies the functions that a digital archive has to perform in order to preserve data and make it understandable to users over time. The DCC Curation Lifecycle Model (used as the structural basis of this book) is another model that provides guidance for planning and carrying out digital curation. The next chapter investigates in more detail what is meant by *data* and other related terms.

References

Constantopoulos, Panos, Costis Dallas, Ion Androutsopoulos, Stavros Angelis, Antonios Deligiannakis, Dimitris Gavrilis, Yannis Kotidis, and Christos Papatheodoro. 2009. "DCC&U: An Extended Digital Curation Lifecycle Model." *International Journal of Digital Curation* 4, no. 1: 34–45. Available: www.ijdc .net/index.php/ijdc/article/viewFile/100/75 (accessed April 26, 2010).

Consultative Committee for Space Data Systems. 2002. *Reference Model for an Open Archival Information System (OAIS): Recommendation for Space Data System Standards.* Washington, DC: CCSDS Secretariat. Available: public .ccsds.org/publications/archive/650x0b1.pdf (accessed April 26, 2010).

Digital Curation Centre. 2008a. "Browse All Standards by Lifecycle Action." Edinburgh: Digital Curation Centre. Available: www.dcc.ac.uk/resources/ standards/diffuse/lifecycle/ (accessed April 26, 2010).

———. 2008b. *The DCC Curation Lifecycle Model.* Edinburgh: Digital Curation Centre, 2008. Available: www.dcc.ac.uk/docs/publications/DCCLifecycle .pdf (accessed April 26, 2010).

———. 2008c. "Frequently Asked Questions about the DCC Curation Lifecycle Model." Edinburgh: Digital Curation Centre (July 2008). Available: www.dcc.ac.uk/digital-curation/digital-curation-faqs/dcc-curation-lifecycle-model (accessed April 26, 2010).

Higgins, Sarah. 2006. "Using OAIS for Digital Curation." Edinburgh: Digital Curation Centre (October 4, 2006). Available: www.dcc.ac.uk/resource/briefing-papers/introduction-curation/using-oais-curation (accessed April 26, 2010).

———. 2007. "Draft DCC Curation Lifecycle Model." *International Journal of Digital Curation* 2, no. 2 (December): 82–87. Available: www.ijdc.net/index.php/ijdc/article/viewFile/46/30 (accessed April 26, 2010).

Humphrey, Charles. 2006. "E-science and the Life Cycle of Research" (March 2006). Available: datalib.library.ualberta.ca/~humphrey/lifecycle-science 060308.doc (accessed April 26, 2010).

International Organization for Standardization. 2003. *Space Data and Information Transfer Systems—Open Archival Information System—Reference Model.* Standard 14721:2003. Geneva: International Organization for Standardization.

Knight, Gareth. 2006. *A Lifecycle Model for an E-print in the Institutional Repository.* Nottingham: SHERPA DP. Available: citeseerx.ist.psu.edu/viewdoc/download?doi=10.1.1.132.1916&rep=rep1&type=pdf (accessed April 26, 2010).

Lavoie, Brian. 2000. "Meeting the Challenges of Digital Preservation: The OAIS Reference Model." Dublin, OH: OCLC. Available: www.oclc.org/research/publications/archive/2000/lavoie/ (accessed April 26, 2010).

National Library of Australia. 2004. "National Library Standards Activities." Available: www.nla.gov.au/services/standards.html (accessed April 26, 2010).

Paradigm Project. 2005–2007a. "Digital Archives & the Records Cycle." In *Workbook on Digital Private Papers.* Paradigm Project. Available: www.paradigm.ac.uk/workbook/introduction/paradigm-lifecycle.html (accessed April 26, 2010).

———. 2005–2007b. *Workbook on Digital Private Papers.* Paradigm Project. Available: www.paradigm.ac.uk/workbook (accessed April 26, 2010).

Research Data Strategy Working Group. 2008. *Stewardship of Research Data in Canada: A Gap Analysis.* Ottawa: National Research Council Canada. Available: data-donnees.gc.ca/docs/GapAnalysis.pdf (accessed April 26, 2010).

RLG-OCLC. 2002. *Trusted Digital Repositories: Attributes and Responsibilities.* Mountain View, CA: Research Libraries Group. Available: www.oclc.org/programs/ourwork/past/trustedrep/repositories.pdf (accessed April 26, 2010).

Defining Data

This chapter investigates in more detail what is meant by the term *data* and by other related terms. The investigation of definitions is necessary because it allows an important question to be better addressed: What exactly is it that we want to curate?

Chapter 1 noted that the definitions of the terms *data*, *digital object*, and *database* (see sidebar) used in this book come from the DCC Curation Lifecycle Model (Digital Curation Centre, 2008). They are located in the innermost of the concentric rings (the bull's-eye) of the lifecycle and apply to all of the lifecycle's actions.

The precise meanings of these definitions need to be teased out. One way of doing this is to seek to answer further questions, such as these: Exactly what kinds of digital objects are the concern of digital curation? All kinds or just certain kinds? Exactly what kinds of databases?

Note that the term *data* as defined by the DCC and as used throughout this book is not limited to scientific data. Rather, it applies to any information in digital form, regardless of the context in which it is created, managed, and used. This could be in scientific and scholarly contexts but equally in libraries and archives, and it also applies to personal information in digital form.

As noted in Chapter 1, knowing the origin of the definitions used in the DCC Curation Lifecycle helps us understand the current concerns and emphases of digital curation better. Because of digital curation's origins in e-science there was initially a heavy focus on scientific data. This focus is now being widened to include humanities and social science data.

Data as Digital Heritage

UNESCO has a longstanding interest in the preservation of digital materials. Its *Charter on the Preservation of the Digital Heritage*, adopted in 2003, encompasses "information created digitally" as well as information "converted into digital form from existing analogue resources" and lists the types of digital materials as including "texts, databases, still and moving images, audio, graphics, software and web-

---

Data refers to "any information in binary digital form." It includes *digital objects* and *databases*.

Digital objects can be simple or complex. "*Simple digital objects* are discrete digital items; such as textual files, images or sound files, along with their related identifiers and metadata. *Complex digital objects* are discrete digital objects, made by combining a number of other digital objects, such as Web sites."

Databases are "structured collections of records or data stored in a computer system."

(*Source*: Digital Curation Centre, 2008.)

---

pages, among a wide and growing range of formats" (UNESCO, 2003a: 1). This list is considerably expanded in UNESCO's *Guidelines for the Preservation of Digital Heritage*. In the *Guidelines* the materials that encompass digital heritage (carefully qualified with the words "at the time of writing"—this work was published in 2003) is wide-ranging and includes:

- **Electronic publications**: "information that is made available for wide readership," such as digital publications distributed via the web, or on carriers (CDs, DVDs, diskettes, e-book devices); they may be in traditional publication forms, such as monographs or serials, or there may be no analog equivalent, such as e-zines or websites.
- **"Semi-published" materials**: examples are pre-print papers and dissertations in e-print archives usually available for restricted use.
- **Organizational and personal records**: business and government records are increasingly created and managed in electronic records management systems.
- **Data sets**: data collected to "record and analyse scientific, geospatial, spatial, sociological, demographic, educational, health, environmental and other phenomena."
- **Learning objects**: developed for and used in educational settings, often in learning management systems.
- **Software tools**: software applications of all kinds.
- **Unique unpublished materials**: a very wide range of materials; research reports are an example.
- **Electronic "manuscripts"**: examples are drafts of works and personal correspondence.
- **Entertainment products**: produced by the film, music, broadcasting and games industries.
- **Digitally generated artworks and documentary photographs**.
- **Digital copies of nondigital materials**: examples of these include images, sound, text, and three-dimensional objects (derived from UNESCO, 2003b: 29–30).

Born-Digital *and* Digitized Data

Born-digital materials are defined by the Digital Preservation Coalition (2008) as materials "which are not intended to have an analogue equivalent, either as the originating source or as a result of conversion to analogue form." (This definition is, perhaps, too narrow. Born-digital materials, that is, materials created using a computer and therefore existing in a digital version, may also have an analog equivalent. The important point is the use of a computer to create the material.) *Digitized* materials are the result of a process of digitizing analog materials.

This distinction, between data that are born digital and data that are the product of a digitizing process, is not usually important for digital curation practice. Digital curation makes little distinction between born-digital and digitized data in most of the curation lifecycle actions—data, whatever their origin, still need to be appraised and selected, ingested, stored, and used and reused. A distinction is, however, made between born-digital and digitized data in the earlier actions of the lifecycle. The *Conceptualise* and *Create or Receive* Sequential Actions are intended to ensure that data are in the best possible shape to be curated; they attempt to ensure that data are preservation-ready. (Chapters 9 and 10 note this in more detail.)

The UNESCO *Guidelines* notes that the quantity of digital copies of analog materials is increasing rapidly but provides a caution—"Having originally been generated from non-digital sources, these might appear to be less vulnerable, but many of them are the only surviving version of originals that have since been damaged, lost or dispersed" (UNESCO, 2003b: 30). We often assume that an original analog version of material resulting from a digitizing project will remain in existence and such material is, therefore, less vulnerable than born-digital data because of the possibility of going back to the original analog version and digitizing it again. However, this assumption is not always correct. Examples abound of the disappearance of analog versions because they have been damaged, lost, deliberately destroyed, or dispersed. One example of such a loss was recently documented in accounts of an attempt to recreate a virtual version of the extensive collection of Islamic manuscripts in the Oriental Institute in Sarajevo after their destruction by Serb nationalists in 1992 (Riedlmayer, 2004). The high cost of digitizing may also be a major factor in determining whether it is possible to go back to an original analog version to digitize it again.

Data—And Much More

Another important consideration is that there is a wide variety of kinds of digital information and digital objects. The preceding example of digital heritage illustrates this point. The following examples of data generated by and used in e-science provide another illustration.

Discussions of digital curation often give the examples of data generated and used in science contexts. This is not surprising given digital curation's origins in e-science, as noted earlier in this chapter, and the increasing use of data in science. A key report from the National Science Foundation (2007: 21) illustrates the increasing use of data in relation to research and education for science and engineering, which are "increasingly data-intensive" because of networks, computers, and digital instrumentation. Each day immense quantities of data are produced, accessed, analyzed, integrated, and stored, as already noted in Chapter 1.

But the phrase "scientific data" used without qualification is not very helpful in getting a sense of its volume and diversity. In the scientific context, data are very diverse indeed. We can, however, identify some generic categories. One taxonomy is:

- **research collections**: for example, local data generated in a laboratory or research project;
- **community collections**: for example, genome databases such as MGI-Mouse Genome Informatics, "the international database resource for the laboratory mouse, providing integrated genetic, genomic, and biological data to facilitate the study of human health and disease" (Jackson Laboratory, accessed 2010); and
- **reference collections**: for example, the Protein Data Bank, containing "information about experimentally-determined structures of proteins, nucleic acids, and complex assemblies" (Research Collaboratory for Structural Bioinformatics, accessed 2010) and providing tools and resources. (From the National Science Foundation taxonomy, as summarized by Liz Lyon, 2007: 15)

Other taxonomies have been developed. One characterizes scientific data as *canonical* or *episodic*. Canonical data does not change; episodic data does (e.g., information about climates). Another considers data as *raw*, *processed*, and *derived* data and *metadata*; yet another considers data in terms of its type: *"omics"* (fields of study in biology, such as proteinomics and genomics), *observational, simulations, multimedia, surveys, performances, computational, software*, and so on (Lyon, 2007: 15). Taxonomies such as these illustrate the variety, range, and different purposes of data. Although these taxonomies have been developed for and applied in science contexts, they can also be applied in other fields.

It is not just the very large and numerous scientific data sets that we wish to curate. Data cannot always be readily separated from the tools that act on them, analyze them, and interpret and present them. (An example in common use is an online currency converter, which manages constantly changing data and presents an analysis of that data on the fly.) Lyon notes that "many layers of subsequent interpretation act upon and transform the data" (Lyon, 2007: 15). New scientific methods are developing to analyze, manipulate, and present these data. New tools are being developed to mine, analyze, and visualize large data sets: examples are DNA sequence analysis, sky surveys, and "monitoring socioeconomic dynamics over space and time" (National Science Foundation, 2007: 21). The National Science Foundation (2007: 22) definition of data encompasses all of these additional layers:

> any and all complex data entities from observations, experiments, simulations, models, and higher order assemblies, along with the associated documentation needed to describe and interpret the data.

Note the words "simulations, models, and higher order assemblies"; that is, the products of manipulating data sets are included in this definition. The definition also includes "the associated documentation needed to describe and interpret the data"; this is noted in detail in Chapter 6. The acceptance of this definition expands the range of data and digital objects we may wish to curate.

Computer simulations are an example of these newer kinds of digital objects. These are computer programs that imitate or represent how something works and are used for purposes such as observing how systems might behave or to find out how a system operates. They are in common use in many scientific contexts. nanoHUB, a web resource for nanotechnology, is one example. It "offers simulation tools which you can access from your web browser, so you can not only learn about but also simulate nanotechnology devices" (Network for Computational Nanotechnology, accessed 2010). Examples of simple online simulations are plentiful, such as a simulation of an early wooden printing press (atlas.lib.uiowa.edu/press-animation.html) and some simple simulations in learning objects developed for grades K–6 (www.eduplace.com/kids/hmsc/content/simulation/).

Visualizations are another example of these newer kinds of digital objects. They apply computer programs to data sets in order to communicate results, summaries, or other characteristics of the data set in a visual form. A simple example of visualization can be seen at the nanoHUB website (nanohub.org/about) where analysis of the usage of this resource over time is presented both on a map of the world and as a graph.

Simulations and visualizations may require curation, and this poses many questions: Do we curate the result of the simulation or visualization, or the application and the data set it was applied to, or just the data set? Do we curate all of the results generated by running simulation or visualization applications? Some visualizations are very large files, so keeping them may not be feasible in terms of the resources that are needed for their curation and for their appraisal (see Chapter 11).

There are other kinds of digital objects to curate, too, such as those that handle the processes of searching, integrating, and analyzing scientific data. Workflow software is increasingly being adopted by scientists. It allows scientists to quickly put together a set of software applications that automates data-handling procedures. Not only do workflows speed up scientific processes by automating repetitive processes, they also provide a means of reliably replicating scientific practice. An example of workflow software is the open source Taverna workbench (taverna.sourceforge.net). This allows scientists using a standard desktop computer (PC, UNIX, or Apple) to develop workflow processes and run them from their desktop. Goble and de Roure (2008: 11) summarize the significance of workflow software as "a reliable and transparent means for encoding a scientific method that supports reproducible science and the sharing and replicating of best-of-practice and know-how through reuse." Workflows, like the data sets on which they operate, also require systematic curation.

Metadata Is Data Too

Metadata, according to the National Science Foundation (2007: 22), "summarize data content, context, structure, interrelationships, and provenance (information on history and origins). They add relevance

---

FURTHER VISUALIZATION EXAMPLES

- "Many Eyes: Listing Visualizations" (manyeyes.alphaworks.ibm.com/manyeyes/visualizations?sort=rating)
- "Flowing Data" (flowingdata.com/category/visualization)

and purpose to data, and enable the identification of similar data in different data collections." In Chapter 6, this list of functions that metadata perform is added to and described in detail. The key point to note at this point is that metadata, too, need curation. The National Science Foundation (2007: 22) also includes in its definition of data that requires curation "the associated documentation needed to describe and interpret the data." In the DCC's Curation Lifecycle this is called *Description Information* and may also need to be curated. Chapter 6 examines metadata in more detail.

Databases

Databases are specifically noted in the DCC Curation Lifecycle as "structured collections of records or data stored in a computer system" (Digital Curation Centre, 2008). Data in databases are structured and controlled by database management software. Databases are widely used in contexts where their preservation is mandatory for a range of reasons, one being compliance with government regulations. Their curation poses many problems, not the least of which is their often constantly changing content.

Curation of databases is carried out in various ways. One of these requires taking snapshots of the database at specified intervals of time and curating these snapshots separately from the database. Another approach is to remove selected records from the live database and curate these separately. This process places a heavy emphasis on appraisal and selection (see Chapter 11) of records in the database in accordance with specified requirements (Müller, 2009).

Summary: New Kinds of Data

We are now in a better position to answer the question posed at the start of this chapter—What exactly is it that we want to curate? As well as data, digital objects, and databases (as defined by the DCC Curation Lifecycle), metadata, documentation, and "higher order assemblies" such as the examples of visualization and workflows noted above need to be curated. This curation will need to take place in all contexts, ranging from the handling of personal digital information to large data sets in science and humanities contexts.

And there will be more. New forms of digital heritage and new uses for already existing types of data will emerge. (Consider how social networking sites such as Facebook and Twitter have altered in a very short time the ways in which people and groups communicate and exchange data). Procedures, practices, and theories of digital curation must be open and flexible enough to accommodate new kinds of data and digital objects and new ways of using them.

The next chapter examines what is involved in digital curation—who is responsible for it and who does it—and considers the different roles of digital curators, archivists, preservation administrators, and other players in the curation arena.

References

Digital Curation Centre. 2008. *The DCC Curation Lifecycle Model*. Edinburgh: Digital Curation Centre. Available: www.dcc.ac.uk/docs/publications/ DCCLifecycle.pdf (accessed April 26, 2010).

Digital Preservation Coalition. 2008. "Introduction." In *Preservation Management of Digital Materials: The Handbook*. York: Digital Preservation Coalition (November 2008). Available: www.dpconline.org/graphics/intro/definitions .html (accessed April 26, 2010).

Goble, Carole, and David de Roure. 2008. "Curating Scientific Web Services and Workflows." *EDUCAUSE Review* 43, no. 5: 10–11.

Jackson Laboratory. "About MGI." Bar Harbor, ME: Jackson Laboratory. Available: www.informatics.jax.org/mgihome/projects/aboutmgi.shtml (accessed April 26, 2010).

Lyon, Liz. 2007. *Dealing with Data: Roles, Rights, Responsibilities and Relationships Consultancy Report*. Bath, England: UKOLN. Available: www.ukoln .ac.uk/ukoln/staff/e.j.lyon/reports/dealing_with_data_report-final.doc (accessed April 26, 2010).

Müller, Heiko. 2009. "Database Archiving." Edinburgh: Digital Curation Centre (February 2, 2009). Available: www.dcc.ac.uk/resources/briefing-papers/introduction-curation/database-archiving (accessed April 26, 2010).

National Science Foundation. 2007. *Cyberinfrastructure Vision for 21st Century Discovery*. Arlington, VA: National Science Foundation. Available: www.nsf.gov/pubs/2007/nsf0728/index.jsp (accessed April 26, 2010).

Network for Computational Nanotechnology. "nanoHUB.org: About Us." West Lafayette, IN: Network for Computational Nanotechnology. Available: nanohub.org/about (accessed April 26, 2010).

Research Collaboratory for Structural Bioinformatics. "PDB: An Information Portal to Biological Macromolecular Structures." Piscataway, NJ: Research Collaboratory for Structural Bioinformatics. Available: www.rcsb.org/pdb (accessed April 26, 2010).

Riedlmayer, A. 2004. "The Bosnian Manuscript Ingathering Project." In *Ottoman Bosnia: A History in Peril* (pp. 27–38), edited by M. Koller and K Karpat. Madison: University of Wisconsin Press.

UNESCO. 2003a. *Charter on the Preservation of Digital Heritage*. Paris: United Nations Educational, Scientific and Cultural Organization. Available: portal.unesco.org/ci/en/files/13367/10700115911Charter_en.pdf/Charter _en.pdf (accessed April 26, 2010).

———. 2003b. *Guidelines for the Preservation of Digital Heritage*. Paris: Information Society Division, United Nations Educational, Scientific and Cultural Organization. Available: unesdoc.unesco.org/images/0013/001300/ 130071e.pdf (accessed April 26, 2010). *Guidelines for the Preservation of Digital Heritage*, March 2003 (pp. 29–30), © UNESCO 2003; used by permission of UNESCO.

Key Requirements for Digital Curation

The four chapters in Part II examine the four Full Lifecycle Actions of the DCC Curation Lifecycle Model. These Full Lifecycle Actions define and describe the essential basic requirements for all aspects of digital curation. They apply to all of the Sequential Lifecycle Actions that are noted in Part III.

Chapter 5 covers the Full Lifecycle Action *Curate and Preserve*. It examines what digital curation aims to do, gives an overview of how these aims are achieved, and notes the roles of data creator, users, and curator.

Chapter 6 examines the Full Lifecycle Action *Description and Representation Information*—the metadata and other information that are essential for effective data curation.

Chapter 7 notes the essential nature of planning in data curation by describing another Full Lifecycle Action, *Preservation Planning*. It describes the need for planning at all stages of curation, notes the importance of developing policy for all aspects of digital curation, and refers to recent research into the costs of digital curation.

Chapter 8 completes the examination of Full Lifecycle Actions by describing the role of and key activities associated with *Community Watch and Participation*—the process of keeping up-to-date and participating in developments to advance and improve curation activities.

Curation and Curators

Chapter 5 examines the Digital Curation Centre (DCC) Curation Lifecycle's Full Lifecycle Action *Curate and Preserve*. The Full Lifecycle Actions, as noted in Chapter 3, apply to all stages of the Lifecycle and in the Lifecycle's diagram are surrounded by the Sequential Actions. They relate not just to the other Full Lifecycle Actions next to them in the Lifecycle diagram. They are also interdependent; for example, although Curate and Preserve is largely concerned with management and administration, it also applies to another Full Lifecycle Action, Description and Representation Information (see Chapter 6), which produces information that needs to be managed and administered. Conversely, Description and Representation Information is also required for effective management of data.

The activities that comprise the Curate and Preserve Full Lifecycle Action are stated in the DCC Curation Lifecycle Model as: "Be aware of, and undertake management and administrative actions planned to promote curation and preservation throughout the curation lifecycle" (Digital Curation Centre, 2008). This chapter examines in more detail what digital curation aims to do, what these management and administrative actions are, and who carries them out.

Aims of Digital Curation

In Chapter 1 the differences between digital preservation and digital curation were noted. In this chapter these differences are revisited, and the aims of digital curation are examined further. *Digital preservation* refers to activities aimed at ensuring that we can access data, digital objects, and databases in the future—for longer than the life span of the software and hardware used in their creation and initial maintenance. Many definitions of digital preservation exist. Here are three of them:

1. "All of the actions required to maintain access to digital materials beyond the limits of media failure or technological change" (Digital Preservation Coalition, 2008: 24).

2. "The managed activities necessary for ensuring both the long-term maintenance of a bytestream and continued accessibility of its contents" (RLG-OCLC, 2002: 3).

3. "The processes of maintaining accessibility of digital objects over time" (UNESCO, 2003: 161).

The key point of these definitions is that digital preservation is a set of managed activities aimed at ensuring that the bit stream is maintained and that data in all forms are accessible for a defined period of time. But digital preservation is not the same thing as digital curation. Chapter 1 noted the brief definition of *digital curation* provided by the DCC, which emphasizes adding value, trusted information, and active management of data in addition to preservation (Digital Curation Centre, "DCC Charter").

Digital preservation is a necessary part of curation, but by itself it is not sufficient. Preserving just the data, for example, copying the bit stream onto new forms of data storage, does not ensure that the digital objects that these data comprise will be usable in the future. This is where digital curation comes into play. It requires that data be actively managed and appraised so that their integrity is protected and their value is enhanced, with the aim of making them useful and usable in the future. To do this, we have to actively manage data over the whole of their life. This is where the Curate and Preserve action in the Curation Lifecycle comes into play. It requires us to know about, and apply, management and administrative actions that promote curation and preservation wherever they apply in the curation lifecycle.

Digital curation aims to produce and manage data in ways that ensure they retain three characteristics: longevity, integrity, and accessibility. *Longevity* refers to the availability of the data for as long as their current and future users (the Designated Community; see Chapter 6) require them. The life span of data is short unless action is taken. The length of time that data need to be maintained varies, but the minimum period of time usually exceeds the life expectancy of the access system (the hardware and software designed to view and/or use the data). *Integrity* refers to the authenticity of data —that they have not been manipulated, forged, or substituted. Because digital preservation techniques such as migration inevitably alter the data, authenticity has to be demonstrated by paying attention to such characteristics as provenance (where the data came from) and context (the circumstances surrounding the creation, receipt, storage, or use of data and their relationship to other data). *Accessibility* requires that we can locate and use the data in the future in a way that is acceptable to their designated community. For example, an image (such as a PDF) may be acceptable for some digital objects (such as documentation), but for other objects (a database, for example) the ability to manipulate or interrogate that object may be required by its Designated Community in the future.

Scope of Digital Curation

How are the aims of ensuring the integrity of digital objects over time and maintaining access to them achieved? To achieve the aims the digital objects need to be managed, and this is the focus of the Curate and Preserve action described in this chapter. Some techniques that are commonly applied are listed here. (This section is based on the National Library of Australia's "Recommended Practices for Digital Preservation," accessed 2010.)

Ensuring Longevity

The main digital curation practices in common use that ensure the long life of digital objects include:

- refreshing data (moving data to a newer version of the same storage medium, or to different storage media, with no changes to the bit stream);
- checking accuracy of the results of refreshing;
- generating metadata that document the processes applied to refreshing data;
- maintaining multiple copies of the bit stream; and
- keeping track of changes (especially obsolescence) in hardware, software, file formats; and standards that might have an impact on digital preservation.

Ensuring Integrity

The main practices in common use that ensure the authenticity of digital objects include:

- refreshing data;
- checking accuracy of the results of refreshing;
- generating metadata that document the processes applied to refreshing data;
- protecting data by managing them in accordance with good IT practices for data security, backups, and error checking;
- maintaining multiple copies of the bit stream; and
- managing intellectual property and other rights.

Maintaining Accessibility

The key practices in current use include:

- maintaining the ability to locate digital materials reliably by assigning persistent identifiers to them to ensure they can be found;
- recording sufficient representation information for digital objects so that the bit stream is still meaningful and understandable in the future;
- producing digital objects in open, well-supported standard formats;
- limiting the range of preservation formats to be managed (often by normalizing data to standard formats);

- keeping track of changes (especially obsolescence) in hardware, software, file formats, and standards that might have an impact on digital preservation; and
- maintaining multiple copies of the bit stream.

There is considerable overlap among the three groups of techniques. Each of these practices can be linked to at least one, and usually more, of the specific actions in the Curation Lifecycle Model. For example, the practices of producing digital objects in open, well-supported standard formats and limiting the range of preservation formats to be managed are included in the Conceptualise and Create or Receive actions (see Chapters 9 and 10); and the practice of keeping track of developments that have an impact on digital preservation is part of the Community Watch and Participation action (see Chapter 8).

Roles of Digital Curators

Whose job is it to apply and manage the actions required for digital curation? What do those people do? Digital curation encompasses a wide range of tasks. The curation of scientific data is well documented. Some of the practical and technical curation tasks for scientists and research groups are:

- applying open-source software and open standards to encourage interoperability among different software and hardware platforms;
- creating metadata and annotations so that digital objects can be reused;
- linking related research materials and making sure the links are persistent;
- using persistent identifiers;
- being consistent about citation formats;
- deciding which digital objects need to be curated over the longer term;
- keeping data storage devices current; and
- validating and authenticating migrated data. (For a more detailed listing of these tasks, see Pennock, 2006.)

Several DCC case studies describe what curation involves in practice for some areas of science (Digital Curation Centre, "Case Studies"). One of these examines the curation of geospatial data (data that identifies the geographic location of features on the Earth's surface). According to the author of this case study (McGarva, 2006), curators of geospatial data:

- create data in a reliable manner that makes their context clear;
- implement sound creation practices to ensure that their data are reusable and sustainable over time;
- clearly identify any processing the data have undergone;
- establish standards for appraisal and selection of geospatial data;

- appraise and select geospatial data for long-term curation according to standards;
- work with data creators to ensure sufficient metadata is available; and
- maintain a technology watch to ensure that data formats do not become obsolete.

While the preceding curation tasks and activities are based on practice in science contexts, nearly all of them apply more widely. For example, metadata is of equal importance for long-term management of all kinds of digital objects in all contexts.

Digital curation also requires the sharing of responsibilities. It is important to determine who the stakeholders in digital curation are, because each kind of stakeholder is likely to have different knowledge and skills and different understandings about what the digital objects are and how they are used. Several kinds of stakeholders play differing roles in the data curation process: funding bodies, discipline-based groups (e.g., scientific organizations), data creators, data users and reusers, and data curators, each with different skills, understandings, and interests.

Funding Bodies

Funding bodies support data creation by providing money for research projects or digitization projects. These bodies are increasingly concerned with making sure that the data whose creation they fund are available to a wide range of users. More and more of them require grant applications made to them include provision for digital curation (as noted already in Chapter 1). Common examples of these requirements are a data management plan, or a plan for depositing data into a publicly accessible data repository. The process of developing and submitting grant applications, and reporting on progress, generates rich documentation about the purpose of data and their nature, along with other useful information. Documentation of this kind is crucial for the reuse of those data in the future.

Discipline Groups

Groups organized around a particular discipline or set of disciplines, particularly in the sciences, have a strong interest in digital curation. They may, for example, provide software that supports data handling. An example is the Protein Data Bank (www.rcsb.org/pdb), used by biologists in fields such as structural biology, biochemistry, genetics, and pharmacology, which has a "Software Tools" link to tools for data extraction and deposition preparation, format conversion, data validation, and dictionary and data management. Another example is ArchNet, which lists archaeology software tools (archnet.asu.edu/resources/Selected_Resources/Software/general.php). They may also establish and support data repositories, such as the Global Biodiversity Information Facility (www.gbif.org). Conway (2009) notes that stakeholders, while supporting digital curation as it applies to digital objects within their own field, are not usually concerned with other disciplines. She indicates a less positive aspect of their role in digital curation, particularly in "emerging and specialist areas of scientific investigation, where much knowledge was still embedded in the data-using scientific groups, and there tended not to be mature documentation supporting the data" (Conway, 2009: 20–21).

Discipline groups are increasingly recognized as significant stakeholders in digital curation. There is a growing understanding that curation requires significant domain knowledge and that curators with this domain knowledge are more effective than those who do not possess it because they understand and can take account of the diversity of disciplinary cultures and approaches to research. There is, however, a major shortage of domain experts with digital curation expertise, as noted in Chapter 2.

Data Creators

Scientists, scholars, and researchers, singly or as members of research teams, are all involved in some of the processes of digital curation. Data creators, if they are attuned to curation requirements, ensure that the data they bring into being are structured and documented to maintain their longevity and reusability. For digital objects to be usable and reusable, they must be of high quality, well-structured, and adequately documented (Chapter 10 notes these characteristics in more detail). The best time to ensure that these characteristics are present is when the data are created. Their presence makes use and reuse of the data significantly easier. If they are missing, use and reuse becomes exponentially more difficult, if not impossible.

These criteria do not apply only to science data. All digital objects, no matter in what context, will stand a better chance of being long-lived and usable in the future if attention is paid, at the time of their creation, to their structure and to the metadata associated with them.

Adequate documentation is particularly critical for digital curation. To take an example from experimental science—in addition to data sets, information about experiments (such as details of the instrumentation) is usually noted but has not traditionally been considered important for curating the data sets. It is often informally noted in blogs or wikis and is at great risk of being lost (Conway, 2009: 20–21).

Data Users and Reusers

Scientists, scholars, and researchers—in fact anyone who uses and reuses data—are also involved in some of the processes of data curation. Data users and reusers, if aware of digital curation, ensure that any annotations they produce are captured and documented to the extent that they can be understood by other users of those data. Annotation tools are noted in more detail in Chapter 15.

Data Curators

Data curators, whose primary role is managing or looking after data, carry out a wide range of tasks. The tasks of a data curator in the biosciences context, for example, include ongoing data management, intensive data description, ensuring data quality, collaborative information infrastructure work, and metadata standards work. A fuller list of tasks and responsibilities encompassed by digital curation includes the following:

- Developing and implementing policies and services
- Analyzing digital content to determine what it can be used for
- Providing advice to creators and users/reusers of digital objects
- Ensuring submission of digital objects to a repository
- Negotiating agreements
- Ensuring data quality
- Ensuring that digital objects are structured in the best way to provide access, rendering, storage, and maintenance
- Enabling the use and reuse of digital objects
- Enabling discovery and retrieval of digital objects
- Preservation planning and implementation (e.g., ensuring appropriate storage and backup routines, obsolescence monitoring)
- Ensuring that policies and services are in place to make sure that digital objects are viable, able to be rendered, understandable, and authentic
- Promoting interoperability

The DCC website contains transcripts of interviews (Digital Curation Centre, 2004) that provide a helpful overview of the concerns and tasks of data creators, reusers, and curators. A more recent account of the work of digital curators is available in Whyte's (2008) study *Curating Brain Images in a Psychiatric Research Group*. Karasti, Baker, and Halkola (2006) discuss in detail what digital curation involves in the domain of ecological research.

The major shortage of domain experts with digital curation expertise is noted in Chapter 2. One domain, biocuration, is well advanced in both the development of its curation practice and in establishing groups for its professionals. Biocuration is "the activity of organizing, representing, and making biological information accessible to both humans and computers" (Howe et al., 2008: 47–50). In this domain there is a heavy reliance on large, complex databases that are annotated with new data by biocurators, for example, UniPROT (www.uniprot.org) for protein structures. These annotated databases link the data sets with writings on research based on these data and in some domains have become essential to scientists. The curators are typically qualified, experienced scientists who carry out tasks such as extracting knowledge from scientific papers, linking information, inspecting and correcting gene structures and protein sequences, developing and managing controlled vocabularies, ensuring clean data, assisting data users with their research, advising on the design of web-based resources, and encouraging submission of data to databases (Howe et al., 2008: 48). In 2009 a new professional body, the International Society for Biocuration, was established. Their website (www.biocurator.org) gives further information about this newly formed organization.

Summary: Managing Curation

The importance of managing curation throughout the lifecycle of data is acknowledged in the Full Lifecycle Action *Curate and Preserve*. Digital curation aims to produce and manage digital objects with the characteristics of longevity, integrity, and accessibility. The actions required to achieve this aim are the concern of a wide range of stakeholders, from individual data creators to the bodies that fund research.

The next chapter is about another Full Lifecycle Action, *Description and Representation Information*. It examines the importance of metadata (administrative, descriptive, technical, structural, and preservation metadata), standards for metadata, and why metadata is essential for adequate description and control of data over the long term. It also describes representation information, which is required to understand and render both the digital object and its associated metadata.

References

Conway, Esther. 2009. *Curating Atmospheric Data for Long Term Use: Infrastructure and Preservation Issues for the Atmospheric Sciences Community.* Edinburgh: Digital Curation Centre. Available: www.dcc.ac.uk/webfm_send/112 (accessed April 26, 2010).

Digital Curation Centre. "Case Studies." Edinburgh: Digital Curation Centre. Available: www.dcc.ac.uk/resources/case-studies (accessed April 26, 2010).

———. "DCC Charter and Statement of Principles." Edinburgh: Digital Curation Centre. Available: www.dcc.ac.uk/about-us/dcc-charter (accessed April 26, 2010).

———. 2004. "Interviews." Edinburgh: Digital Curation Centre (September–October 2004). Available: www.dcc.ac.uk/community/interviews-setting-scene (accessed April 26, 2010).

———. 2008. *The DCC Curation Lifecycle Model.* Edinburgh: Digital Curation Centre. Available: www.dcc.ac.uk/docs/publications/DCCLifecycle.pdf (accessed April 26, 2010).

Digital Preservation Coalition. 2008. *Preservation Management of Digital Materials: The Handbook.* York: Digital Preservation Coalition (November 2008). Available: www.dpconline.org/advice/digital-preservation-handbook.html (accessed April 26, 2010).

Howe, Doug, Maria Costanzo, Petra Fey, Takashi Gojobori, Linda Hannick, Winston Hide, David P. Hill, Renate Kania, Mary Schaeffer, Susan St Pierre, Simon Twigger, Owen White, and Seung Yon Rhee. 2008. "The Future of Biocuration." *Nature* 455 (4 September): 47–50.

Karasti, Helena, Karen S. Baker, and Eija Halkola. 2006. "Enriching the Notion of Data Curation in E-science: Data Managing and Information Infrastructuring in the Long Term Ecological Research (LTER) Network." *Computer Supported Cooperative Work* 15: 321–358.

McGarva, Guy. 2006. "Curating Geospatial Data." Edinburgh: Digital Curation Centre (April 5, 2006). Available: www.dcc.ac.uk/resources/briefing-papers/introduction-curation/curating-geospatial-data (accessed April 26, 2010).

National Library of Australia. "Recommended Practices for Digital Preservation." Canberra, ACT: National Library of Australia. Available: www.nla.gov.au/preserve/digipres/digiprespractices.html (accessed April 26, 2010).

Pennock, Maureen. 2006. "Curating E-science Data." Edinburgh: Digital Curation Centre (August 25, 2006). Available: www.dcc.ac.uk/resources/briefing-papers/introduction-curation/curating-e-science-data (accessed April 26, 2010).

RLG-OCLC. 2002. *Trusted Digital Repositories: Attributes and Responsibilities.* Mountain View, CA: Research Libraries Group. Available: www.oclc.org/programs/ourwork/past/trustedrep/repositories.pdf (accessed April 26, 2010).

UNESCO. 2003. *Guidelines for the Preservation of Digital Heritage.* Paris: Information Society Division, United Nations Educational, Scientific and Cultural Organization. Available: unesdoc.unesco.org/images/0013/001300/130071e.pdf (accessed April 26, 2010).

Whyte, Angus. 2008. *Curating Brain Images in a Psychiatric Research Group: Infrastructure and Preservation Issues.* Edinburgh: Digital Curation Centre. Available: www.dcc.ac.uk/webfm_send/111 (accessed April 26, 2010).

Description and Representation Information

This chapter notes *Description and Representation Information*, one of the four Digital Curation Centre (DCC) Curation Lifecycle's Full Lifecycle Actions. The activities that comprise this action are stated in the DCC Curation Lifecycle Model in these words: "Assign administrative, descriptive, technical, structural and preservation metadata, using appropriate standards, to ensure adequate description and control over the long-term. Collect and assign representation information required to understand and render both the digital material and the associated metadata" (Digital Curation Centre, 2008a). What does this mean in practice?

Higgins (2006) notes, "Metadata is the backbone of digital curation. Without it a digital resource may be irretrievable, unidentifiable or unusable." Effective digital curation relies heavily on information that is added to or associated with the digital object that is being preserved. These additions and associations occur at all points in the curation lifecycle. Maintaining just the data or the digital objects will not ensure that they are preserved, nor will it mean that they will be usable in the long term. What is needed is additional information about the data or digital objects. The key to identifying, locating, accessing, understanding, and using data and digital objects in the future is to add information about them that provides a context and, if required, provides the tools to use those data. This added information comes in several varieties:

- Metadata that describes digital objects and refers to where they are located
- Metadata that provides the technical information needed to use the digital objects
- Metadata that describes what has happened to the digital objects as they move through the curation lifecycle

The DCC Curation Lifecycle Model refers to this added information as *description information* and *representation information*. Description information is added "to ensure adequate description and control over the long term"; representation information is added "to understand and render both the digital material and the associated metadata" (Digital Curation

Centre, 2008a). The terms *description information* and *representation information* come from the Open Archival Information System (OAIS) Reference Model (see Chapter 3). Essential to OAIS is the concept of information package—a container of the digital object plus information about that object (i.e., description and representation information), which, together, allow the object to be understood and used. The OAIS Reference Model defines the kinds of description and representation information that is needed to archive and use digital objects over the long term.

The Curation Lifecycle Model's statement about the Full Lifecycle Action *Description and Representation Information* indicates that for descriptive information (or metadata) there are different kinds: administrative, descriptive, technical, structural, and preservation metadata. These types of metadata need to be constructed according to defined and accepted standards, with the aim of making sure that there are adequate descriptions of the data or digital objects to enable them to be located and controlled during the period they are curated. Representation information is different from descriptive information (the metadata) that we add to or associate with data or digital objects. Rather than allowing us to manage the data or digital objects, the role of representation information is to help us to understand data or digital objects and to render them (i.e., display, play, or otherwise use them in ways originally intended).

A further distinction between the two categories of added information—description information and representation information—is significant. The added information is developed in different ways, depending on what kind it is. It may be assigned by people (such as catalogers, curators, or data creators), or it may be automatically generated. For example, descriptive metadata is typically assigned, whereas technical metadata is typically derived from data using a computer program. This distinction is significant because constructing description and representation information is resource intensive when carried out manually, so automating this process wherever possible is considered essential in handling large quantities of data.

The key activities associated with the Description and Representation Information action are:

- appreciating the need for description and representation information;
- being aware of where description and representation information is required;
- understanding the key standards that exist for description and representation information; and
- developing policies for applying description and representation information.

The Need for Description and Representation Information

Curating digital objects is not about just the data that comprise the objects. It requires that information about the digital objects is generated and is also curated. Description and representation information allows the curator to:

- persistently identify digital objects;
- maintain reliable links to the digital objects;
- clearly describe what the digital objects are;
- clearly identify the technical characteristics of the data comprising the digital objects;
- identify who is responsible for the management and preservation of the digital objects;
- describe what can be done to the digital objects;
- describe what is needed to re-present the digital objects at the standard required by users;
- record the history of the digital objects; and
- document the authenticity of the digital objects.

This information also allows users to understand the context of digital objects and their relationship to other digital objects (National Library of Australia, accessed 2010).

The converse situation—when there is insufficient and appropriate description and representation information—is that digital objects can neither be effectively managed nor accessed by those who seek to use them in the future. We may be unable to locate digital objects because the metadata is not specific enough to differentiate among them or because the location of a digital object has changed and there is no record of where it was moved to. We may not be able to read and use the digital objects because we lack sufficient knowledge about their technical properties or structure. We may not be able to understand the digital objects because we don't know enough about the context in which they were created. We may not be able to verify that the data comprising the digital objects are authentic and that we can rely on them (Cunningham, 2008).

Definitions

Administrative, descriptive, technical, structural, and preservation metadata have already been briefly mentioned. It is useful to define these and other terms associated with the Description and Representation Information action.

Description information is descriptive metadata that describes a digital object. *Metadata* is "structured information that describes, explains, locates, or otherwise makes it easier to retrieve, use, or manage an information resource" (National Information Standards Organization, 2004: 1). For our purposes, it comprises the following:

- **Administrative metadata**: metadata related to the use, management, and encoding processes of digital objects over a period of time. Includes the subsets of technical metadata, rights management metadata, and preservation metadata.

- **Descriptive metadata**: metadata that describes a work for purposes of discovery and identification, such as creator, title, and subject.
- **Technical metadata**: a form of administrative metadata dealing with the creation or storage encoding processes or formats of the resource.
- **Structural metadata**: metadata that indicates how compound objects are structured, provided to support use of the objects.
- **Preservation metadata**: administrative metadata dealing with the provenance of a resource and its archival management. (National Information Standards Organization, 2004: 15–16)

This list can be expanded with respect to curation activities. Using metadata we can note information about the controlled vocabularies applied to a digital object to classify or index its content, about other digital objects it is related to, about what processes (and hardware and software) were used to produce it, and about what processes are required to use it. There is much more: metadata records information we need for curation purposes about intellectual property rights associated with digital objects, about how they were acquired and where from, about users (who can access them, who has accessed them), about which version of the digital object is to hand, about checks of data integrity (such as checksum calculations), and about the preservation actions applied to the digital object, such as migrations. Metadata is also used to record information about the metadata itself, such as how it was created or when it was altered (Higgins, 2006).

Representation information is different. It is "either information which describes how to interpret a data object (such as a format specification), or a component of a technical environment which supports interpretation of that object (such as a software tool or hardware platform)" (Adrian Brown, cited in Rusbridge, 2008). Representation information is explained in more detail later in this chapter.

Standards for Description and Representation Information

Standards are essential for description and representation information. As indicated in other chapters (and especially in Chapter 8), data sharing and reuse, which are at the heart of digital curation, requires interoperability, which in turn requires adherence to standards. Standards that apply to description and representation information are no exception to this requirement.

Standards for description and representation information are listed and described on several websites. The DCC DIFFUSE Standards Frameworks (www.dcc.ac.uk/diffuse) include several subsections, such as standards for metadata content, metadata description, metadata structure, and thesauri and word lists. The large number of standards relevant to this topic is indicated by the further subdivision into standards for authentication, authorities, metadata content, metadata description, metadata structure, reference models and frameworks, searching protocols, thesauri and word lists, and XML DTD and schemas. The "Data Documentation & Standards" topic on the Preserving Access to Digital Information (PADI) website (www.nla.gov.au/padi/topics/29.html) notes many standards relevant to description and representation information. The Library of Congress has a "Standards" page (www.loc.gov/standards) that is also helpful.

Description Information

Metadata (which can be equated with description information) is defined formally as "structured information that describes, explains, locates, or otherwise makes it easier to retrieve, use, or manage an information resource" (National Information Standards Organization, 2004: 1). Digital objects without associated description information are impossible to curate, because not enough is known about them to ascertain what they are or whether it is worth expending resources on their curation.

Description information for curation purposes comes in several varieties:

- Metadata that describes digital objects and their location (the *descriptive metadata* and *structural metadata* noted in the Curation Lifecycle Model)
- Metadata that provides the technical information needed to use digital objects (the *technical metadata* noted in the Model)
- Metadata that describes what has happened to digital objects as they move through the curation lifecycle (the *administrative metadata* and *preservation metadata* in the Model).

Metadata that describes digital objects and indicates where they are located consists of descriptive and structural metadata. *Descriptive metadata* is information that allows digital objects to be identified so they can be linked with requests. The name of the creator of the data set and the author of a document are examples of this type of information. This category also includes *structural metadata*, which describes how compound digital objects are organized.

Metadata that provides the technical information needed to use digital objects is *technical metadata*: information about technical characteristics of them such as their format, compression or encoding algorithms, encryption and decryption keys, or software (including the release number) used to create or update the data. Technical metadata also includes information about the overall system environment: the hardware, operating systems, and application software in which the data were created. This metadata enables digital objects to be identified and processed.

Metadata that describes what has happened to digital objects as they move through the curation lifecycle consists of administrative and preservation metadata. *Administrative metadata* is information about the use, management, and encoding processes of digital objects over a period of time; in other words, lifecycle data. It includes information about the creation of digital objects, subsequent updates, transformation, versioning, summarization, and descriptions of migration and replication. This kind of metadata is necessary to enable data, databases, and digital objects to be managed effectively.

Definitions of the different varieties of metadata vary according to the context and there is sometimes overlap, especially about what kinds of metadata are described as preservation metadata. This is illustrated in Figure 6.1.

Preservation Metadata

Preservation metadata is defined on the PADI website as "structured ways to describe and record information needed to manage the preservation of digital resources." It is used to store "technical details on the format, structure and use of the digital content, the history of all actions performed on the resource including changes and decisions, the authenticity information such as technical features or custody history, and the responsibilities and rights information applicable to preservation actions" (National Library of Australia, 2007).

Preservation metadata is essential for ensuring the long-term accessibility of digital objects. It does this by providing a mechanism to record information about the digital objects so that they are described in sufficient

Figure 6.1. Description Information and Its Functions

	Broad Function	Type	Specific Function	Examples
Descriptive Information	Describes data and their location	Descriptive metadata	Allows data to be identified so they can be linked with requests	Name of the creator of the data set Name of the author of a document
		Structural metadata	Describes how compound digital objects are organized	Relationship of TIFF page image to other page images
	Provides the technical information needed to use data	Technical metadata	Provides the technical information needed to use data	Format Compression or encoding algorithms Encryption and decryption keys Software (including release number) used to create or update the data
			Provides information about the overall system environment	Hardware, operating systems, application software in which the data were created
	Describes what has happened to data as they move through the curation lifecycle	Administrative metadata	Provides information about the use, management, and encoding processes of digital objects over a period of time	Information about data creation, subsequent updates, transformation, versioning, summarization Descriptions of migration and replication
		Preservation metadata	Records the preservation actions that have been applied to data over time	File format Significant properties Technical environment Fixity information

detail to identify them and to record information about the requirements that must be met to use them. It also provides a way of recording the preservation actions that have been applied to the digital objects over time. More specifically, preservation metadata:

- Identifies the material for which a preservation programme has responsibility
- Communicates what is needed to maintain and protect data
- Communicates what is needed to re-present the intended object (or its defined essential elements) to a user when needed, regardless of changes in storage and access technologies
- Records the history and the effects of what happens to the object
- Documents the identity and integrity of the object as a basis for authenticity
- Allows a user and the preservation programme to understand the context of the object in storage and in use. (UNESCO, 2003: Section 14.20)

What kind of information is commonly recorded in preservation metadata? The file format of a digital file is one kind. This often consists of a reference to a unique identifier for the format in a format registry (format registries are noted in Chapter 13). Significant properties (the properties or characteristics of a digital object that must be maintained over time; see Chapter 10) are another. An important kind of preservation metadata is environment information, recording the technical environment in which a digital object is used, such as the hardware, software, and other files required to use it. Fixity information, indicating whether a file has changed, is recorded usually in the form of a checksum calculation and the algorithm used to produce it. (This and the following paragraph are based on Priscilla Caplan's [2006] installment on preservation metadata in the *DCC Curation Reference Manual*, recommended for further study of preservation metadata.)

Technical metadata, another kind of preservation metadata, describes the technical characteristics of files and bit streams. Some of these characteristics are required for all files, for example, size, format, and fixity information. Other characteristics are relevant only to specific file types or formats; audio files, for example, require information about duration of the sound recording, sampling frequency, bit rate, compression, and the number of tracks and their relationships. Details of a digital object's provenance (see Chapter 15) are also recorded in the preservation metadata. Provenance information could include where a digital object originated and who has had custody of it, who created it, who owns the rights to it, and what preservation actions have been applied to it (with details of what the preservation action was, when it was applied, who and what was involved, and the result). The way in which metadata is associated with the content (digital object) to create an information package is also recorded in preservation metadata.

All digital curation actions require metadata. Providing adequate quantities of appropriate metadata is a major challenge. The ideal is to collect metadata by automated processes close to the point of data creation

> A **format registry** is an online listing of definitive technical information about file formats. Format registries play an important role in supporting long-term access to digital objects. Examples of format registries include the Global Digital Format registry (www.gdfr.info) and PRONOM (www.nationalarchives.gov.uk/PRONOM), in 2010 in the process of being combined to form the Unified Digital Format Registry (www.udfr.org).

Automated software tools for extracting technical metadata from digital objects, and tools for converting this extracted metadata into XML schema elements, are available. Examples include the National Library of New Zealand's Metadata Extraction Tool, and the Ecological Metadata Language editor. These are noted further in Chapter 13.

so that the need for costly human input is minimized. For example, all the information about an experiment, the environment, the people, as well as the data flowing from the equipment and samples should ideally be captured through automated processes without human intervention. Automated software tools for extracting technical metadata from digital objects, and tools for converting this extracted metadata into XML schema elements, are available and are noted in Chapter 13.

Persistent Identifiers

Persistent identifiers are labels for digital objects that remain the same regardless of where the object is located. They allow us to refer to a digital object and locate it even when it moves to other servers or to other repositories or archives. Reliable identification of data and digital objects is essential for providing long-term access to them and ensuring their reliability and authenticity, thus enabling their reuse over time. We need to know where to find the data or digital object, and persistent identifiers help us do so. If a digital object is moved, it can always be located through its persistent identifier, which does not change. A persistent identifier is also a unique identifier, one that refers to only a single digital object and can, therefore, help reduce confusion if there are several versions of a resource.

Much of the discussion of persistent identifiers has been about their application to web resources. The normal way of identifying web material is to use a Uniform Resource Locator (URL). However, a URL points to only one web location and, if the location of material at the URL changes (e.g., if the material is moved from one domain name to another), the URL changes and the material becomes inaccessible. Many schemes exist for application to web resources. Those encountered most frequently include the Uniform Resource Name (URN), the Persistent Uniform Resource Locator (PURL), and the widely used Digital Object Identifier (DOI) which has achieved National Information Standards Organization (NISO) standard status as ANSI/NISO Z39.84. The "Persistent Identifiers" page on the PADI website provides a summary of the major persistent identifier schemes for web resources and gives a comprehensive list of publications about the topic (National Library of Australia, 2002). The use of persistent identifiers is not limited to web material; it is equally essential for linking and citation of primary research with data sets. (Two good sources of further information about persistent identifiers have been written by Joy Davidson [2006] and Emma Tonkin [2008].)

Metadata Schemas and Standards

Metadata schemas are the formal expressions of the individual kinds of metadata (or elements). These are often adopted as metadata standards that, because they provide standardized ways of selecting metadata and of expressing it, allow the results to be shared among more than one organization. Sharing is essential for effective curation, as noted elsewhere in this book (especially in Chapter 8). Using standards for metadata ensures that the description information created is consistent and indicates the elements that are required to manage and curate the digital objects they describe.

Metadata standards provide standards in three areas: structure, semantics, and syntax. How the metadata is structured is indicated by noting the elements that are described; the semantics describe the meanings of each element; and the syntax indicates how to write the metadata.

Different kinds of metadata standards are available and are often used in combination in curation contexts. Some of the widely applied standards for preservation metadata are noted next. There are many such standards, some of which are discipline specific. The aim here is to indicate examples to illustrate how they work, not to offer a comprehensive listing.

One characteristic of many of the metadata standards used in digital curation is that they are XML based. Using standards based on XML has numerous advantages. XML is an open (nonproprietary), well-supported, and widely adopted standard for encoding textual data, designed to be used regardless of the hardware platform. It is well supported by open software applications, and, because it has been in use since 1996 and was based on SGML (Standardized General Markup Language), an ISO standard that predates XML by ten years, it is widely understood. The use of XML allows metadata to be exchanged and reused by different archives because the way the metadata is expressed is standardized. Other advantages are that data in XML are human readable and structured hierarchically, making them easier to check if the data become corrupted. Reese and Banerjee (2008: 97–107) provide an informative section in their book on this topic titled "Why Use XML-Based Metadata?"

The most common metadata standards applied to digital curation are Preservation Metadata: Implementation Strategies (PREMIS), Metadata Encoding and Transmission Standard (METS), Metadata Object Description Schema (MODS), and Metadata Authority Description Schema (MADS), noted in more detail in the following sections. These are all related to XML, although in different ways. PREMIS exists independently of XML but is often used in conjunction with METS, which is a standard for expressing descriptive information in XML. MODS and MADS combine XML and guidelines for developing metadata. Underlying all of these standards is XML, which allows the metadata developed to be expressed in a standardized way.

PREMIS

Several preservation metadata schemas have been developed, PREMIS being one of the most widely adopted. The *PREMIS Data Dictionary for Preservation Metadata* (2008) defines a core set of preservation metadata elements that has wide applicability in the preservation community. It defines preservation metadata as metadata that:

- supports the viability, renderability, understandability, authenticity, and identity of digital objects in a preservation context;
- represents the information most preservation repositories need to know to preserve digital materials over the long-term;
- emphasizes "implementable metadata": rigorously defined, supported by guidelines for creation, management, and use, and oriented toward automated workflows; and
- embodies technical neutrality: no assumptions made about preservation technologies, strategies, metadata storage and management, etc. (*PREMIS Data Dictionary for Preservation Metadata*, 2008: 1)

The PREMIS data model defines relationships between digital preservation "entities":

- **Intellectual Entities**: not defined in PREMIS. Users are expected to apply other relevant metadata standards. Examples are a particular book, map, photograph, database, or website.

- **Objects** (divided into three types: representation, file, and bit stream): what the repository preserves. Examples are a PDF file, an audio stream in uncompressed PCM, and a video stream in MJPEG.

- **Events**: actions on an object in the preservation repository. These document provenance and track the history of the object. Examples are the action of verifying that a file is well formed and creating a new version of an object in a more contemporary format (i.e., migration).

- **Agents**: people, organizations, or software programs associated with preservation events in the life of an object.

- **Rights**: an agreement with a rights-holder that allows a repository to take actions in relation to objects in the repository. An example is an organization giving permission to make copies of an object.

PREMIS is used in conjunction with other applicable metadata standards where appropriate. The PREMIS schema has been endorsed for use with METS. PREMIS maintenance is sponsored by the Library of Congress.

METS

METS (www.loc.gov/standards/mets) is a standard for encoding in XML the metadata describing or characterizing digital objects. It provides a means of associating all the metadata about a digital object with the object—that is, it is a "container format" specifying how different kinds of metadata can be packaged together (Caplan, 2008: 16). METS was developed with reference to the OAIS Reference Model's information package concept. The Library of Congress supports METS by acting as its maintenance agency.

METS encourages interoperability by providing a standard for exchanging digital materials among institutions. As the quantity of digital objects being curated increases, so too does the amount of metadata required for curation. When digital objects are shared between repositories, the metadata about them is also shared, so a common data transfer standard greatly increases the effectiveness of this sharing process. METS is designed to provide this interoperability.

A METS XML document has five major sections (based on the Library of Congress's "METS: An Overview & Tutorial," accessed 2010):

- **Descriptive metadata**: contains pointers to external descriptive metadata (e.g., a MAchine Readable Cataloging [MARC] record in a library catalog) or contains descriptive metadata, or both.

- **Administrative metadata**: provides information about how the files were created and stored, intellectual property rights, the original source object, and the provenance of the files comprising the digital object.

- **File groups**: lists all files comprising all versions of the digital object.

- **Structural map**: outlines a hierarchical structure of the digital object, linking the parts of that structure to content files and metadata about each element.

- **Behavior**: used to associate executable behaviors with content in the METS object.

MODS and MADS

MODS (www.loc.gov/standards/mods) is a standard developed by the Library of Congress for encoding descriptions of information resources. It consists of a bibliographic element set expressed in XML so that metadata developed using this schema can be readily shared. MODS is designed to allow the importing of existing catalog data that is in MARC 21 format, so it is especially valuable if there is legacy metadata in MARC format that needs to be moved to another metadata standard.

Associated with MODS is MADS (www.loc.gov/standards/mads). MADS is also an XML schema, developed to complement MODS and to use data in MARC 21 format. It is used to describe and provide authority control for names of people, organizations, events, and terms. MADS can be used independently of MODS but is designed to work well with it.

Metadata standards are often used in combination in curation contexts. Dappert and Enders (2008) illustrate how three metadata standards, METS, MODS, and PREMIS, each with different aims, work together in a system for archiving e-journals. Some elements can be expressed in more than one standard; for example, both METS and PREMIS provide for file format information, but PREMIS allows linking to the PRONOM format registry while METS does not. Both were used. Dappert and Enders (2008) conclude that "no single existing metadata schema accommodates the representation of descriptive, preservation and structural metadata."

However, the use of XML-based standards such as METS, PREMIS, and MODS cannot be assumed in all contexts. There are many metadata standards in widespread use that have been developed for specific communities. As one example, geospatial data uses metadata schemas developed specifically for it, such as ISO 19115 *Geographic Information—Metadata* and extensions based on it, but these do not accommodate some preservation metadata. In particular, these geospatial metadata standards "do not provide a wrapper function that would allow additional technical or administrative metadata elements to be associated with . . . the data producer-originated metadata," such as administrative metadata noting information about the acquisition of the data, technical metadata related to data integrity, or metadata recording preservation actions applied to the data by the archive. The geospatial community has not to date sought to combine metadata developed according to its standards with preservation metadata based on the METS and PREMIS standards (McGarva, Morris, and Janée, 2009: 22–25).

Representation Information

Representation information is a key concept in curation but one that is "often misunderstood" according to Rusbridge (2007). Representation information is the information required to make a bit stream retrievable as a meaningful digital object. It describes how to interpret a digital object (such as a format specification) or a component of a technical environment that supports interpretation of that object (such as a software tool or hardware platform; as noted by Chris Rusbridge [2008] in a Digital Curation Blog posting).

Representation information is added to data and digital objects so we can understand and render both the digital material and the associated metadata. We need more than just the information about the file format to ensure that the bit stream is accessible and understandable over time. We also need information about operating system and hardware dependencies, character encoding, and algorithms, among other things. Without representation information, digital objects are just a sequence of meaningless binary information. As the DCC puts it:

> Digital objects are stored as bitstreams which are not understandable to a human being without further data to interpret them. Representation information is the extra structural or semantic information which converts raw data into something more meaningful. For example, structure information could tell a computer to interpret a string of bits as ASCII characters, and semantic information could explain what a particular mathematical symbol means. (Digital Curation Centre, accessed 2008b: Q6)

A case study of curation in the eCrystals Data Repository emphasizes the need for adequate representation information. Representation information is collected and maintained because it reduces the risks of not being able to understand information in the future. Documentation for data formats, software, standards, and programming languages that become obsolete is needed, as is documentation of the specialized knowledge about how to manipulate the data (Patel and Coles, 2007). Another example of representation information (RI) is provided by Rusbridge (2007), who asks us to "imagine a social science survey dataset encoded with SPSS [common statistical software]. We may have all the capabilities required to interpret SPSS files, but still not be able to make sense of the dataset if we do not know the meaning of the variables, or do not have access to the original questionnaires. Both the latter would qualify as RI."

OAIS and Representation Information

The concept of representation information is derived from the OAIS Reference Model (see Chapter 3), which categorizes the information required for preservation as Content Information, Representation Information, Preservation Description Information (broken down into Reference, Context, Provenance, and Fixity Information), and Packaging Information. The representation information category is divided into three classes: Structure Information, Semantic Information, and Other Representation Information.

Representation information is required to "understand and render" the digital material. How is "understandable" defined? Understandable to whom? The answer to these questions lies in the OAIS Reference Model. The information being preserved should be "independently understandable to the Designated Community"; that is, members of the Designated Community do not require expert assistance to understand and use the information of that community. The archive needs to understand the knowledge and requirements of the Designated Community in order to ensure that appropriate representation information is available. This is further examined in "Appendix 2: Understandability & Use" in *Trustworthy Repositories Audit & Certification: Criteria and Checklist* (RLG-NARA Task Force on Digital Repository Certification, 2007: 77–80).

Representation information takes various forms. *Structure Information* describes the formats and data structures relevant for processing and rendering digital objects. Structure information is usually information about file formats. File formats used for processing are often open standards, and formal descriptions of these formats assist in automated processing. File formats for rendering are, by comparison, more likely to be commercially based and proprietary formats, making it more difficult or impossible to record their structure. If the file formats and data structures of digital objects created by proprietary software cannot be recorded, it may be necessary to keep the original software or other software that provides access to the digital object.

Semantic Information provides additional information about the content of a digital object, particularly information that defines relationships among objects or parts of objects. Examples include data dictionaries, ontologies, and thesauri. For a spreadsheet, for example, semantic information could indicate which units of measurement have been used for which data values.

Other Representation Information is any other kind of representation information thought necessary to interpret the digital object. It could be information about relevant software, hardware, and storage media, encryption or compression algorithms, or documentation. Time-dependent information is another example; some data sets change over time, and it may be important to record the state of a data set at specific points in time, such as on a particular date or when a specific action has occurred.

Two examples illustrate these points. The first is of a binary file produced by Portable Document Format (PDF) software, containing information in English describing a medical procedure. For this the Designated Community is defined as having a knowledge base typical of second-year medical students who read English; if they are to understand the file they need to see it rendered in the same way it was rendered when it was originally submitted to the archive. To achieve this, the representation information needed is information about the PDF-A format. The archive curates and provides to the Designated Community the binary file, preservation description information about the file, and a PDF-A rendering application. The second example is of a musical score for a synthesizer, in a nonproprietary binary format. The Designated Community is defined as German readers who wish to generate music from a digital representation of the score, using a computer and synthesizer. To understand the score they need the binary bit stream, plus information about the PDF-A format, both in German. In both cases the archive may not itself curate the PDF-A specifications and rendering application but may instead provide a link to a repository where these are available. (These examples come from "Appendix 2: Understandability & Use" in *Trustworthy Repositories Audit & Certification: Criteria and Checklist* [RLG-NARA Task Force on Digital Repository Certification, 2007: 77–80] where more examples can be found.)

Sharing Representation Information

Representation information needs to be curated in its own right. It needs to be stored in association with the digital object and other metadata so that the digital object can be understood and rendered in the future. It may be stored by the repository that stores the digital objects or stored externally by another reliable repository. Much representation information is not unique and can be applied to many digital objects—it can be reused. One way to do this is to establish repositories of representation information. These help to reduce duplication of effort in developing representation information and to share knowledge and expertise (Brown, 2008: 10).

Collecting and maintaining adequate representation information is a major endeavor. One example of a repository to assist this undertaking is the Representation Information Repository established by the Cultural, Artistic and Scientific Knowledge for Preservation, Access and Retrieval (CASPAR) project and the DCC (registry.dcc.ac.uk:8080/Registry Web/Registry/index.jsp). Representation information can be deposited in the registry so that it becomes an authoritative source of representation information for the data curation community. Format registries such as PRONOM (developed by The National Archives [United Kingdom]) and the Unified Digital Format Registry (formed by the merger of the Global Digital Format Registry and PRONOM from 2010) can also be considered as representation information repositories. They provide details about file formats, which are essentially the Structure Information category of representation information. Adrian Brown's (2008) paper is a useful source of further information.

Policies for Description and Representation Information

As is the case for all aspects of curation, policies are needed to guide the use of description and representation information. The key aspects that policy should address are the determination of who has access to description and representation information and under what conditions, reuse, the kinds of description and representation information that are required, and the metadata standards and schemas that will be applied. (This section is based on *Policy-making for Research Data in Repositories: A Guide* [Green, Macdonald, and Rice, 2009], a compilation of considerations that have been aggregated from numerous sources, as stated and listed in the guide.) A policy relating to who has access to description and representation information and under what conditions might, for example, specify that description and representation information is available without charge to anyone. A policy about reusing description and representation information could consider whether prior permission is needed, whether it can be reused for commercial purposes, or whether it should be made available for harvesting by other organizations.

Policies and their associated procedures for the kinds of description and representation information that are required and where such information is drawn from are likely to be very detailed. They could include statements about what description and representation information must be supplied to the archive and by whom; for example, the data creator may be required to provide a codebook for statistical data, or a format specification, or an explanation of the research protocol or methodology. Procedures that specify what metadata standards are used in the provision of description information might, for example, prescribe that descriptive metadata is created using MODS.

Summary: Curation Needs Metadata

Description and representation information is commonly considered to be essential for curation but is also, perhaps, the factor that restricts effectiveness the most. There are limits to the human resources that can be applied to curation, given the massive quantities of data that are involved, so automation of as many of the curation processes as possible is necessary. Metadata is critical to support this high level of automation. Ideally it is automatically created when the data are created and is then available when the data are ingested into the long-term archive. There has, however, been very little progress toward achieving this ideal.

Much effort has been expended on aspects of description and representation information, but there is more to be done. Caplan's (2006: 23) comments about preservation metadata are apposite:

> Many specifications for preservation metadata have been published and significant progress has been made towards standardizing a core set of preservation metadata elements. However…the success of preservation metadata in supporting long-term preservation is largely untried. The metadata recorded today is our best guess of what will be useful tomorrow. As more experience is gained with various preservation strategies and different preservation repository systems, we can expect our understanding of preservation metadata to grow increasingly more sophisticated in the future.

Librarians and archivists are very familiar with the need for metadata to support curation activities, but for curating digital objects the requirements are more extensive, especially those for preservation metadata. For individuals who create digital objects, metadata is equally important. Consider, for example, the difficulty of searching through hundreds of digital photographs labeled JPEG1, JPEG2, JPEG3, and so on.

The next chapter describes *Preservation Planning*, another Full Lifecycle Action. It notes the need for planning for preservation throughout the curation lifecycle of data and digital objects and also notes the importance of policy for curation.

References

Brown, Adrian. 2008. *White Paper: Representation Information Registries*. London: PLANETS. Available: www.planets-project.eu/docs/reports/Planets _PC3-D7_RepInformationRegistries.pdf (accessed April 26, 2010).

Caplan, Priscilla. 2006. *DCC Digital Curation Manual: Instalment on Preservation Metadata*. Edinburgh: Digital Curation Centre. Available: www.dcc.ac.uk/ resources/curation-reference-manual/completed-chapters/preservation-metadata (accessed April 26, 2010). Used by permission of Priscilla Caplan.

———. 2008. *The Preservation of Digital Materials* (Library Technology Reports 44, no. 2). Chicago: ALA TechSource.

Cunningham, Adrian. 2008. "The Uses of Metadata in Public Administration." Glasgow: Digital Preservation Europe (November 7, 2008). Available: www.digitalpreservationeurope.eu/publications/briefs/uses_of_metadata_in _public_administration.pdf (accessed April 26, 2010).

Dappert, Angela, and Markus Enders. 2008. "Using METS, PREMIS and MODS for Archiving eJournals." *D-Lib Magazine* 14, no. 9/10 (September/ October). Available: www.dlib.org/dlib/september08/dappert/09dappert .html (accessed April 26, 2010).

Davidson, Joy. 2006. "Persistent Identifiers." Edinburgh: Digital Curation Centre (October 18, 2006). Available: www.dcc.ac.uk/resources/briefing-papers/ introduction-curation/persistent-identifiers (accessed April 26, 2010).

Digital Curation Centre. 2008a. *The DCC Curation Lifecycle Model*. Edinburgh: Digital Curation Centre. Available: www.dcc.ac.uk/docs/publications/ DCCLifecycle.pdf (accessed April 26, 2010).

———. 2008b. "Frequently Asked Questions about the DCC Curation Lifecycle Model" (July 2008). Edinburgh: Digital Curation Centre. Available: www .dcc.ac.uk/digital-curation/digital-curation-faqs/dcc-curation-lifecycle-model (accessed April 26, 2010).

Green, Ann, Stuart Macdonald, and Robin Rice. 2009. *Policy-making for Research Data in Repositories: A Guide*. Version 1.2. Edinburgh: EDINA and University Data Library. Available: www.disc-uk.org/docs/guide.pdf (accessed April 26, 2010).

Higgins, Sarah. 2006. "What Are Metadata Standards?" Edinburgh: Digital Curation Centre (August 30, 2006). Available: www.dcc.ac.uk/resources/ briefing-papers/standards-watch-papers/what-are-metadata-standards (accessed May 6, 2010).

Library of Congress. "METS: An Overview & Tutorial." Washington, DC: Library of Congress. Available: www.loc.gov/standards/mets/METSO verview.v2.html (accessed April 26, 2010).

McGarva, Guy, Steve Morris, and Greg Janée. 2009. *Preserving Geospatial Data* (Technology Watch Report). York: Digital Preservation Coalition. Available: www.dpconline.org/technology-watch-reports/download-document/363-preserving-geospatial-data-by-guy-mcgarva-steve-morris-and-gred-greg-janee.html (accessed April 26, 2010).

National Information Standards Organization. 2004. "Understanding Metadata." Bethesda, MD: NISO Press. Available: www.niso.org/publications/press/ UnderstandingMetadata.pdf (accessed April 26, 2010). Reprinted with permission from the National Information Standards Organization (NISO). Original text © NISO Press, 2004.

National Library of Australia. "Digital Preservation: Critical Elements of Preserving Digital Collections." Canberra, ACT: National Library of Australia. Available: www.nla.gov.au/preserve/digipres/elements.html (accessed April 26, 2010).

———. 2002. "PADI—Persistent Identifiers." Canberra, ACT: National Library of Australia. Available: www.nla.gov.au/padi/topics/36.html (accessed April 26, 2010).

———. 2007. "PADI—Preservation Metadata." Canberra, ACT: National Library of Australia (July 2007). Available: www.nla.gov.au/padi/ topics/32.html (accessed April 26, 2010). Used by permission of the National Library of Australia.

Patel, Manjula, and Simon Coles. 2007. *A Study of Curation and Preservation Issues in the eCrystals Data Repository and Proposed Federation*. Bath: UKOLN. Available: www.ukoln.ac.uk/projects/ebank-uk/curation/eBank 3-WP4-Report (Revised).pdf (accessed April 26, 2010).

PREMIS Data Dictionary for Preservation Metadata. 2008. Version 2.0. Washington, DC: PREMIS Editorial Committee. Available: www.loc.gov/ standards/premis/v2/premis-2-0.pdf (accessed April 26, 2010).

Reese, Terry, and Kyle Banerjee. 2008. *Building Digital Libraries: A How-To-Do-It Manual*. New York: Neal-Schuman.

RLG-NARA Task Force on Digital Repository Certification. 2007. *Trustworthy Repositories Audit & Certification: Criteria and Checklist*. Chicago: Center for Research Libraries. Available: www.crl.edu/sites/default/files/attachments/ pages/trac_0.pdf (accessed April 26, 2010).

Rusbridge, Chris. 2007. "Representation Information: What Is It and Why Is It Important?" Digital Curation Blog, comment posted July 6, 2007. Available:

digitalcuration.blogspot.com/2007/07/representation-information-what-is-it.html (accessed April 26, 2010).

———. 2008. "Representation Information from the Planets?" *Digital Curation Blog,* comment posted April 14, 2008. Available: digitalcuration.blogspot.com/2008/04/representation-information-from-planets.html (accessed April 26, 2010). Used by permission of Chris Rusbridge, Digital Curation Centre.

Tonkin, Emma. 2008. "Persistent Identifiers: Considering the Options." *Ariadne* 56 (July). Available: www.ariadne.ac.uk/issue56/tonkin (accessed April 26, 2010).

UNESCO. 2003. *Guidelines for the Preservation of Digital Heritage.* Paris: Information Society Division, United Nations Educational, Scientific and Cultural Organization. Available: unesdoc.unesco.org/images/0013/001300/130071e.pdf (accessed April 26, 2010). © UNESCO 2003; used by permission of UNESCO.

Preservation Planning and Policy

This chapter investigates *Preservation Planning*, one of the four Full Lifecycle Actions in the Digital Curation Centre (DCC) Curation Lifecycle Model. Preservation planning is the ongoing process of planning data curation activities. The activities contained in the Preservation Planning action are referred to in the DCC Curation Lifecycle Model in these words: "Plan for preservation throughout the curation lifecycle of digital material. This would include plans for management and administration of all curation lifecycle actions" (Digital Curation Centre, 2008). The key activities encompassed by Preservation Planning are:

- appreciating the need for planning at all stages of curation,
- developing plans for all stages of curation, and
- periodically reviewing and updating curation procedures.

This chapter notes the need for planning throughout the curation lifecycle of digital material. It also describes the importance of developing policy for all aspects of digital curation and refers to the findings of recent research into the costs of digital curation.

Risk Management as the Context for Preservation Planning

To ensure their long-term accessibility, authenticity, and integrity, digital objects need to be managed over the whole of their lifecycle, beginning at the point when they are created. To achieve the active management of data throughout their lifecycle, "constant maintenance and elaborate 'lifesupport' systems' must be planned" (Hedstrom, 2002: 3). Planning is intrinsic to the OAIS Reference Model on which most digital archives are based (see Chapter 3). In the OAIS Reference Model, the *Preservation Planning* function covers the development of preservation strategies, undertaking technology watch and other planning and policy activities.

One way of thinking about the planning process is to consider it as proactive preservation activities aimed at minimizing risks. The active

RISK MANAGEMENT: MORE EXAMPLES

Information storage media failure—affects ability to access digital objects

Equipment obsolescence—affects ability to access digital objects

Insufficient metadata—makes digital objects more difficult to preserve

Inadequate ongoing resourcing—threatens the viability of an organization

Physical disasters—threaten digital objects and storage

management of risks over time is essential to preserve digital objects and to ensure that they remain usable in the future. A risk management approach is increasingly common in the preservation of both digital and nondigital materials.

Risk management is aimed at reducing the likelihood that compromising events will occur and at limiting their impact when they do occur. A straightforward example is the reduction of risk from virus attack by using virus protection software and ensuring it is regularly updated. Another example is making regular backups and checking the integrity of the backups to minimize the risks of loss if data become corrupted. Planning for risk reduction activities and their implementation is critical.

One major area where planning is required is during the creation of digital objects—for example, planning to create them in open, well-supported, uncompressed, and stable file formats. (This is noted further in Chapters 9 and 10.) Planning to do this reduces the risk, later in the digital object's life, that file formats will become obsolete, thereby decreasing the odds of being able to use those digital objects in the future.

Broad principles of risk management have become standard practice for digital preservation. They include protecting data by implementing a regular backup procedure; maintaining multiple copies of the bit streams; having disaster recovery contingencies in place; providing secure and stable media storage conditions; copying data to more stable media at defined intervals; and ensuring data security by implementing procedures for virus protection and unauthorized access. To these can be added maintaining ongoing access to digital materials by ensuring sufficient relevant metadata is associated with data sets, possibly limiting the range of formats that the archive manages, community watch activities to monitor for obsolescence and applicable new developments, and collaboration to develop solutions. Applying a risk management approach requires planning at all stages of the curation lifecycle. Planning provides information about digital objects that are at risk, determines the actions required to reduce risk, and ascertains the resources required (Clifton, 2005).

Risk management is not the only context in which planning for digital curation takes place. The requirements of research funding bodies also specify that a data management plan and plans for data sharing, curation and preservation be included in applications for funding. (An indication of these requirements can be seen in "Table 2: Summary of Research Data Policies of Research Funders" of a report on the establishment of a research data service for the United Kingdom [Serco Consulting, 2008: 9–12]). For example, the Wellcome Trust (accessed 2010), a major funder of medical research, expects researchers to "plan at the proposal stage how they will manage and share their data."

Key Planning Steps

Planning for each Sequential Action of the Curation Lifecycle Model, and also for some of the Full Lifecycle Actions, is essential.

Planning for Sequential Actions

The design of data and representation information is planned at the *Conceptualise* stage so that the data can be preserved and reused in optimal ways. Collecting data needs planning (in the *Create or Receive* action of the Lifecycle) to ensure that they, together with relevant description and representation information, are collected in ways that ensure their accuracy. To ensure that decisions are consistent, *Appraise and Select* requires planning and the development of selection and retention policies. Preparing digital objects to add to a digital archive and adding them to a digital archive (the *Ingest* activities) require planning the procedures for assigning persistent identifiers, for virus checking, for authenticity checks such as checksums, and for many other processes. Planning to store digital objects so that they retain their authenticity is essential in the *Preservation Action* stage. In *Store*, planning to develop sustainable models and long-term institutional commitment to preserving digital objects is necessary. Planning to ensure that digital objects are accessible to users and reusers is the basis of the *Access, Use, and Reuse* action; examples are planning to provide multiple access methods to digital objects, to heighten their visibility and enable reuse, and determining metadata that assists in their discovery.

Planning for Full Lifecycle Actions

The *Curate and Preserve* Full Lifecycle Action is concerned with the management and administration of curation and preservation (see Chapter 5) and focuses on actions that ensure the longevity of digital objects, their authenticity, and that they remain accessible. Planning is a prerequisite for all of these. For example, planning is needed to manage multiple copies of a bit stream (where they are stored, how their authenticity is checked, and so on). The *Description and Representation Information* Full Lifecycle Action (see Chapter 6) necessitates planning to ensure that sufficient and appropriate representation information to describe the digital objects and record their storage and manipulation is available, that digital objects are consistently cited according to relevant standards so they can be analyzed and reused, and that relevant metadata are added so the digital objects are discoverable.

Steps to take in planning for curation have been codified. One example is the British Atmospheric Data Centre (BADC) *Data Management Plan Template* (British Atmospheric Data Centre, 2008?). Application of this template helps ensure that the aims of curation are achieved through defining responsibilities, creating a high-quality archive, supporting data creators and users, and adhering to conditions associated with the use and deposition of the data. The template poses questions under these topics:

- Rights and responsibilities
- What is the dataset
- Format of dataset
- Metadata—information about the data

- Ownership of data
- Data archiving
- Storage and backup
- Data distribution
- Access to third-party data
- Publications
- Liaison between data repository and dataset users/program participants

The questions relating to the "Ownership of data" section ask "Who has ownership of the data? Is it copyrighted/protected? What is the source of the data?" In the "Storage and backup" section, the questions are:

> Who is responsible for the integrity of the data? Is this the primary archive of this data or is it mirrored from elsewhere? How difficult would it be to replace and would it be important to replace it? How often should it be backed up? . . . And onto what medium—disc, tape, . . . How long should the archive keep the data? What should we do with it after this time? (British Atmospheric Data Centre, 2008)

Appendixes to the data management plan that is developed by applying the template cover conditions for depositing data in the archive, for using data from the archive, and for accessing those data; a list of data sets is also attached to the data management plan. (Chapter 10 is also relevant to planning curation processes.) The DCC also released for consultation in 2009 a draft template of a "Data Management Plan Content Checklist" (Donnelly and Jones, 2009).

Planning for active management of data and digital objects over the whole of their lifecycle is based on evaluating potential solutions or sets of actions against the requirements of an archive, then developing a plan based on this evaluation. To date there are relatively few software tools to assist in this process, so it continues to be largely manual. One software tool that has been developed is Plato, an outcome of the Preservation and Long-Term Access through Networked Services (PLANETS) project (www.planets-project.eu). The background to the PLANETS project's preservation planning interests and Plato's development has been summarized by Martin Donnelly (2008). Plato is a decision support tool that assists in making decisions about which preservation actions best suit the digital objects that planners are interested in preserving. It is available as open-source software (www.ifs.tuwien.ac.at/dp/plato/intro.html).

Policy for Curation

What Policies Address

Developing policies for all aspects of digital curation is vital for its effectiveness. This section notes the kinds of policies that are required and what they contain. Policies relating to specific actions in the curation lifecycle are noted in other chapters: for example, Chapter 9, "Creating Data," includes a section about policies for creating and receiving data.

Policies provide clear, long-term direction and guidance and are regularly reviewed and updated. They provide long-term guidance by unambiguously stating principles, values, and intentions. Their value lies in the clear articulation of these so that expectations are confirmed and explicit and consistent decisions can be made on the basis of the statements they contain.

Having policies about curation in place assists an organization to develop a digital curation strategy and to plan coherent digital curation programs. They ensure and reinforce accountability: for instance, they serve to demonstrate that funds can and will be used responsibly and ensure consistency in this. Other benefits of having policies in place include protecting organizations if they are accused of any wrongdoing, indicating clearly to staff what is acceptable practice and what is not, and stating to the rest of the world that the organization takes its curation responsibilities seriously.

In addition to policies about curation, procedures for curation should be in place. Unlike the general statements in policies, the substance of procedures is very specific. Policies are implemented through procedures, which describe the process of implementing policy and work together with policies to achieve the overall goals of an organization. For example, a policy about ingest might state that digital objects are normalized, that the version that precedes the normalized version is also deposited in the archive, that the object is given a unique identifier and checked for viruses before ingest. The procedures related to this policy will document in more detail what happens: for example, the range of file formats that are accepted, the range of file formats they are normalized to and the steps to take in the normalization process, the steps to take to capture the version before it is normalized, the naming conventions used to provide a unique identifier, and the standards and software used to check for the presence of viruses.

Although the contents of policies will clearly differ according to an organization's mission and requirements, good policies usually have elements in common. They state what is allowed and what is not allowed. They indicate how the policy will be monitored and who has the responsibility for ensuring this. They note links to other relevant policies and to statements about procedures. They also note the date when they are to be reviewed and how frequently review should occur.

The central role of policy can be seen in the *Administration* function of the OAIS Reference Model (see Chapter 3). The *Administration* function is carried out through lower-level functions, one of which is *Establish Standards and Policies*. Based on inputs such as budget information and scope of an organization, this function establishes standards and policies that are implemented by other functions in the OAIS Reference Model. For example, this *Establish Standards and Policies* function develops storage management policies that are implemented by the *Archival Storage* higher-level function and policies about format and documentation standards and procedures that are implemented by the higher-level function *Ingest* (International Organization for Standardization, 2003: Figure 4.5).

Kinds of Policies Required

What kinds of policies should be in place? The OAIS Reference Model suggests that policies are required for archival storage (e.g., for managing migration), management (e.g., resource utilization, pricing), disaster recovery, and security (e.g., physical access control).

Examples of policies developed for digital curation are available on the PADI website (www.nla.gov.au/padi/topics/172.html). One of these is the UK Data Archive's Preservation Policy. Section 5.3.1 notes the policy for *Physical data preservation and storage* and illustrates how policies are written and what they contain:

> In order to best safeguard long-term preservation, the UKDA follows a policy of multiple copy resilience. Five versions of the complete preservation system are held: main near-line copy (on the main preservation server) and a shadow copy (on main preservation server). Both are held on the main area on the Hierarchical Storage Management (HSM) system and are presently accessed only by the dedicated preservation user. The storage media used for this copy is SDLT and disc cache area. The access online copy (on the mirror preservation server) is held in a RAID 5 disc system and copies are generated for user access and dissemination. There are also a near-site online copy kept on a RAID 5 disc system on a server located in another building within the University of Essex, and an off-site online copy. Finally a disc-based offline copy exists, which are held in either DVD-R or CD-R copy. The UKDA follows best practice in the storage and housing of magnetic and optical media. In particular, for environmental conditions for storage media (BS 4783, ISO/IEC22051, BS ISO 18921:2002 and BS ISO 18925:2002) and for the storage of archival materials (BS 5454). (Woollard, 2009: 10)

The Trusted Digital Repository certification places heavy emphasis on policies (see Chapter 14). The requirements for achieving Trusted Digital Repository status state that policies must be in place. One of the requirements is A3.2: "Repository has procedures and policies in place, and mechanisms for their review, update, and development as the repository grows and as technology and community practice evolve." These policies need to be complete, readily available, and kept up to date and evolve as circumstances change. They should address at least the core areas of "transfer requirements, submission, quality control, storage management, disaster planning, metadata management, access, rights management, preservation strategies, staffing, and security." These are accompanied by documented procedures about "day-to-day practice and procedure" (RLG-NARA Task Force on Digital Repository Certification, 2007: 13). Specifically noted in Appendix 3, which lists the minimum documentation required (RLG-NARA Task Force on Digital Repository Certification, 2007: 81), are policies for legal permissions, policies and procedures relating to feedback, recording access actions and access, as well as documented procedures and disaster plans.

An essential guide to developing policy is *Policy-making for Research Data in Repositories* developed by the DISC-UK Data Share Project (Green, Macdonald, and Rice, 2009). Its valuable guidance covers six key areas where policies are helpful. The first of these areas relates to the content of the archive: its scope, the kinds of data it handles, file formats it will accept, and so on. The second area is policy relating to metadata: who has access to it, its reuse, types required, and sources and metadata schemas adopted. Third is policy relating to the ingest of data: who is eligible to deposit it, the quality requirements for that data, policy around confidentiality of data, and rights relating to that data. The fourth area is policy about access, use, and reuse of data. Fifth is policy applying to preservation of data: retention periods, fixity, and authenticity are included. Finally, policy about the withdrawal of data from the archive is important.

Although the importance of policy for digital curation is well recognized, policies are not as widespread as their significance warrants. Digital preservation policies were examined in a study commissioned by JISC in 2008. This study identified the lack of digital preservation policies and the resulting low priority paid to it in strategic planning. The two volumes of this study present an analysis of existing policies and offer excellent advice to developers of preservation policies through a model and numerous examples (Beagrie et al., 2008).

Costs of Curation

Planning for curation calls for estimates of the resources required and identification of where these resources will come from. Planning is difficult because the costs of curating data are not yet fully understood, despite considerable research into determining them and into the development of cost models.

Two British research projects that are investigating costs are the Life Cycle Information for E-Literature (LIFE) project and the Keeping Research Data Safe project. The LIFE project (www.life.ac.uk) has produced a model of the digital lifecycle and a methodology for estimating costs based on that lifecycle. The LIFE model establishes the costs associated with each phase of the lifecycle: creation or purchase; acquisition; ingest; metadata creation; bit stream preservation; content preservation; and access. It also acknowledges costs outside the lifecycle that need to be considered, such as costs of management and administration, systems and infrastructure, and economic adjustments such as inflation (Wheatley et al., 2007). A later phase of this project, under way in 2009–2010, is developing the model further by analyzing more examples and is producing a software tool for the prediction of costs.

The first phase of the Keeping Research Data Safe project investigated the costs of preserving research data in British universities (www.jisc.ac .uk/publications/documents/keepingresearchdatasafe.aspx). The second phase (www.beagrie.com/jisc.php) builds on this work by identifying long-lived data sets and analyzing the costs of preserving them.

The costs of digital preservation are being investigated by the Blue Ribbon Task Force on Sustainable Digital Preservation and Access (brtf.sdsc.edu). Economic sustainability is its focus—how to determine costs and then ensure that the resources are available for preservation activities by identifying sustainable economic models. Its interim report identified barriers to achieving economic sustainability. These included the inadequacy of current funding models that are often for one-off projects and not sustained, lack of recognition of the urgency of the issues, and fear that digital access and preservation are too hard to take on (Blue Ribbon Task Force, 2008).

Costs of ensuring accessibility to research data are also being actively investigated by other bodies. The Alliance for Permanent Access, whose aim is to "foster the development of an ecosystem of trusted digital repositories to enable Europe to fully exploit the potential of European scientific collaboration," made the theme of its 2008 conference *Keeping the Records of Science Accessible: Can We Afford It?* (Alliance for Permanent Access, 2008). The conference report noted that precise costing of digital preservation is not possible, as there are too many variables depending on such factors as the type, quality, and quantity of data and the access required to them. However, factors that influence costs can be determined. Also noted was the importance of timeliness as a factor influencing costs. It is far cheaper to properly curate data at the creation stage; adding or changing "bad" metadata is prohibitively expensive after time has passed. The experience of the Archaeology Data Service (ads.ahds.ac.uk), it was noted, is that the highest percentage of overall costs occur at the Acquisition and Ingest stages rather than the Storage and Preservations stages—42 percent and 23 percent, respectively (Alliance for Permanent Access, 2008: 3). Clearly, then, planning *before* curation activities begin is well worthwhile.

Even though the costs of digital curation are not yet fully known, practitioners are able to report costs in some areas from their experience. Costs of storage were the subject of recent postings on e-mail lists. These noted that costs of ingest and data management can dominate storage costs, and, as the quantities of data stored increase, the cost of power becomes a significant factor in overall costs. "And as the cost of purchasing storage goes down, the cost of managing it goes up" (Ashley, 2009).

The costs of preserving RAW file versus Tagged Image file Format (TIFF) files (both used to store data about images) were explored in a series of postings (e.g., Rusbridge, 2008). For image files, the compression used in the format is a factor; a JPEG 2000 file takes about one-third of the storage space as an uncompressed TIFF file. This makes a sizeable difference in costs of storage if large numbers of files are being considered. But the answer is not so simple. For example, because files formats act differently their choice has consequences for curation. The example was cited of a one-byte error having only a minimal effect on an uncompressed TIFF, but the same one-byte error could affect 17 percent of a JPEG 2000 file because of the way the file is constructed. Other factors noted were the costs of labor, hardware maintenance, software maintenance, media replacement at specified intervals, capital equipment replacement, software licenses, and electricity. The frequency of data migrations also affects cost, as they involve intervention by people, so, no matter how much migration processes are automated, their labor costs are unlikely to decrease.

Ways to measure the costs of digital curation are not yet clearly established. It should not be forgotten, however, that many other factors besides costs play a role in determining the economic sustainability of digital curation. These include developing and maintaining secure business models, presenting compelling business cases, and collaborating in networks of preservation partners (LeFurgy, 2009: 425). All of these require considerable planning.

Summary: Planning for Active Management

The planning of digital curation activities occurs at every stage of the curation lifecycle. It should be based on policy, which also needs to be articulated for every stage of the curation lifecycle. The costs of curation should be considered when planning, but the current state of our understanding of costs makes such consideration problematic.

Planning of digital curation is not the prerogative of those who work with scientific or scholarly data. It is, of course, highly essential for libraries and archives that manage digital objects both for immediate access and for longer-term storage and later reuse, as the previous examples show. Planning is also highly applicable to many aspects of curating personal data. An obvious example is planning a regular backup regime for personal data—and implementing it!

The next chapter describes the fourth Full Lifecycle Action of the DCC Curation Lifecycle, *Community Watch and Participation*. It notes the reasons for and processes involved in keeping up-to-date and participating in developments to advance and improve curation activities.

> ### PRESERVATION PLANNING: REVIEW
>
> **Key points:** *Preservation Planning* is the ongoing process of planning data curation activities.
>
> **Key activities:**
> - Appreciate the need for planning at all stages of curation
> - Develop plans for all stages of curation
> - Periodically review and update curation procedures

References

Alliance for Permanent Access. 2008. *Keeping the Records of Science Accessible: Can We Afford It?* The Hague: Alliance for Permanent Access. Available: www.alliancepermanentaccess.eu/index.php?id=3 (accessed April 26, 2010).

Ashley, Kevin. 2009. "Cost of Digital Archiving." The dcc-associates Listserv, comment posted June 5, 2009. Available: www.mail-archive.com/dcc-associates @lists.ed.ac.uk/msg00175.html (accessed April 26, 2010).

Beagrie, Neil, Najla Semple, Peter Williams, and Richard Wright. 2008. *Digital Preservation Policies Study. Part 1, Final Report.* Salisbury: Charles Beagrie Ltd. Available: www.jisc.ac.uk/media/documents/programmes/preservation/ jiscpolicy_p1finalreport.pdf (accessed April 26, 2010).

Blue Ribbon Task Force. 2008. *Sustaining the Digital Investment: Issues and Challenges of Economically Sustainable Digital Preservation.* Washington,

DC: Blue Ribbon Task Force. Available: brtf.sdsc.edu/biblio/BRTF_ Interim_Report.pdf (accessed April 26, 2010).

British Atmospheric Data Centre. 2008. "DMP Template." Didcot, UK: BADC.

Clifton, Gerald. 2005. "Risk and the Preservation Management of Digital Collections." *International Preservation News* 36 (September): 21–23. Available: www.ifla.org/VI/4/news/ipnn36.pdf (accessed April 26, 2010).

Digital Curation Centre. 2008. *The DCC Curation Lifecycle Model.* Edinburgh: Digital Curation Centre. Available: www.dcc.ac.uk/docs/publications/ DCCLifecycle.pdf (accessed April 26, 2010).

Donnelly, Martin. 2008. "PLANETS Testbed." Edinburgh: Digital Curation Centre (September 4, 2008). Available: www.dcc.ac.uk/resources/briefing-papers/technology-watch-papers/planets-testbed (accessed April 26, 2010).

Donnelly, Martin, and Sarah Jones. 2009. "Data Management Plan Content Checklist: Draft Template for Consultation." Edinburgh: Digital Curation Centre (June 17, 2009). Available: www.dcc.ac.uk/docs/templates/DMP_ checklist.pdf (accessed April 26, 2010).

Green, Ann, Stuart Macdonald, and Robin Rice. 2009. *Policy-making for Research Data in Repositories: A Guide.* Version 1.2. Edinburgh: EDINA and University Data Library. Available: www.disc-uk.org/docs/guide.pdf (accessed April 26, 2010).

Hedstrom, Margaret. 2002. "Research Challenges in Digital Archiving and Long-Term Preservation." Address to the Workshop on Research Challenges in Digital Archiving and Long-Term Preservation, Washington, DC, April 12–13, 2002. Available: www.sis.pitt.edu/~dlwkshop/paper_hedstrom.doc (accessed April 26, 2010).

International Organization for Standardization. 2003. *Space Data and Information Transfer Systems—Open Archival Information System—Reference Model.* Standard 14721:2003. Geneva: International Organization for Standardization.

LeFurgy, William G. 2009. "NDIIPP Partner Perspectives on 'Economic Sustainability.'" *Library Trends* 57, no. 3 (Winter): 413–426.

RLG-NARA Task Force on Digital Repository Certification. 2007. *Trustworthy Repositories Audit & Certification: Criteria and Checklist.* Chicago: Center for Research Libraries. Available: www.crl.edu/sites/default/files/attachments/ pages/trac_0.pdf (accessed April 26, 2010).

Rusbridge, Chris. 2008. "Responses to RAW versus TIFF: Compression, Error and Cost-Related." Digital Curation Blog, comment posted July 2, 2008. Available: digitalcuration.blogspot.com/2008/07/responses-to-raw-versus-tiff.html (accessed April 26, 2010).

Serco Consulting. 2008. "UKRDS Interim Report." London: Serco Consulting (July 7, 2008). Available: ukrds.ac.uk/resources/download/id/17 (accessed April 26, 2010).

Wellcome Trust. "Q&A: Wellcome Trust Policy on Data Management and Sharing." London: Wellcome Trust. Available: www.wellcome.ac.uk/About-us/Policy/Spotlight-issues/Data-sharing/Data-management-and-sharing/ WTX035045.htm (accessed April 26, 2010).

Wheatley, Paul, Paul Ayris, Richard Davies, Rory Mcleod, and Helen Shenton. 2007. *The LIFE Model.* v1.1. London: LIFE Project. Available: eprints.ucl.ac .uk/4831 (accessed April 26, 2010).

Woollard, Matthew. 2009. *UK Data Archive Preservation Policy.* Version 03.10. Colchester: UK Data Archive. Available: www.data-archive.ac.uk/news/ publications/preservationpolicy.pdf (accessed April 26, 2010). Used by permission of the UK Data Archive, University of Essex.

Sharing Knowledge and Collaborating

This chapter investigates the Full Lifecycle Action *Community Watch and Participation*—the process of keeping up-to-date and participating in developments to improve and advance curation activities. In practice, this means that digital curators participate actively in collaborative activities. The key activities encompassed by Community Watch and Participation are:

- keeping up-to-date with digital curation activities and with developments in related areas,
- sharing data and participating in other activities underpinning data reuse,
- participating in the development of standards for digital curation, and
- participating in the development of tools and toolkits for digital curation.

Keeping Up-to-Date

The "Community Watch" part of *Community Watch and Participation* refers to being fully aware of other activities in the digital curation community on an ongoing basis. There are many ways to maintain such an awareness.

Digital curation is a field about which a wealth of high-quality information is available on the web. It is also a field that changes rapidly and has few common understandings so far. These factors make it very important to keep up-to-date. Online materials may be the best source of information, but they vary in quality and currency. The quantity of printed material is increasing; at least four books on digital preservation were published between 2005 and 2007, and numerous journal articles are being published. These issues of quality and quantity have been recognized by organizations involved in digital curation and digital preservation. Consequently, there is now a curated database of

IN THIS CHAPTER:
✔ Keeping Up-to-Date
✔ Collaboration: Intrinsic to Digital Curation
✔ Standards: Essential for Digital Curation
✔ Tools and Toolkits
✔ Summary: Collaboration Is the Key
✔ References

high-quality resources, and some websites also provide authoritative advice and guidance that has been reviewed and approved by knowledgeable practitioners. Some of these resources are listed later. The intention of this list, which is limited to English-language resources, is to indicate the types of resources that are available to digital curators, not to provide an authoritative comprehensive list of resources.

Starting Points

PADI: Preserving Access to Digital Information (www.nla.gov.au/padi/index.html), an essential starting point for all areas of digital curation, is a database established by the National Library of Australia. Its products include a quarterly newsletter about recent developments, *DPC/PADI: What's New in Digital Preservation* (www.dpconline.org/graphics/whatsnew/), produced in conjunction with the United Kingdom's Digital Preservation Coalition. Understanding the terminology used in digital curation is assisted by glossaries that include the Arts and Humanities Data Service's (2007) "AHDS Preservation Glossary" and the Society of American Archivists' "Glossary of Archival and Records Terminology" (Pearce-Moses, 2005). Authoritative guidance on specific topics is found in the *Curation Reference Manual* (Digital Curation Centre, accessed 2010). Produced by the Digital Curation Centre (DCC), this manual provides installments by experts in the field on a range of topics relevant to digital curation. The UNESCO (2003) *Guidelines for the Preservation of Digital Heritage* also provide authoritative advice. The Digital Preservation Coalition (2008) maintains the influential publication *Preservation Management of Digital Materials: A Handbook*.

Online Tutorials

Several online tutorials about digital preservation are available, although none of these covers digital curation in its entirety. Among them are the following:

- *Digital Preservation Management* (Cornell University Library, 2003–2007). This highly recommended tutorial is an essential introduction to digital preservation.
- The Canadian Heritage Information Network (CHIN) provides a number of tutorials related to creating and managing digital content (www.chin.gc.ca).
- The Joint Information Systems Committee (JISC) Digital Media's cross-media advice documents (www.jiscdigitalmedia.ac.uk/crossmedia) include "An Introduction to Digital Preservation" (accessed 2010) and "Establishing a Digital Preservation Strategy" (accessed 2010).

There are many tutorials on specific technical topics on the web, for example, *OAI for Beginners: The Open Archives Forum Online Tutorial* (Open Archives Forum, 2003).

Project Websites

The websites of digital curation and digital preservation projects are a fruitful source of useful material. These must be used with care, as the information they present is not always current. Project funding may have ended and work ceased, but the website may still be available.

- Cultural, Artistic, and Scientific Knowledge for Preservation, Access, and Retrieval (CASPAR; www.casparpreserves.eu). CASPAR recently added Training Lectures, "a collection of videos of talks and screen captures of software—all about digital preservation."

- Digital Preservation Coalition (DPC; www.dpconline.org/ graphics/index.html). This is not a project but is included here because its website contains useful reports, including a series of Technology Watch reports.

- Digital Preservation Europe (DPE; www.digitalpreservation europe.eu). Links to reports, briefing papers, and position papers are in the "DPE Publications" pages of the website.

- Electronic Resource Preservation and Access Network (ERPANET; (www.erpanet.org). This project ended in 2007 but during its existence produced a wide range of materials that are still useful, although some are now outdated.

- National Digital Information Infrastructure & Preservation Program (NDIIPP; (www.digitalpreservation.gov). This is "a Collaborative Initiative of the Library of Congress."

- Paradigm Project (www.paradigm.ac.uk). This project, funded from 2005 to 2007, produced a workbook that covers many aspects of curation.

- PLANETS (www.planets-project.eu) provides reports on aspects of its toolkit development.

- Sustaining Heritage Access through Multivalent ArchiviNg (SHAMAN) (shaman-ip.eu/shaman). This project is aimed at developing a long-term digital preservation framework.

Blogs and E-mail Lists

Among blogs that are specifically about digital curation are the Digital Curation Blog (digitalcuration.blogspot.com), "inspired by the Digital Curation Centre to discuss issues relating to the curation and long term preservation of digital science and research data," and the DCC Blawg (dccblawg.blogspot.com), which focused on the legal aspects of digital curation. Postings about digital curation appear regularly in many other blogs. E-mail lists whose primary interest is digital curation include DIGITAL-PRESERVATION List (www.jiscmail.ac.uk/cgi-bin/webadmin? A0=digital-preservation), operated by JISC, a major U.K. funding body for higher education that has had a major role in promoting digital preservation, and padiforum-l (www.nla.gov.au/padi/forum), owned by the National Library of Australia and affiliated with the PADI web portal for digital preservation resources. PADI identifies other discussion lists (www.nla.gov.au/padi/format/list.html) relevant to digital curation.

Online Journals

Articles about digital curation appear in a wide range of journals and can be located using indexing and abstracting databases available through libraries. Journals that regularly publish articles about digital curation include *Ariadne* (www.ariadne.ac.uk), which notes current digital library initiatives and technological developments; *D-Lib Magazine* (www.dlib.org), which focuses on "digital library research and development, including . . . new technologies, applications, and contextual social and economic issues"; and the *International Journal of Digital Curation* (www.ijdc.net/index.php/ijdc/issue/current), published by the DCC. The DCC website provides a list of curation- and preservation-related journals (www.dcc.ac.uk/IJDC). PADI also provides a list of journals and newsletters (www.nla.gov.au/padi/format/journal.html).

Other Sources

The DPE website provides an annotated list of online resources (www.digitalpreservationeurope.eu/registries/resources) of relevance and importance to a wide range of digital curation activities. Discipline-specific websites also contain relevant resources. An example is the list of digital curation resources (nssdc.gsfc.nasa.gov/nost/curation.html) available on the NASA/Science Office of Standards and Technology (NOST) website. The number of training opportunities in digital curation is increasing. One of DPE's aims is to coordinate training opportunities, and to this end it maintains a Registry of Digital Preservation Trainers (www.digitalpreservationeurope.eu/registries/trainers) and an events register (www.digitalpreservationeurope.eu/events/events).The DCC also maintains lists of forthcoming events (www.dcc.ac.uk/events) that can help locate training opportunities.

Collaboration: Intrinsic to Digital Curation

The "Participation" part of *Community Watch and Participation* refers to the need for collaboration in the digital curation community. Collaboration is one of the keys to effective curation. All communities involved in curation—data creators, users, and in fact all stakeholders—should participate in discussions about the challenges posed and in creating helpful responses to these challenges. Collaborative efforts are, in fact, "more the norm than the exception" (Jordan et al., 2008: 6).

Collaboration is, in fact, firmly embedded in digital curation practice. Active management of data for current and future use relies on effective sharing of data, which, in turn, relies on agreement on and adoption of standards. Partnerships have been important in digital curation from its inception, because it was quickly realized that no single organization could adequately archive, preserve, and provide access to digital materials. The reasons for this include the scale of digital curation issues, uncertainty about how to address them, and the high cost of digital curation in relation to the financial resources available. Collaboration ensures the best use of resources through sharing expertise and experience and through developing and building technical resources and solutions that can be shared.

The benefits of collaboration have been rehearsed in many publications and are well understood. The UNESCO (2003) *Guidelines for the Preservation of Digital Heritage* identify many of them, specifically in relation to digital curation. These include access to a wider range of expertise; sharing of the costs of developing software and systems; access to tools and systems of other organizations; the sharing of learning opportunities; encouragement of influential stakeholders to take digital curation seriously; increased ability to influence data producers and system developers; joint research and development of standards and practices; and enhanced ability to attract resources and other support for well-coordinated curation programs at regional, national or sectoral levels (UNESCO, 2003: 64–65).

Examples of collaboration in digital curation are easy to find. Websites such as PADI and that of the DCC, noted in "Keeping Up-to-Date" earlier in this chapter, indicate one mechanism by which expertise is shared. International conferences such as the DCC's series of International Digital Curation Conferences also provide forums where expertise can be shared. The DPE project was established specifically to share European expertise in the field of digital curation by "pooling of the complementary expertise that exists across the academic research, cultural, public administration and industry sectors in Europe" (Digital Preservation Europe, "DPE: Digital Preservation Europe," accessed 2010). Both the DCC and DPE have as stated aims the sharing of learning opportunities, with the DPE, for example, running the "Digital Preservation Exchange Programme" (Digital Preservation Europe, accessed 2010).

The DCC's series of international conferences on digital curation are not the only conferences where expertise is shared. Others held on a regular basis include the International Conference on Digital Preservation (iPres). Most conferences of professional library and archives organizations now include sessions about digital curation, such as the conferences held by national bodies (the Society of American Archivists and the American Library Association) and by regional organizations. Many conferences that focus on digital libraries, such as the Joint Conference on Digital Libraries (JCDL), the European Conference on Digital Libraries (ECDL) and the International Conference on Asian Digital Libraries (ICADL), also include sessions or streams devoted to digital curation.

Sharing of the costs of developing software and systems is practiced through the adoption of open-source concepts. For example, two of the key digital preservation repository systems, Fedora (www.fedora.info) and DSpace (www.dspace.org), are open source and have a large international community of participants who contribute to their development.

AN EXAMPLE OF COLLABORATION

Some material quoted in this book has a Creative Commons Non-Commercial (CC-NC) license. This means it can be used without permission for noncommercial purposes, and readers may reuse it, provided they attribute the original source in the manner specified by the author or licensor. (The Creative Commons website provides more information: creativecommons.org.)

This willingness to share published information about digital curation illustrates the international and collaborative nature of digital curation. Developments and practice in one region are keenly observed and adopted and modified to suit local requirements in other regions. Many digital curation projects funded by public money are required to make documentation of their activities freely available.

Persistent lobbying of influential stakeholders to take digital curation seriously is carried out by groups such as the DPC and the DCC in the United Kingdom, both of which have lobbying as a stated objective, and the NDIIPP in the United States, also with a strong lobbying role. Joint research and development is evident in the development of key standards used in digital curation. An example is METS, whose Editorial Board has members from Germany, the United Kingdom, and the United States (www.loc.gov/standards/mets/mets-board.html); another is the development of the Trusted Digital Repository concept (see Chapter 14) by a working group with members from the United Kingdom, Germany, the United States, France, and Australia. These two examples are by no means unusual in digital curation.

Projects that aim to make data sharing easier also demonstrate high levels of collaboration. The sharing of expertise is fully demonstrated in the DISC-UK DataShare project (www.disc-uk.org/datashare.html), which ran from 2007 to 2009. It involved the collaboration of partners to develop new models, workflows, and tools for sharing research data sets.

Projects that share archival storage resources, such as MetaArchive, also demonstrate collaboration. The MetaArchive Cooperative (www .metaarchive.org), established in 2003 with funding from the Library of Congress's NDIIPP, is a coalition of universities and research libraries that provides "low-cost, high-impact preservation services to help ensure the long-term accessibility of the digital assets of universities, libraries, museums, and other cultural heritage institutions" (Meta-Archive Services Group, accessed 2010). It is based on the open-source Lots of Copies Keep Stuff Safe (LOCKSS) software, which allows digital preservation to be carried out collaboratively at a series of geographically distributed sites. In addition to providing an affordable service to its members, MetaArchive assists other groups to create similar collaborative digital preservation networks, hosts activities to support and train groups wishing to establish networks, and fosters awareness of digital preservation issues (Halbert and Skinner, 2008: 5).

Standards: Essential for Digital Curation

Effective digital curation requires the development and implementation of standards. (Chapter 3 noted one important standard, the OAIS Reference Model, formalized as ISO standard 14721:2003, which is widely used as the basis of planning digital archives.) A fundamental aspect of digital curation is the sharing and reuse of data. This implies interoperability of systems—the ability of software and hardware to exchange and use information. For reliable and consistent interoperability, standards are essential. They are the basis upon which digital curation systems that work are built. Standards, however, require consensus among all who apply them so that confusion and misunderstanding are reduced; achieving consensus, in turn, requires knowledge of what is happening in digital curation—in other words, maintaining a community watch.

Standards apply to all digital curation activities: data capture; citation; annotation; classification; achieving interoperability; software integration; representation information—the list is long. The chapters in Part III note which standards are relevant to each activity of the curation lifecycle.

The first step is to identify (or develop if they don't already exist) the standards that are relevant for curation activities. Many standards for digital curation were developed by the DIFFUSE project, funded by the European Union (EU), which was concerned with standards relevant to the information society. The DCC continues to maintain and update the registry of these standards (Digital Curation Centre, "DCC DIFFUSE Standards Frameworks," accessed 2010). It can be searched through the DCC Curation Lifecycle actions. Standards have not yet been developed for all aspects of digital curation, and digital curators may find themselves involved in developing new standards.

Three examples illustrate the significance of standards for digital curation and of participating in standards development.

A standard for exporting data: The instrumentation used in creating data in research experiments is typically commercially manufactured. Many of these instruments use data-capture tools specific to a manufacturer, which are based on data standards developed by that manufacturer. There is little uniformity, even for similar types of instrumentation. The scientific community is increasing pressure on manufacturers to conform to standards, at least in the way that data that they create and collect can be exported from the software used for creation and collection (e.g., enabling XML output) so that data from a wide range of instruments can be combined.

A standard for stable data formats: Using standard data formats that will remain accessible over time is a commonly applied digital preservation strategy. Standards that are stable and have been widely adopted are much more likely to be supported over a long period. Standards that are open (i.e., not proprietary) are less likely to become obsolete in a short period, because there is a large user base willing to participate in ensuring that the standards are maintained. XML is often adopted, as it is a stable standard with a very good track record, is in increasingly widespread use, and has a large user base. Chapter 10 notes in more detail the requirements for stable data formats.

A standard for sharing data: One requirement for interoperability is that data and their associated metadata are expressed in a standard format so that different software can recognize them and then act on them. For metadata, METS (Library of Congress, accessed 2010) provides a standard for encoding metadata for digital objects. It is widely used in digital curation environments.

Tools and Toolkits

Digital curation processes are often characterized as "artisan" or "hand-crafted," referring to their labor-intensive nature. This limits considerably the quantities of data that can be curated using these processes. Automation of curation workflows and processes is commonly understood to be essential for improving digital curation, because it increases the ability to curate larger quantities of data and reduces the costs of doing so. Automated workflows and procedures need software tools—tools that can be applied in many areas of digital curation. Some curation actions where software tools can be applied include the following:

- Identification of digital objects (e.g., where they are located, what formats they are in)
- Describing digital objects (e.g., automated metadata creation)
- Manipulating data (e.g., data management, data storage, repositories)
- Preserving data (e.g., migration)
- Rights management and access control (e.g., restricting access to authorized users of a system)

Tools are being developed by many digital curation research and development projects. Recent EU-funded projects such as CASPAR and PLANETS are developing tools to advance automation in digital curation. CASPAR (www.casparpreserves.eu) aims to "produce tools and techniques to support digital preservation and make it easier to share the cost" (Giaretta, 2007). These tools must be useful and usable, easy to use, requiring little effort to adopt, sustainable after the CASPAR project ends, and open source. PLANETS (www.planets-project.eu) has developed prototype tools and services for preservation planning, preservation action, and preservation characterization. It has made available Plato, a preservation planning workflow tool based on a toolkit of other preservation planning tools, such as PLANETS-compliant migration tools for digital objects, emulation tools for specific environments, and characterization tools that extract significant properties from digital objects. In the United States, NDIIPP provides a long list of tools and services designed, developed, or used by NDIIPP partners (www.digital preservation.gov/partners/resources/tools/index.html). These tools cover most curation activities.

If they are to be adopted widely, the tools developed for digital curation must be *usable* and *useful*. These characteristics and tools that are in common use are described in more detail in Chapter 13. Community watch activities monitor the development of curation tools on an ongoing basis to determine whether new tools are applicable to local data curation activities. In addition, input into tool development, where feasible, as part of collaborative approaches to digital curation will ensure that they are usable and useful.

Summary: Collaboration Is the Key

Engaging with the wider digital curation community has many positive benefits. The first step is to become aware of current thinking and practice in the field so that local practice develops as best practice. For example, monitoring changes in technology indicates when hardware and software are in danger of becoming obsolete. (This is known as *technology watch*.) Participating in some of the many collaborative activities that characterize digital curation and in the development of standards in the field provides more effective outcomes.

The next chapter is the first in Part III, "The Digital Curation Lifecycle in Action." This section of the book examines the DCC Curation Lifecycle's Sequential Actions. First, Chapter 10 notes the development and planning of data creation procedures with digital curation activities and outcomes in mind.

References

Arts and Humanities Data Service. 2007. "AHDS Preservation Glossary." London: Arts and Humanities Data Service (October 17, 2007). Available: ahds.ac.uk/exec/creating/glossary.htm (accessed April 26, 2010).

Cornell University Library. 2003–2007. *Digital Preservation Management: Implementing Short-Term Strategies for Long-Term Problems.* Ithaca, NY: Cornell University Library. Available: www.icpsr.umich.edu/dpm/dpm-eng/eng_index.html (accessed April 26, 2010).

Digital Curation Centre. *Curation Reference Manual.* Edinburgh: Digital Curation Centre. Available: www.dcc.ac.uk/resources/curation-reference-manual (accessed April 26, 2010).

———. "DCC DIFFUSE Standards Frameworks." Edinburgh: Digital Curation Centre. Available: www.dcc.ac.uk/resources/standards/diffuse (accessed April 26, 2010).

Digital Preservation Coalition. 2008. *Preservation Management of Digital Materials: A Handbook.* York: Digital Preservation Coalition (November 2008). Available: www.dpconline.org/advice/digital-preservation-handbook.html (accessed April 26, 2010).

Digital Preservation Europe. "Digital Preservation Exchange Programme (DPEX)." Glasgow: DPE. Available: www.digitalpreservationeurope.eu/exchange (accessed April 26, 2010).

———. "DPE: Digital Preservation Europe." Glasgow: DPE. Available: www.digitalpreservationeurope.eu (accessed April 26, 2010).

Giaretta, David. 2007. "The CASPAR View on What Digital Curators Do and What They Need to Know." Paper presented at DigCCurr 2007, Chapel Hill, NC, April 18–20, 2007. Available: www.casparpreserves.eu/Members/cclrc/Presentations/the-caspar-view-on-what-digital-curators-do-and-what-they-need-to-know-research-perspectives/at_download/file (accessed April 26, 2010).

Halbert, Martin, and Katherine Skinner. 2008. "The MetaArchive Cooperative: A New Collaborative Service Organization Providing a Distributed Digital Preservation Infrastructure." *CLIR Issues* no. 66. Available: www.clir.org/pubs/issues/issues66.html (accessed April 26, 2010).

Joint Information Systems Committee. "Establishing a Digital Preservation Policy." Bristol: JISC Digital Media. Available: www.jiscdigitalmedia.ac.uk/crossmedia/advice/establishing-a-digital-preservation-policy (accessed April 26, 2010).

———. "An Introduction to Digital Preservation." Bristol: JISC Digital Media. Available: www.jiscdigitalmedia.ac.uk/crossmedia/advice/an-introduction-to-digital-preservation (accessed April 26, 2010).

COMMUNITY WATCH AND PARTICIPATION: REVIEW

Key points: *Community Watch and Participation* is the ongoing process of keeping up-to-date with data curation activities and developments in related areas, and participating in developments to advance and improve curation activities.

Key activities:
- Keep up-to-date with data curation activities and developments in related areas
- Share data and participate in activities underpinning data reuse
- Participate in standards development
- Participate in the development of tools and toolkits for data curation

Jordan, Christopher, Ardys Kozbial, David Minor, and Robert H. McDonald. "Encouraging Cyberinfrastructure Collaboration for Digital Preservation." Paper presented at iPres 2008, British Library, London, September 30, 2008. Available: www.bl.uk/ipres2008/presentations_day2/39_Jordan.pdf (accessed April 26, 2010).

Library of Congress. "METS: Metadata Encoding & Transmission Standard." Washington: Library of Congress. Available: www.loc.gov/standards/mets (accessed April 26, 2010).

MetaArchive Services Group. "About MetaArchive." Atlanta: MetaArchive Services Group. Available: www.metaarchive.org/about (accessed April 26, 2010).

Open Archives Forum. 2003. *OAI for Beginners: The Open Archives Forum Online Tutorial.* Bath: OA-Forum and UKOLN. Available: www.oaforum.org/tutorial (accessed April 26, 2010).

Pearce-Moses, Richard. 2005. "Glossary of Archival and Records Terminology." Chicago: Society of American Archivists (2005). Available: www.archivists.org/glossary (accessed April 26, 2010).

UNESCO. 2003. *Guidelines for the Preservation of Digital Heritage.* Paris: Information Society Division, United Nations Educational, Scientific and Cultural Organization. Available: unesdoc.unesco.org/images/0013/001300/130071e.pdf (accessed April 26, 2010).

The Digital Curation Lifecycle in Action

The seven chapters in "Part III. The Digital Curation Lifecycle in Action" follow the Digital Curation Centre (DCC) Curation Lifecycle Model's Sequential Actions. Also noted are the model's Occasional Actions. Together these chapters outline the reasons for and activities associated with each of the Sequential and Occasional Actions.

Chapter 9 notes the first Sequential Action, *Conceptualise*. It emphasizes the need to think about curation at the very first stages of planning research, digitizing, or any other data creation activity that is carried out with digital curation processes and outcomes in mind.

Chapter 10 examines the second Sequential Action, *Create or Receive*, noting the requirements for curation-ready data. Whereas Chapter 9 outlines the nature of the planning required to ensure that we have "good" data and comprehensive data management plans so that curation is effective, this chapter explains the principles and practices of making data curation-ready.

Chapter 11 describes *Appraise and Select*, the third Sequential Action, noting the importance of selection of the digital objects to be curated. It examines the processes of developing criteria for the determination of which data sets and digital objects should be kept for the long term and which should be discarded, and then applying those criteria. This chapter also notes the Occasional Actions *Reappraise* and *Dispose*, both closely related to the *Appraise* action.

The fourth Sequential Action, *Ingest*, is the topic of Chapter 12. Ingest refers to the processes of preparing digital objects for adding to a digital archive and of adding them to the digital archive.

Chapter 13 discusses the preservation strategies and actions associated with *Preservation Action*, the fifth Sequential Action. This is the process of ensuring long-term preservation and retention of digital objects and includes activities aimed at ensuring that they are authentic, reliable, and usable over time, and at the same time retain their integrity. Also included in this chapter is the Occasional Action *Migrate*.

Chapter 14 focuses on the sixth Sequential Action, *Store*, which is concerned with what is required to provide acceptable data storage in the archiving system.

Chapter 15 covers *Access, Use, and Reuse*, the seventh Sequential Action, and *Transform*, the eighth and final Sequential Action. Access, Use, and Reuse is the process of ensuring that data is accessible to authorized users for use and also later reuse. Transform, most frequently the outcome of the Access, Use, and Reuse action, refers to the process of creating new data from the original data.

Designing Data

This chapter investigates the first of the Sequential Actions of the DCC Curation Lifecycle Model, *Conceptualise*—the process of conceiving and planning the creation of data, including capture method and storage options. It is, to put it simply, the planning of research, digitizing, or any other data-creation activity that is done with digital curation processes and outcomes in mind.

The key activities encompassed by Conceptualise aim to ensure that curation is made easier at later stages of the curation lifecycle, through careful planning when a research project or digitization project is being designed. These key activities include planning for:

- data capture and storage in curation-friendly file formats,
- recording sufficient information at the time of data capture to assist with ongoing management of those data and with their use,
- scrupulous identification of files,
- data storage on appropriate media, and
- identification of a safe place for the data and ensuring that an archive will take them.

Another important activity in Conceptualise is the design of systems used to create and manage data to best effect for digital curation. Chapters 14 and 15 note the design of systems so that they are suitable for managing data over time and re-presenting them in the future.

All the evidence to date indicates that the earlier the involvement of curation in the data lifecycle, the better the results for long-term curation. For example, a focus on user requirements during the conceptualization and planning of a research project or of a digitization program will highlight the information that significantly assists users to access and use the data that are captured. The costs of digital curation are contained more effectively as a result of early decision making, as most of them are incurred at the early stages of the lifecycle, up to and including the Ingest phase.

IN THIS CHAPTER:

✔ Designing Curation-Ready Data

✔ Importance of Standards

✔ Designing Projects with Curation in Mind

✔ Three Examples

✔ Summary: Planning Data for Curation

✔ References

What does this entail in practice? In a blog posting, Chris Rusbridge (2008) identifies the stages of a research project and the curation activities that are required at each of them. The two earliest stages are the *pre-proposal* stage and the *proposal* stage. During the pre-proposal stage discussions are likely to be general, exploring the feasibility of the project and the resources that might be needed. Curation-related thinking could be about identifying the data that are already available and the data that the project needs to generate, which includes thinking about legal and ethical issues affecting use of the data.

During the proposal stage the project is planned in detail. Funding bodies increasingly require that requests for research funds include a data management plan. Curation concerns during this stage are decisions about standards for the collection, analysis, management, and storage of data, which must be made with the usual norms and standards of the scientific discipline in mind. Without adherence to these, data are much less likely to be shareable and reusable. Rusbridge (2008) comments: "This stage begins to have a significant effect on curation, as the decisions that are fore-shadowed here will have major effects later on. Repeat after me: curation begins before creation!"

Curation concerns that relate primarily to these two early planning stages may also arise later in the project. For example, the data management plan may need to be revised; if this is the case, the changes made and their curation implications should be documented. Another example: it is useful to test any procedures for depositing data that are part of your data management plan. Rusbridge (2008) concludes:

> So: the message is that curation should be a constant theme, albeit as background during most of the project execution. But the decisions taken during pre-proposal, proposal and establishment phases will have a big effect on your ability to curate your data, which may affect your research results, and will certainly affect the quality and re-usability of the data you deposit.

Designing Curation-Ready Data

Consider this scenario, which demonstrates ways that digital objects are lost or become unusable. A project is being planned that involves digital objects being created—let's say a project to digitize library materials in paper form. At the planning stage, there is much thinking about the standards that will be used—the resolution quality required, the file formats that will be used, the equipment available, the metadata that will be added. The project goes ahead; all is well—so far. As time passes, what happens to the knowledge about the data produced during the project and about their metadata? Immediately after the end of the project, knowledge levels about all of these things are high, but, as time passes, problems arise; details of how the data were collected, or about the equipment and software used to digitize, are lost. More time passes. An accident may destroy the digital objects and/or documentation. The retirement or resignation of key personnel (the head of the imaging unit, perhaps) makes access to that person's knowledge more difficult. The result? The digital objects become significantly less usable and less useful, perhaps even to the extent of being completely unusable. (This scenario is adapted from the description of a research project given by Gail Steinhart and Brian Lowe [2007].)

This scenario relates to digital objects from a library-based digitizing project. Lynch makes a similar point about scientific data. Scientists have the primary responsibility to curate data at the start of the lifecycle, but Lynch (2008: 28) observes that "scientists are not necessarily good data managers and can more fruitfully spend their time doing science. Moreover, it is unfair and unreasonable—and increasingly ineffective—to assign long-term information management tasks to a rotating staff of students and postdocs." The loss of access to data and to their information content in this scenario can be minimized if digital curation principles are considered when the research is conceptualized and planned. Data creators will benefit greatly from planning their project or their research from the start so that good curation is a more likely outcome.

What does this mean in practice? At the start of this chapter the key activities involved in conceptualizing data creation with curation in mind were noted as:

- capturing and storing data in curation-friendly file formats,
- recording sufficient information at the time of data capture,
- scrupulously identifying files,
- storing data on appropriate media, and
- identifying a safe place for the data and making sure that an archive will take them.

Applying these to the scenario, actions could be the following:

- Decide to use an open file format to ensure it is curation friendly (open file formats are described in more detail in Chapter 10).
- Decide, at the time of creating the digital images, the metadata that need to be collected, including metadata about the equipment and software used; develop a workflow that ensures that metadata is collected; and identify the resourcing needed for its collection.
- Decide how files will be named and how directories will be structured to ensure that each file is uniquely identified and can be located easily.
- Determine what media will be used to store the data generated.
- Identify a trusted archive to store the data, and negotiate storage requirements with that archive.

This list is by no means comprehensive. For example, in some projects it might be necessary to ensure that the digital objects produced are authorized and ethically sound—that is, they contain only information that has been collected or created according to ethical standards and do not allow identification of individuals or transgress any privacy or data protection laws.

Importance of Standards

Standards are essential for reliable digital curation—sharing and reuse of data, for instance, requires interoperability, which in turn depends on adhering to standards. Standards should be identified (or developed, if they don't already exist) for most digital curation actions, as noted in Chapter 8. Standards are particularly relevant in the Conceptualise action of the DCC Curation Lifecycle Model: file format standards, metadata standards, and file identification standards are examples.

Two examples illustrate the importance of standards when planning data creation. The first comes from scientific research. Commercially manufactured instrumentation used in experimental research comes with manufacturer-specific data-capture tools that use data standards specific to that manufacturer (i.e., they are proprietary standards). These do not necessarily follow a common standard beyond the context of that manufacturer's products. This means that data created by tools developed by different manufacturers cannot be combined. Manufacturers need to conform to standards, at the very least in the way that the data collected can be exported from their software (e.g., data in XML). Smith (2008: 100–101) illustrates this by referring to architectural three-dimensional (3D) CAD models:

> 3D models are created in proprietary software using non-standard native formats, and each product uses different techniques for capturing a model's shape information via designer-specified parameters, storing geometry and other properties attached to the geometry, and rendering the model on the computer screen. Each software product's method of doing this uses different, very complex mathematical techniques.... These different methods are the differentiators that define competitive advantages among such products; there are few incentives in the industry to define standard parametric data formats.

The consequence is that 3D CAD file formats need the original software package (and version of that package) that was used to create them for the models to be rendered accurately. There is no standard format for creating these data. Data export is, however, another matter; there are standards for transferring data from one 3D CAD software product to another, but Smith indicates that the application of any of them results in loss of information. As a result, for the curation of 3D CAD models, it is at present necessary to maintain the original proprietary software in which they were created.

The second example is the common use of standard data formats in order to ensure digital objects remain accessible over time. Standard data formats are stable, have been widely adopted, and have a large user base. Many of them are open source. Using standard data formats reduces the risk of data becoming obsolescent.

Designing Projects with Curation in Mind

Planning for curation takes place at most stages of project design. Chris Rusbridge has this to say about building curation and reusability into a project. After reminding the reader that, during the period a project is active, "all the information anyone would ever need to re-use your data is all around you," he indicates that this state of affairs soon changes: "some is never written down until near or after the end of the project, when the post-doc has left for that great job." His advice is:

> make sure you capture everything you can while it's easily accessible; this might include some of the text and key parameters of the proposal to your funders, or items as apparently unconnected as health and safety plans and records (which may record who was doing what, where and when). You must of course keep and manage your experimental parameters and calibrations, your data file descriptions, database designs and schemas, tag libraries, questionnaires, etc etc. (Rusbridge, 2007: 6–7)

Lynch indicates some of the kinds of information whose identification and collection need, ideally, to be planned early. *Appropriate metadata* is one category: for example, experimental parameters and set-up, necessary so that the data collected can be interpreted in the future. This kind of metadata is most readily captured at the same time the data are captured. *Provenance* information is a second category: this refers to information about the source or sources of the data, how they were derived from their sources, the extent to which they depend on other data that are external to the immediate context, and any changes to the data since their initial capture. The *storage formats* in which the data are stored, too, need to be documented. This is especially important for data that are developed for a particular project and associated with software that has also been developed for the purposes of a particular project (Lynch, 2008: 28).

Research funding agencies increasingly require that aspects of digital curation, in particular data sharing, are built into grant proposals. The requirements typically include a plan that is practical, allows data sharing, and plans for what happens to the data at the end of the project. Note particularly the requirement that data can potentially be shared. This requirement implies interoperability—that digital objects can be successfully exchanged between computer systems and successfully used in computer systems other than the systems within which they were created and initially used.

In the United Kingdom, the Research Information Network (RIN), an organization that provides guidance and support for researchers and information management professionals, articulates some of the requirements for sharing, access, and use of data in its *Framework of Principles*. Principle 2 considers standards and quality assurance, emphasizing the need to apply standards when creating and collecting data to ensure that they are usable and to ensure the quality of data so that users of those data can use them with confidence. Principle 3 is about access, usage, and credit. The data should be easy to find and to use. The roles of data creators and those who have gathered data should be credited and their legitimate rights protected. Data creators and collectors must ensure that they indicate clearly details such as who owns the data, how they were collected, rights connected with those data, and who can have access (Research Information Network, 2008: 2).

Another example from the United Kingdom is the Biotechnology and Biological Sciences Research Council (BBSRC) requirements for data management and data sharing to be included in research grant proposals. The Biotechnology and Biological Sciences Research Council's (2007) *Data Sharing Policy: Guidance for Applicants* requires applicants for the research grants that it awards to submit either a data-sharing plan or an explicit argument about why data sharing is not possible or appropriate. It specifies that these plans should be based on established standards and existing resources wherever possible. The plan must include detailed information about:

- Data areas and data types—the volume, type, and content of data that will be generated, for example, experimental measurements, records, and images;
- Standards and metadata—the standards and methodologies that will be adopted for data collection and management and why these have been selected;
- Relationship to other data available in public repositories;
- Secondary use—further intended and/or foreseeable research uses for the completed dataset(s);
- Methods for data sharing—planned mechanisms for making these data available, for example, through deposition in existing public databases or on request, including access mechanisms where appropriate;
- Proprietary data—any restrictions on data sharing due to the need to protect proprietary or patentable data;
- Timeframes—timescales for public release of data; and
- Format of the final dataset. (Biotechnology and Biological Sciences Research Council, 2007: 6)

It may not always be possible to plan all aspects of curation in the Conceptualise action of the Curation Lifecycle. The example of architectural 3D CAD models, described earlier in this chapter (Smith, 2008), reminds us that for some materials there is no choice but to use proprietary software.

Three Examples

A considerable amount of advice is available through the Internet to help with planning for data management and curation. Three examples from the United Kingdom are noted here for their practical advice.

The first example is the Rural Economy and Land Use Programme Data Support Service's (2006) *Guidance on Data Management*, which offers useful practical advice, arranged in sections relating to data management strategies, digital preservation, making backups, format translation and choice of formats, data quality, ensuring authenticity and controlling access, version control, data storage, and security. For example, the section on making backups suggests that specific attention must be given to the frequency of backup; rolling backup copies (i.e., not overwriting old backups with new copies automatically); having at least one offsite backup copy; being aware of institutional backup policies; keeping independent backups of critical files; validating backup copies using checksums (and store the checksum results); choosing robust and reliable backup media regularly; and following manufacturers' recommendations for storage of backup media.

Another illustrative section is "Format Translation and Choice of Formats" (Rural Economy and Land Use Programme Data Support Service, 2006: 6–7), which presents a useful table that compares types of data, preferred format for management backup and submission to data centers, and the formats for long-term preservation used by data centers. For example, for tabular data with extensive metadata, such as "a survey dataset with variable labels, code labels, and missing values in addition to the matrix of data," the preferred formats for management backup and submission to data centers are SPSS portable (.por) or delimited text and command file (SPSS, Stata, SAS, etc.) containing metadata information or binary formats of statistical packages (SPSS, Stata, SAS, etc.—even though these offer less long-term security; the usual formats for long-term preservation by data centers are delimited text and command file [SPSS, Stata, SAS, etc.] and other structured text/markup files containing metadata information [e.g., DDI XML file]). *Guidance on Data Management* concludes with a "Checklist for Data Management" (see sidebar).

The second example is actually a set of examples in the "AHDS Guides to Good Practice" (Arts and Humanities Data Service, accessed 2010). Although these are dated (the Arts and Humanities Data Service [AHDS] ceased operation in 2008, and the guides were usually produced before then), they provide helpful guidance in areas of the arts and humanities about applying standards and good practice to creating and using data. AHDS also provided general introductory information on creating digital resources (James, 2005), as well as the specific good practice guides for creating a variety of materials in particular arts and humanities disciplines. The range of disciplines and data types covered is extensive: archaeology (aerial photography and remote sensing data, geophysical data in archaeology, computer-aided design data sets and images, records produced during excavation and field work archiving, geographic information systems [GIS] data sets, virtual reality); history (GIS data in historical research); performing arts (data produced by collaborative working methods and new media tools, digital resources in the performance arts, digitized audio materials); literature, language, and linguistics (linguistic corpora, electronic texts); and visual arts (virtual reality). These guides are especially valuable, because most other guidance that is available has been developed for the creation and management of scientific data.

CHECKLIST FOR DATA MANAGEMENT

- Have you gained written consent?
- Are you sure about who owns the IPR [Intellectual Property Rights] of your data?
- Have you used standardised and consistent measures and procedures to collect and check and verify data?
- Have you provided enough documentation to inform a secondary user about project methods, data collection and data preparation?
- Are your data and files labelled sufficiently?
- Are you using up-to-date recommended data formats?
- Do you need to anonymise data?
- Are your copies of data—digital and non-digital—held in a safe location?
- Are your files backed up sufficiently?
- Do you know which is the master version of your data?
- Have you included analytic information too, for example, derived variables or interview summaries?

(*Source:* Rural Economy and Land Use Programme Data Support Service, 2006: 21.)

The third example is not really an example of consolidated advice, but it is included here because of its close relationship to the Conceptualise action of the DCC Curation Lifecycle. The DCC's website includes "Frequently Asked Questions about Submitting Funding Proposals to the Medical Research Council (MRC)" (Digital Curation Centre, 2007), which provide advice intended to assist applicants for Medical Research Council funding about the points that need to be considered in the planning of curation. The answers provide guidance on important aspects of developing a curation-focused data management plan. Advice is first offered about prerequisites for sharing data, information relating to that data, including metadata and details of tools, methods, and workflows. Attention is paid to the kinds of data that will be conceptualized and developed during the project, such as semantic information about data sets (e.g., a copy of the questionnaire, as well as the responses to it), and to the need to ensure continuing access to them. Another area of advice is about the legal implications of collecting certain kinds of data. Data sets may need to be anonymized (by removing data that enables identification of individuals)—awareness of data protection legislation is important here. Data sharing agreements that identify how issues such as consent, confidentiality, ethical and legal considerations, access rights, and intellectual property will be managed are required. There is much more useful advice in this set of questions.

Summary: Planning Data for Curation

This chapter notes the planning that is needed to ensure that "good" data are created and that data management plans are put in place that make effective curation more likely. What, then, are "good" data? What should data to be able to do, in digital curation terms? At the very least three requirements need to be met: to keep data and the ability to process them; to make ownership and the allowable usage of those data clear; and to make them citable (Rusbridge, 2007). This is done by planning when the projects that create data are conceptualized and developed. In particular, planning to ensure data are created in standard data formats and file types that can be processed with open, well-documented programs, planning to keep documentation about the data, formats, software, and agreements about its use, and planning to apply standards for how data are cited are essential. The next chapter notes the characteristics of "good" data and how to create curation-friendly data.

References

Arts and Humanities Data Service. "AHDS Guides to Good Practice." London: Arts and Humanities Data Service. Available: ahds.ac.uk/creating/guides/index.htm (accessed April 26, 2010).

Biotechnology and Biological Sciences Research Council. 2007. *Data Sharing Policy: Guidelines for Applicants*. Swindon: Biotechnology and Biological Sciences Research Council. Available: www.bbsrc.ac.uk/publications/policy/

CONCEPTUALISE: REVIEW

Key points: *Conceptualise* is the process of developing and planning data creation procedures with digital curation processes and outcomes in mind.

Key activities:
- Plan for curation at the research design stage:
  - Capture and store data in curation-friendly file formats
  - Record sufficient information at the time of data capture to assist with ongoing management and use
  - Scrupulously identify files
  - Store data on appropriate media
  - Identify a safe place for the data and make sure that an archive will take them

data_sharing_policy.html (accessed April 26, 2010). (c) 2007 Biotechnology and Biological Sciences Research Council; used by permission.

Digital Curation Centre. 2007. "Frequently Asked Questions about Submitting Funding Proposals to the Medical Research Council (MRC)." Edinburgh: Digital Curation Centre (June 29, 2007). Available: www.dcc.ac.uk/digital-curation/digital-curation-faqs/submitting-funding-proposals-medical-research-council (accessed April 26, 2010).

James, Hamish. 2005. "Introduction to Creating Digital Resources." London: Arts and Humanities Data Service (October 10, 2003, revised December 15, 2005). Available: ahds.ac.uk/creating/information-papers/creating-introduction/index.htm (accessed April 26, 2010).

Lynch, Clifford. 2008. "How Do Your Data Grow? Scientists Need to Ensure That Their Results Will Be Managed for the Long Haul. Maintaining Data Takes Big Organization." *Nature* 455, no. 7209 (September 4): 28–29.

Research Information Network. 2008. *Stewardship of Digital Research Data: Summary of the RIN's Framework of Principles.* London: Research Information Network. Available: www.rin.ac.uk/system/files/attachments/Stewardship-data-briefing.pdf (accessed April 26, 2010).

Rural Economy and Land Use Programme Data Support Service. 2006. *Guidance on Data Management.* Colchester: Rural Economy and Land Use. Available: www.data-archive.ac.uk/relu/RELUaug2006.pdf (accessed April 26, 2010). Used by permission of the UK Data Archive, University of Essex.

Rusbridge, Chris. 2007. "Create, Curate, Re-Use: The Expanding Life Course of Digital Research." Paper presented at EDUCAUSE Australasia 2007. Available: hdl.handle.net/1842/1731 (accessed April 26, 2010). Used by permission of Chris Rusbridge, Digital Curation Centre.

———. "Project Data Life Course." 2008. Digital Curation Blog, comment posted November 17, 2008. Available: digitalcuration.blogspot.com/2008/11/project-data-life-course.html (accessed April 26, 2010). Used by permission of Chris Rusbridge, Digital Curation Centre.

Smith, MacKenzie. 2008. "Curating Architectural 3D CAD Models." *International Journal of Digital Curation* 4, no. 1: 99–106. Available: www.ijdc.net/index.php/ijdc/article/viewFile/105/80 (accessed April 26, 2010). Used by permission of MacKenzie Smith.

Steinhart, Gail, and Brian Lowe. 2007. "Data Curation and Distribution in Support of Cornell University's Upper Susquehanna Agricultural Ecosystems Program." Paper presented at DigCCurr, Chapel Hill, NC, April 18–20, 2007. Available: ils.unc.edu/digccurr2007/papers/steinhartLowe_paper_4-3.pdf (accessed April 26, 2010).

Creating Data

The previous chapter outlined the nature of the planning required to ensure that we have "good" data and comprehensive data management plans so that curation is effective. This chapter notes the next Sequential Action in the DCC Curation Lifecycle, *Create or Receive*.

Scientists, researchers, scholars, private individuals—most of us, in fact—create data. Ideally these data will be created with their curation in mind so that they are accessible in the future and can be shared and reused. Archivists, data curators, librarians, and others who receive digital objects into an archive are keenly interested in ensuring that these digital objects are accessible in the future and can be shared and reused: that is, that they are curation ready. This chapter explains the principles and practices of making digital objects that are curation ready.

Create or Receive is the second stage of the DCC Curation Lifecycle. The activities that it comprises are:

- create data, including administrative, descriptive, structural, and technical metadata (preservation metadata may also be added at the time of creation); and

- receive data, in accordance with documented collecting policies, from data creators, other archives, repositories, or data centers and if required assign appropriate metadata.

In other words, there are two processes in the Create or Receive Sequential Action: (1) creating data and their associated description and representation information so that they are curation ready and (2) receiving data from external sources and making them curation ready. These processes ensure that curation is made easier at later stages of the curation lifecycle. The key activities encompassed by Create or Receive are:

- develop, document, and apply policies about creating and receiving data;

- influence data creators to create data that is curation friendly;

- create data in standard data formats and file types that can be processed with open-source, well-documented programs;

- collect and keep documentation about the data, formats, software, agreements about its use, and provenance; and
- develop and implement procedures for receiving data.

Policies for Creating and Receiving Data

Policies for creating and receiving digital objects are valuable for data curators because they delineate clearly the requirements and responsibilities of creators and curators. Effective curation requires that policies about data formats and quality, the deposit process, and rights and ownership are developed, clearly documented, and then applied (and revised when necessary).

Policies are required in these areas:

- Who is eligible to deposit data in the archive
- The data quality requirements that are in place
- The metadata that needs to be submitted
- Confidentiality and disclosure
- The access status of the data (whether or not there are embargos on them)
- Rights and ownership
- Data file formats: which formats will be accepted for deposit, which are preferred, whether the files will be normalized (converted to another format that the archive can manage better)
- Any volume and size limitations on the data received by the archive

Other areas where policies about creating and receiving digital objects may be useful depend on the nature of the digital objects, the archive, and the discipline. The DISC-UK DataShare Project's publication *Policy-Making for Research Data in Repositories: A Guide* (Green, Macdonald, and Rice, 2009) provides excellent advice on policies for creating and receiving data and is applicable to a wide range of contexts.

The topics and questions that policies should address are indicated in the following list. More comprehensive lists are provided by Green, Macdonald, and Rice (2009).

- **Eligible depositors**: Who is eligible to deposit data in the archive? What kind of data will be received? What procedure is in place for providing a receipt to the depositors of data?
- **Data quality requirements**: What criteria do the data need to meet in terms of quality? Is the coverage complete? Have they been checked for validity?
- **Metadata**: What metadata (descriptive, structural, and administrative) should be supplied by the creator? What happens if this required metadata is not supplied? What metadata will the archive supply?

- **Confidentiality and disclosure**: What requirements must data creators meet regarding confidential data? Does data, for example, identify people? Will the archive anonymize data?

- **Embargo status**: Will an embargo be placed on the data that makes it unavailable for use? How long will the embargo last? What will trigger the lifting of the embargo?

- **Rights and ownership**: What rights relating to the data are retained by the creator? What rights are transferred to the archive? What limitations are placed on the way the archive can use the data? Can the archive change the data at all (e.g., during processing data for preservation)? Does the creator certify that the data do not infringe the copyright of others or certify that permission from the rights-owner has been received?

- **Data file formats**: Which formats will be accepted for deposit? Which formats are preferred? Will the formats be normalized? Will compression formats (e.g., zipped files) be accepted? Will the archive retain the original bit stream as well as the normalized files? Is there a limit to the size and number of files the archive will accept?

Having policies about creating digital objects and receiving them into the archive is good practice. Such policies assist the curation process by spelling out clearly what is required of data creators and what is required of the archives that receive the digital objects. The rest of this chapter examines these requirements in more detail.

Creating Data for Curation

In this chapter these questions are posed: What are "good" data? What should data be able to do, in digital curation terms? Three requirements are suggested: to keep data and the ability to process them; to make ownership and the allowable usage of those data clear; and to make them citable. The techniques to fulfill these are noted as creating data in standard data formats and file types that can be processed with open-source, well-documented programs; keeping documentation about the data, formats, software, and agreements about its use; and applying standards for how data are cited. In all of these techniques, application of standards is essential—standards for data structure, data quality, citation, and annotation and provenance.

The rest of this chapter explores these requirements and techniques. The next sections look at how "good" data are structured for three purposes:

- **Their use and reuse**—so they can be kept and processed

- **Their management**—to ensure that they can be accessed, used and reused over time

- **Their discoverability**—so they can be identified and located

There is one notable omission from this chapter, and that is metadata. Metadata requirements are noted at many points, but only briefly. More about metadata and its importance in successful curation is found in Chapter 6 and at relevant points in subsequent chapters.

Structuring Data for Use and Reuse

To keep data and to keep the ability to process data, they need to be authentic (the data are what they claim to be), accurate (they haven't been tampered with), renderable (they can be used in the ways for which they were intended or viewed as originally intended), and in a form that best ensures their longevity. (See Chapter 5 and also later in this chapter for further discussion of these concepts.) One way to achieve these aims is to use file formats that stand a good chance of being understood in the future. These file formats are likely to be in widespread use and very likely to be open (i.e., not proprietary). Criteria to use to predict the ongoing viability of a file format include the following (based on Clausen, 2004: 11–12):

- **Openness**: Is there an open, publicly available specification for the format? Are its specifications in the public domain? Is it unencrypted?

- **Portability**: Is the format independent of particular hardware, operating system, or other software? Is it independent of particular institutions, groups, or events? Is it in widespread and current use? Does it contain little or no built-in functionality?

- **Quality**: Is it robust, simple, thoroughly tested, and loss-free?

Two examples of the kinds of files formats that are preferred are taken from the UK Data Archive's (2009) *Managing and Sharing Data: A Best Practice Guide for Researchers.* These preferences are based on criteria such as the file formats are widely adopted, are *de facto* standards, and are nonproprietary and well documented.

The first example is qualitative textual data, for which the preferred formats are (1) eXtensible Markup Language (XML) marked-up text according to an appropriate Document Type Definition (DTD) or schema; (2) Rich Text Format (.rtf); (3) plain text data; and (4) ASCII (.txt). Also acceptable are Hypertext Markup Language (HTML), widely used proprietary formats such as MS Word (.doc/.docx), and proprietary or software-specific formats such as NUD*IST, NVivo, and ATLAS.ti. The second example is digital audio data, where the preferred formats are Free Lossless Audio Codec (FLAC) (.flac), and WAV file (.wav) but also acceptable are MPEG-1 Audio Layer 3 (.mp3), and Audio Interchange File Format (AIFF; .aif). In general, the simplest formats possible are preferred for long-term preservation, such as RTF, ASCII, PDF, and XML.

Many other recommendations about the file formats for preservation are available. Some are the Florida Digital Archive's "Supported and Recognized File Formats" (accessed 2010) and its "Recommended Data Formats for Preservation Purposes in the Florida Digital Archive" (2008), and The National Archives' (United Kingdom) *Selecting File Formats for Long-Term Preservation* (Brown, 2008).

An e-mail list discussion in August 2008 about preferred formats for archiving images illustrates some of the requirements and practices of curating image data. The preservation format used by one archive is TIFF; that archive also keeps the source RAW format (the unprocessed data produced by the digital camera) as part of the AIP (see Chapter 3). While the TIFF format is well defined, a wide variety of proprietary RAW formats are created by cameras from different manufacturers. The photographers are interested in the RAW image being kept so that a different final product can be produced at a later date. (This is analogous to keeping negatives and photographic prints in the predigital era.) It may also be necessary to capture information about how the RAW file was processed to TIFF (Ferrante, 2008).

Open Formats and Open Source

Curation-ready digital objects should be created in standard data formats and in file types that can be processed with well-documented software programs. The file formats and software should, if possible, be open: that is, a publicly available specification for the format should exist, which is available in the public domain and not encrypted. Why is there such a strong emphasis on openness?

Rusbridge (2008) proposes a spectrum of file format obsolescence. At one end of his spectrum, files are completely usable and not at risk; they are in widespread use, are fully and openly documented, do not contain any proprietary content in terms of intellectual property restrictions, and exist in several versions, at least one of which is open source. At the other end of the spectrum, the files are completely inaccessible, with no known way to interpret them. Between these two points of the spectrum lie three other points: currently usable, at risk; currently unusable, at significant risk; and currently inaccessible, migration path not known. These three contain significant proprietary content for which documentation is not available.

Open file formats and open-source software assist curation by allowing curators to have control over software source code and to see how file formats are structured. The availability of access to the source code for file formats, and to documentation about them, allows the future possibility of developing tools to migrate the open formats. Curation is made difficult or impossible if proprietary file formats are used, because their structure cannot be accessed for preservation purposes. Although many software packages are backwards compatible—that is, they can import and handle data created in earlier versions of that software—there is no guarantee that they will continue to do this over the long term. (It is common for backwards compatibility to function effectively for only a few versions back.) In addition, there is no guarantee of interoperability; data created in one software package may not be accessible and usable in other similar software packages. Rather than rely on backwards compatibility, it is better curation practice to convert data to standard formats that can be interpreted by a range of software packages. In practice this usually means using open formats—formats where the specifications are publicly available—rather than proprietary formats. Figure 10.1 summarizes features for selecting file formats for data curation.

These are the key characteristics of open file formats:

- They are based on freely available standards.
- They are developed by a community rather than by a single entity.
- They can be used in multiple software packages, not just one.
- They do not contain any intellectual property restrictions, such as patented components. (Rusbridge, 2008)

Two examples of formats with these characteristics are JPEG and PDF. JPEG is a label applied to a file format for images. Defined by an international standard (ISO 10918), it exists in several profiles, of which the lossless version is preferred for preservation purposes; JPEG 2000, Part 1, Core Coding Version with lossless compression is also acceptable. The other example, PDF, is widely used for document exchange. This format allows users to exchange and view documents independently of the software, hardware, and operating system in which they were created. PDF was originally proprietary software developed by Adobe Systems, which relinquished its interest in it to the ISO and it is now an international standard, ISO 32000-1:2008.

Open-source software programs are increasingly being developed and used for digital curation. It is no exaggeration to state that most curation-specific software is open source. An example is Xena (XML Electronic Normalizing for Archives; xena.sourceforge.net), software developed by the National Archives of Australia for the preservation of digital records. It detects the file format (including proprietary formats) of a digital object and converts it to an open format. This free, open-source software is written in Java and, consequently, runs on three operating systems: Linux, Windows, and Mac OS X. Xena requires the open-source OpenOffice suite of software (www.openoffice.org) to run. Initiatives such as the Open Source Initiative (www.opensource.org) and SourceForge (sourceforge.net), a repository of open-source software, illustrate the increasing popularity of the open-source concept, which is a key aspect of digital curation.

Significant Properties and Authenticity

To keep digital objects, make them accessible, and be able to process and use them over time, we need to know precisely what it is we want to keep. More specifically, we need to know which of the properties or characteristics of the digital objects we must maintain over time. These properties or characteristics are known as *significant properties*.

Significant properties are defined by the InSPECT Project (Arts and Humanities Data Service, accessed 2010) as "those aspects of the digital object or database which *must* be maintained over time in order for the digital object to remain accessible, usable and meaningful." The significant properties of digital objects and databases are typically categorized as the following: *(continued p. 122)*

Figure 10.1. Selecting File Formats for Data Curation

NA	Paradigm	Arms and Fleischhauer
Open standards	Is it defined by an international, national, or publicly available standard? Is the quality of the specification adequate?	Disclosure: the degree of access to full specifications and tools for validating technical integrity Impact of patents: the degree to which digital preservation will be inhibited by patents
Ubiquity	How widely has the format been adopted as a preservation format? How proven is it in terms of longevity?	Adoption: the degree to which the format is already used
Stability	How stable is the format? Is it backwards compatible?	
Metadata support	Does it have good metadata support?	Self-documentation: easier to manage digital objects that contain basic descriptive, technical, and administrative metadata
Feature set	Does it have a good range of functionality without being too complex for the purpose?	
Interoperability	Is it independent of any specific hardware or software environment?	External dependencies: the degree to which a format depends on particular hardware, operating system, or software for rendering or use
Viability	Does it include an error-detection facility?	
Authenticity (broadly, the format must preserve the content (data and structure) of the record, and any inherent contextual, provenance, referencing and fixity information)		
Processability (certain types of data must retain their processability to have any reuse value)		
Presentation	How well does it retain the formatting and other significant properties of converted digital objects?	Quality and functionality factors that are genre specific and pertain to the ability of a particular format to represent the significant characteristics required or expected by current and future users of a given content item
		Technical production mechanisms: the implementation of mechanisms like encryption that might prevent the preservation of content by the digital repository
	Is it easily convertible into other formats (for migration purposes)?	
		Transparency: the degree to which the digital representation is open to direct analysis with basic tools; this is enhanced if textual content employs standard character encodings
Support by software tools		
Ease of identification and validation of the format		

Source: NA: The National Archives, *Selecting File Formats for Long-Term Preservation* (Brown, 2008); Paradigm: Paradigm Project (2008a), *Workbook on Digital Private Papers*, Chapter 8; Arms and Fleischhauer (2005), "Digital Formats: Factors for Sustainability, Functionality, and Quality."

- **Content**: for example, text, image, slides
- **Context**: for example, who, when, why
- **Appearance**: for example, font and size, color, layout
- **Behavior**: for example, hypertext links, updating calculations, active links
- **Structure**: for example, embedded files, pagination, headings

Determining the significant properties of digital objects is also an important factor when deciding on the best file formats to use for the required outcome. A simple example is the very stable file format ASCII, which does not allow any formatting beyond a basic level to be captured.

The concept of *authenticity* has become central to digital curation. Authenticity is defined as "The quality of being genuine, not a counterfeit, and free from tampering" and is determined from evidence such as the characteristics, structure, content, and context of a digital object or database (Pearce-Moses, 2005). Authenticity is closely linked with significant properties; preserving a digital object's significant properties helps to ensure that it retains its authenticity over time.

Significant properties are determined by the requirements of the community for whom the digital objects are being preserved. Digital preservation usually involves some change to the digital objects (this point is noted further in Chapter 13). Although some change may be acceptable to some communities, it is not acceptable to others. For example, for some categories of word-processed documents, the content (the text) may be the most significant characteristic, and other characteristics (such as layout or font size) are not essential to its use in the future; for statistical data sets, the ability to manipulate the data is likely to be essential to future users and must be retained.

Considerable research has been carried out into significant properties; it is summarized by Knight and Pennock (2008). However, significant properties are still to be defined for most formats or data types. The InSPECT Project (Arts and Humanities Service, accessed 2010) is determining the significant properties for four types of digital objects: vector images, moving images, learning objects, and software. It is also developing a generalized methodology for determining the significant properties of other digital object types. Andrew Wilson (2007) provides a thorough examination of the state of understanding about significant properties in the Project's *Significant Properties Report*.

Documentation

Another key requirement for digital objects to be usable over time is access to documentation about those digital objects. This documentation provides detailed description of the digital objects. It indicates how they were digitized or created, provides information that allows the user to understand the meaning of them, and notes their structure and content. Any actions applied to the digital objects are also documented. The aim is to make sure that digital objects are understandable both now and in the future. Documentation of digital objects is best carried out when they are created and then as an ongoing part of the curation process.

The UK Data Archive's (2009: 6) *Managing and Sharing Data* specifies what should be documented:

- the context of data collection: project history, aims, objectives, hypotheses, etc.;
- data collection methods: data collection process, sampling design, instruments, hardware and software used, questionnaire used, scale and resolution, temporal coverage, and geographic coverage;
- dataset structure: data files, cases, relationships between files, etc.;
- data sources used;
- data validation, checking, proofing, cleaning, and other quality assurance procedures carried out;
- modifications made to data over time since their original creation and identification of different versions of datasets; and
- where applicable, information on data confidentiality and consent agreements made.

Different kinds of data have different documentation requirements. In the context of a research project, for example, qualitative data may require a list and description of sound files or image files. Documentation for numerical data in tables requires careful noting of the variables, fields, and records, together with their values. Coding of the values, and details of how any derived data created from the data set were constructed, are examples of other documentation that is needed.

Influencing Data Creators

In some circumstances there are opportunities to influence the creators of data. The aim is to work, either directly or indirectly, with data creators and provide them with the knowledge they need to create curation-friendly data. This is not always feasible. A library that collects personal manuscripts in digital form may not have any influence on the creators of those manuscripts and perhaps may not be able even to identify potential donors. By comparison, a government archive has the potential to influence creators of electronic records within its jurisdiction by issuing guidelines for best practice, and it may even mandate adherence to these guidelines. In some situations direct influence is possible—for example, in a digitization project where file formats and other standards can be mandated. More commonly, though, influence is possible only indirectly through the development and dissemination of guidelines, such as guidelines for the submission of digital objects to an archive.

An example of detailed guidance about creating digital objects is the Association of Recorded Sound Collections Technical Committee's (2009) *Preservation of Archival Sound Recordings*. It advocates that archival copies of sound recordings must be digital and indicates some of the requirements when creating digital copies for archival purposes.

Attention is paid to data quality ("The transfer process should not add any artifacts or subjective changes," p. 3) and file formats ("The digital archival master file format should be widely used, self-documenting, with publicly accessible specifications, and it should not depend on a specific operating system or type of equipment," p. 3). Metadata requirements are noted ("Keep detailed notes about the digital transfer, including the date and location, the make and models of the equipment used, the settings on the equipment...," p. 5). There is considerable comment on what is required of the file formats used, such as that no compression should be used.

Other examples of guidelines that offer advice about data creation are plentiful. Here are four of them. The National Archives of Australia (2004) provides advice on the web in its *Digital Recordkeeping: Guidelines for Creating, Managing and Preserving Digital Records*, aimed at Australian federal government agencies. For creators of personal records, the Paradigm Project's (2008b) *Guidelines for Creators of Personal Archives* offer useful practical advice, as also do the InterPARES Project's (2007) *Creator Guidelines: Making and Maintaining Digital Materials: Guidelines for Individuals*. An unusual example, possibly unique, is advice offered at the national level in Archives New Zealand's (2009a) *Digital Continuity Action Plan*, which includes general "action tips for maintaining digital information" such as "use recordkeeping metadata for digital recordkeeping" and "target specific record formats that are causing problems" (Archives New Zealand, 2009b).

Structuring Data for Management

Data Management

Data need to be managed to ensure that they can be processed, accessed, and reused over time. Processes such as data cleaning, storage, and maintenance are applied. Selection of viable file formats (noted earlier) is essential. Three characteristics of file formats that are particularly helpful for managing data are metadata support, interoperability, and viability.

- **Metadata support**: Description and representation information are essential for curation (see Chapter 6). Some software applications generate description and representation information automatically, which is then added to by data creators or data managers. Some file formats accommodate metadata. As one example, metadata fields in a TIFF file record details about the make and model of scanner, software and operating system, creator's name, and a description of the image. Another example is Exif (Exchangeable Image File Format), an image-file format that embeds metadata derived from a digital camera, such as date and time information, camera settings including camera model and ISO speed information, and a thumbnail for previewing the image. It can also accommodate information about geographic location from a global positioning system (GPS) receiver.

- **Interoperability**: Managing data over time will almost certainly require its migration from one technical environment to another. File formats that are platform independent and/or are supported by a wide range of software are easier to migrate, as noted earlier in this chapter.

- **Viability**: Some file formats are "stronger" than others in the sense that they can still be accessed and used even though parts of the data may have been damaged. The robustness of the file format is seldom taken into account when drawing up lists of recommended file formats, which more usually focus on characteristics such as the openness of the file format (see Figure 10.1 for a list of these characteristics). How files behave under stress, for instance, when there is a loss of bits because of media deterioration, determines their robustness. Recommended file formats based on the characteristics usually applied are not necessarily robust file formats.

File formats that have in-built mechanisms for error checking can assist data management by indicating when files have become corrupted. An example is the Portable Network Graphics (PNG) format, which allows PNG decoders to detect errors (W3C, 2003). There are, however, relatively few file formats with this capability.

Data Quality

Ensuring the quality of data is an important early step in the curation process. Data quality is important in all research and in all other activities that generate data. The best outcomes in managing data over time and reusing data are achieved when they are of high quality. There are three critical points for data quality in the digital curation process: when data are collected, when they are prepared for analysis, and when they are verified.

The first critical point is the point at which data are collected. The quality of data collection methods used has a significant bearing on data quality. For scientific data, quality is usually achieved by a combination of automated and manual processes that calibrate the data created by scientific instruments and then validate, verify, and clean those data. For example, with experimental data the instrumentation generating the data is calibrated after the measurements have been taken in order to check characteristics of the data gathered; data are validated by checking for equipment errors and transcription errors; and data are verified by checking the veracity of the data, for instance, by taking multiple samples. Another example: the quality of the data collected during sound recordings of interviews depends on the quality of the recording equipment used.

The second critical point is data preparation. During this stage data are transcribed, coded, and so on. Rigorous adherence to standardized procedures helps to achieve data quality.

Data verification, the third critical point, entails cleaning, editing, and checking data. When data are cleaned, incomplete, noisy, and inconsistent data (data that for various reasons fall outside the norms or standards of that project) are identified and actions applied to rectify these issues by filling in missing values, smoothing out noisy data, and detecting outliers. The checking of data can be automated or manual—taking a random sample of the data and checking them against the original data, for instance, or keying in data twice, or checking data for values that are out of the expected range and removing or otherwise accounting for them. An example from bioinformatics describes this process in more detail. Data cleaning, the process of detecting and removing errors and discrepancies, is essential to ensure data quality. It is carried out both manually and using proprietary programs. Manual curation of the data improves the quality of data that comes from other public domain databases or is submitted by individual researchers. "Using data analysis and visualisation tools, curators inspect and correct the data for consistency, accuracy, completeness, correctness, timeliness, relevance, and uniqueness" (Koh and Brusic, 2005: 58).

Another aspect of data quality is the extent of the metadata provided by the data creator. Insufficient descriptive, structural, and administrative metadata can compromise an archive's ability to effectively curate digital objects.

Structuring Data for Discoverability

Digital curation requires that data are discoverable, that is, they can be located. Standardized methods of describing and identifying resources are applied. Discoverability of resources is closely associated with metadata, especially descriptive metadata. Metadata is noted in detail elsewhere in this book (in Chapter 6 and at relevant points in other chapters). This section is concerned with one aspect of discoverability—standardized methods of identifying the location of digital objects.

Reliable long-term access is based on persistent identification of data, databases, and digital objects. If these cannot be reliably identified and located, they are effectively lost, and any curation and preservation activities applied to them will have been in vain. A related concern is the increasingly linked nature of digital objects, which are increasingly available online and often cite other online data, databases, and digital objects. If the locations of these change then links are broken and the data, databases, or digital objects cannot be located and referred to. This raises several questions: Do the data exist? If so, where are they? If data that look similar are located, can we be sure they are the same?

Another reason for being concerned about identifying and locating data is controlling those who can access data. Automated transactions that allow access only to authorized users require unambiguous identification of data, database, or digital object for computer processing.

A *persistent identifier* is an identifier that does not change, even if the locations of the data or digital objects change. Reliable identification of data is essential for providing long-term access to them and ensuring their reliability and authenticity. A persistent identifier—"a name for a resource which will remain the same regardless of where the resource is located" (National Library of Australia, 2002)—provides this reliable identification.

Although much of the discussion about persistent identifiers has been about their application to web resources, the use of persistent identifiers is not limited to web material. They are equally essential for linking and citation of primary research to data sets. Chapter 6 provides more information about persistent identifiers.

Receiving Data for Curation

Archivists, data curators, librarians, and others who receive data, databases, and digital objects into an archive are keenly interested in ensuring that these are curation ready. If they have been created using the criteria noted earlier in this chapter, the curator is more likely to be successful in ensuring long-term access.

The data, databases, and digital objects considered for ingesting (taking into an archive) may come directly from data creators such as scientists or may come from other archives, repositories, or data centers. Whatever their source, they will be considered for ingest according to documented policies for what the archive collects. (This is noted further in Chapter 11.) Ideally the data, digital objects, and databases received are of high quality, created in curation-friendly open formats using open-source software, able to run on a variety of hardware platforms, and fully documented with administrative, descriptive, structural, and technical metadata. If required, the curator will assign appropriate metadata to ensure that the data can be successfully maintained and accessed.

Specific actions that are carried out when data are received by an archive include the following:

- Sort, identify, and list the data to be transferred. Information should be available about file formats present, media, operating system and version, programs and versions used to create the data, who created the data (and for what reason, and when), the quantity of material, and the metadata present. Hard copies of supplementary material may also be present.

- Ensure that a depositor agreement has been completed.

- Ascertain how the data are to be transferred: for example, by FTP or on physical media (and if so, what type), and effect the transfer.

- Review data received for their relevance to the scope of the archive, whether file formats are acceptable to the archive, whether spam has been excluded.

- Determine whether the integrity of the data has been maintained during the submission process.

- Check whether the metadata records supplied are accurate.

- Add persistent identifiers.
- Assess the quality of the data (e.g., that the required metadata has been provided by the data creator or depositor and that variable names in a data set match up with the variable names in a codebook).

The activities that are needed when data are received by an archive are also noted in Chapter 12.

As with other digital curation tasks, receiving data into an archive is increasingly automated. An example is the software released by the Library of Congress in 2009 as part of its Transfer Tools project:

> The software tools developed are based on BagIt, which specifies how to package files for the purposes of exchanging data. These tools, which are open source and available through SourceForge, automate part of the process of sending and receiving large quantities of data.

Summary: The Positive Effects of "Good" Data

"Good" data and digital objects are structured for good curation and are accompanied by metadata and other relevant documentation. This ensures that they are curation ready or at least curation friendly. The choice of open file formats, attention to significant properties, documentation, and the existence and implementation of policies for creating and receiving data and digital objects are key ingredients in the recipe for curation-ready data.

Although the examples in this chapter largely come from the science data environment, they are equally applicable to all contexts, including individuals who wish to curate their personal data. The same principles apply; attention to choice of file formats and ensuring documentation is available are, for example, crucial to ensure that curation of digital objects is made easier in later stages in their lifecycle.

The next chapter notes the next Sequential Action in the DCC Curation Lifecycle, *Appraise and Select*, and two related Occasional Actions, *Reappraise* and *Dispose*.

References

Archives New Zealand. 2009a. *Digital Continuity Action Plan*. Wellington, NZ: Archives New Zealand Available: archives.govt.nz/advice/digital-continuity-action-plan (accessed April 26, 2010).

———. 2009b. "Digital Continuity Action Plan—Questions and Answers." Wellington, NZ: Archives New Zealand (August 7, 2009). Available: archives.govt.nz/advice/digital-continuity-action-plan/digital-continuity-action-plan-questions-and-answers (accessed April 26, 2010).

Arms, Caroline R., and Carl Fleischhauer. 2005. "Digital Formats: Factors for Sustainability, Functionality, and Quality." Paper presented at IS&T Archiving

---

CREATE OR RECEIVE: REVIEW

Key points: *Create or Receive* is the process of creating data and their associated description and representation information so they are curation-ready (i.e., accessible in the future and can be shared and reused), or of receiving data from external sources and making them curation-ready.

Key activities:
- Develop, document, and apply policies about creating and receiving data
- Influence data creators to create data that is curation-friendly
- Create data in standard data formats and file types that can be processed with open source, well-documented programs
- Collect and keep documentation about the data, formats, software, agreements about its use, and provenance
- Develop and implement procedures for receiving data

Conference, Washington DC (April 29, 2005). Available: memory.loc.gov/ammem/techdocs/digform/Formats_IST05_paper.pdf (accessed April 26, 2010).

Arts and Humanities Data Service. "InSPECT." London: Arts and Humanities Data Service. Available: www.significantproperties.org.uk/about.html (accessed April 26, 2010).

Association of Recorded Sound Collections Technical Committee. 2009. *Preservation of Archival Sound Recordings*. Annapolis, MD: ARSC. Available: www.arsc-audio.org/pdf/ARSCTC_preservation.pdf (accessed April 26, 2010).

Brown, Adrian. 2008. *Selecting File Formats for Long-Term Preservation*. London: The National Archives (Digital Preservation Guidance Note: 1). Available: www.nationalarchives.gov.uk/preservation/advice/digital.htm (accessed April 26, 2010).

Clausen, Lars R. 2004. *Handling File Formats*. Århus: Statsbiblioteket. Available: netarchive.dk/publikationer/FileFormats-2004.pdf (accessed April 26, 2010).

Ferrante, Riccardo. 2008. "Re: Archiving Images: RAW or TIFF?" The dcc-associates Listserv, comment posted August 15, 2008. Available: www.mail-archive.com/dcc-associates@lists.ed.ac.uk/msg00131.html (accessed April 26, 2010).

Florida Digital Archive. "Supported and Recognized File Formats." Gainesville, FL: Florida Center for Library Automation. Available: www.fcla.edu/digitalArchive/formatInfo.htm (accessed April 26, 2010).

———. 2008. "Recommended Data Formats for Preservation Purposes in the Florida Digital Archive" (August 2008). Gainesville, FL: Florida Center for Library Automation. Available: www.fcla.edu/digitalArchive/pdfs/recFormats.pdf (accessed April 26, 2010)

Green, Ann, Stuart Macdonald, and Robin Rice. 2009. *Policy-Making for Research Data in Repositories: A Guide*. Version 1.2. Edinburgh: EDINA and University Data Library. Available: www.disc-uk.org/docs/guide.pdf (accessed April 26, 2010). Used by permission of Robin Rice.

InterPARES Project. 2007. *Creator Guidelines: Making and Maintaining Digital Materials: Guidelines for Individuals*. Vancouver, BC: InterPARES Project. Available: www.interpares.org/ip2/display_file.cfm?doc=ip2(pub)creator_guidelines_booklet.pdf (accessed April 26, 2010).

Knight, Gareth, and Maureen Pennock. 2008. "Data Without Meaning: Establishing the Significant Properties of Digital Research." Paper presented at iPres 2008, London, September 29–30, 2008. Available: www.bl.uk/ipres2008/presentations_day1/16_Knight.pdf (accessed April 26, 2010).

Koh, J.L.Y., and V. Brusic. 2005. "Database Warehousing in Bioinformatics." In *Bioinformatic Technologies*, edited by Y.-P.B. Chen. Berlin: Springer.

Library of Congress. 2009. "Library Releases Software Tools." Washington, DC: Library of Congress (January 9, 2009). Available: www.digitalpreservation.gov/news/2009/20090109news_article_Sourceforge.html (accessed April 26, 2010).

National Archives of Australia. 2004. *Digital Recordkeeping: Guidelines for Creating, Managing and Preserving Digital Records*. Canberra, ACT: National Archives of Australia. Available: www.naa.gov.au/Images/Digital-recordkeeping-guidelines_tcm2-920.pdf (accessed April 26, 2010).

National Library of Australia. 2002. *Managing Web Resources for Persistent Access*. Canberra, ACT: National Library of Australia. Available: www.nla.gov.au/guidelines/persistence.html (accessed April 26, 2010).

Paradigm Project. 2008a. "File Formats." Chapter 8 in *Workbook on Digital Private Papers*. Oxford: Paradigm Project. Available: www.paradigm.ac.uk/workbook/preservation-strategies/file-formats.html (accessed April 26, 2010).

———. 2008b. *Guidelines for Creators of Personal Archives*. Oxford: Paradigm Project. Available: www.paradigm.ac.uk/workbook/appendices/guidelines.html (accessed April 26, 2009).

Pearce-Moses, Richard. 2005. "A Glossary of Archival and Records Terminology." Chicago: Society of American Archivists (2005). Available: www.archivists.org/glossary (accessed April 26, 2010).

Rusbridge, Chris. "Comments on an Obsolescence Scale, Please." Digital Curation Blog, comment posted November 20, 2008. Available: digitalcuration.blogspot.com/2008/11/comments-on-obsolescence-scale-please.html (accessed April 26, 2010). Used by permission of Chris Rusbridge, Digital Curation Centre.

UK Data Archive. 2009. *Managing and Sharing Data: A Best Practice Guide for Researchers*. Colchester: UK Data Archive. Available: www.data-archive.ac.uk/news/publications/managingsharing.pdf (accessed April 26, 2010). Used by permission of the UK Data Archive, University of Essex.

W3C. 2003. *Portable Network Graphics (PNG) Specification* (Second Edition): *Information Technology—Computer Graphics and Image Processing—Portable Network Graphics (PNG): Functional Specification. ISO/IEC 15948:2003 (E), W3C Recommendation*. Available: www.w3.org/TR/PNG (accessed April 26, 2010).

Wilson, Andrew. 2007. *Significant Properties Report*. London: Arts and Humanities Data Service. Available: www.significantproperties.org.uk/documents/wp22_significant_properties.pdf (accessed April 26, 2010).

Deciding What Data to Keep

This chapter investigates the third of the Sequential Actions of the DCC Curation Lifecycle Model, *Appraise and Select*—the processes of developing criteria for determining what data and digital objects should be kept for the long term and what should be discarded and then applying those criteria. It also notes two of the Occasional Actions, *Reappraise* and *Dispose*, which are closely related to the *Appraise and Select* Sequential Action. The activities that comprise Appraise and Select are stated in the Curation Lifecycle Model as:

- evaluate data and select for long-term curation and preservation; and
- adhere to documented guidance, policies, or legal requirements. (Digital Curation Centre, 2008)

The key activities encompassed by Appraise and Select are:

- developing, documenting, and applying policies about appraisal and selection, including: (a) defining the designated community—the people who will use the data and digital objects in the future, (b) identifying properties of the data and digital objects to preserve, and (c) deciding how long the data or digital objects need to be maintained;
- developing appraisal criteria; and
- determining whether to keep data by evaluating them against the appraisal criteria.

Dispose is a potential outcome of the appraisal process. *Reappraise* refers to the process of appraisal, the difference being that it is carried out at a later stage in the lifecycle in response to some trigger.

What Is Appraisal?

Appraise and Select is referred to immediately above as the processes of developing criteria for determining what data and digital objects should be kept for the long term and then applying those criteria. But there is more to it than that. It is worth looking more closely at some definitions of the term *appraisal* (and also the term *selection*) and dipping into the history of appraisal so that we can understand better how it applies to data.

Definitions of the term *appraisal* are easy to find. A concise example defines appraisal as "the process of determining significance of any information object" (Oliver et al., 2008: 5). Appraisal is a term originating from archival practice, "the process of evaluating records to determine which are to be retained as archives, which are to be kept for specified periods and which are to be destroyed" (Ellis, 1993: 461). Faundeen and Oleson (2007: 2) note several more definitions and conclude that they focus on "the theme of usefulness or value that we place on something." *Selection* is a more general term, usually applied when deciding what materials will be added to a repository, and it is typically used in the library context. Both appraisal and selection rely on criteria for determining what is considered worthy of preservation or of adding to a repository.

There is no single approach to appraisal in the archives context; nor is there a single approach to selection in the library context. Cox (2007: 5) notes that archival appraisal models and methodologies include "the Schellenberg framework of values, the articulation of institutional collection policies, archival documentation strategies, and macro-appraisal approaches such as functional analysis." He also notes that these models and methodologies are likely to be different from the appraisal approaches that are developed for data and digital objects to accommodate new "information forms" such as instant messaging and text messaging and other forms not yet envisaged.

What is the intention of appraisal? At its heart is the determination of significance; in fact, appraisal can be considered as a methodology developed by archivists to do just this. Its outcome is the designation of some records as warranting long-term preservation. Determining what is significant cannot be an absolute; it is influenced by a wide range of factors—economic, political, ideological, cultural, and social. Based on this designation of an information object or a data set as significant, a series of other decisions about it are then made, such as whether to acquire it and, at a later stage, whether to retain it in a collection. This determination of significance, and revisiting it at a later date (or dates), is especially important because of the resourcing implications that the addition of material to a collection has (Oliver et al., 2008: 8).

Cox (2007: 4) also makes the same pragmatic point—that appraisal is "an effort to look at a vast universe of documentation (and a universe that is expanding quite rapidly) and then to shrink it down in some strategic, planned, or rational fashion that allows archivists to administer it and researchers to access it.... This means that we select the right materials to digitize and pick from the digitally born records the most critically important to our researchers and society." For scientific data, Faundeen and Oleson (2007) suggest that "determination" is what appraisal is all about, determining the data sets to which resources are committed in order to preserve them and make them accessible.

What Data Do We Want to Keep?

What data (used in its broad sense to include digital objects and databases) do we want to keep? Sometimes this is the wrong question. In some contexts, and for some kinds of data, the question posed should be do we *need* to keep the data? Data might be selected for long-term curation because they have to be kept for legal reasons or because not keeping them presents too high a risk to the organization generating those data. Other data we might *want* to keep. The key questions that arise then are: Why do we want to keep them? How do we decide what data are likely to be useful or reusable? In addition, there are key questions common to both cases. How long should we plan to keep the data? Do we want them to be fully functional (e.g., with all linked data also available) in the future? These and other questions can be addressed by developing and applying policies for appraisal and selection—policies that help in deciding what data are worth keeping or need to be kept, why, and for how long.

An element of selection or appraisal is commonly understood to be part of most data preservation activities. The need for selection (with its corollary, the need to discard some data) is commonly recognized, even at the personal and popular levels. Newspaper columnist Chris O'Brien (2009) suggests that it is "Time to clean up your digital closet," and to do so "You will need to start thinking like a librarian and become an active curator of your files. . . . The first and most important thing to do is to begin deleting files. Whittle things down to the essentials. What do you really want to maintain and pass along? You must be ruthless and vigilant."

The question "What data do we want to keep for the future?" has two dimensions: (1) Which data sets or digital objects do we want to keep? (2) Which characteristics or elements of those data sets or digital objects do we want to keep? Finding answers to these questions becomes increasingly necessary as the rate of data production continues to outstrip the rate at which resources for digital curation are made available.

To answer both of these questions requires knowledge of the designated community—the people who will understand and use the data in the future (noted further in Chapters 3 and 6). It is not just the data themselves that are selected but also *representation information*—the information about the data that is needed to make the data understandable in the future (see Chapter 6). There is also a need to think about what the designated community will consider sufficient in the future; for instance, will it be sufficient to keep just the information content of a database, without keeping the ability to search and manipulate that content? The difficulties of defining the designated community do, however, need to be acknowledged. There may not be, perhaps, any truly valid way to determine what data properties future users might deem significant.

There are exceptions to the expectation that appraisal is required. Appraisal and selection practices differ from discipline to discipline largely because the nature and quantity of data handled in each discipline varies. We are inclined to generalize about scientific data, assuming they are, by and large, similar. But different disciplines show significantly different data creation and management practices. For a start, the amounts of data generated vary: in astronomy, very large quantities (terabytes each day) are collected from sophisticated, expensive equipment; field researchers in biology generate comparatively small quantities of data about individual specimens; some disciplines, such as the space sciences, have a well-developed history of selection and appraisal and of establishing and using metadata and software standards. These differences are reflected in selection, appraisal, and retention policies and practices, which are different for different disciplines (Esanu et al., 2004). The disciplinary differences are highlighted by a 2009 study of researchers in the life sciences, which concluded that there are significant differences in information use and exchange patterns in different areas of the life sciences. In relation to appraisal and selection, the report noted that "The sheer volume of data and information that is now being produced, and expected to be produced in the future, is a cause for concern. Researchers fear that there will be too much data to handle, process, or even look at" (Research Information Network and British Library, 2009: 44).

Determining which data sets or digital objects to retain is not the end of appraisal and selection. They must be accompanied by relevant description and representation information (see Chapter 6)—that is, the information about them needed to make them understandable in the future. Successful curation involves more than just a concern with the data set or digital object.

Drivers for Keeping Data

The point was made earlier that, in some contexts, the key question is: Do we *need* to keep the data? What are the drivers? Why is it necessary to keep those data?

Chapter 1 noted some compliance reasons for keeping data. There may, for instance, be pressure from community groups, such as taxpayers' groups, to keep and make available data whose creation involved expenditure of public funds. Compliance with the requirements of funding bodies and the requirements of publishers is increasingly a driving force for digital curation. There may also be the need to comply with specific legal requirements, such as data protection acts and freedom of information acts. On the other side of the coin, there may be legal restrictions that prevent the curation of data. An example is copying data, which is the basis of the digital preservation strategies of refreshing, migration, and emulation without the specific approval of the copyright owner; copying for preservation purposes may not be covered by copyright legislation. Another example is the data owner who may not allow his or her data to be reused; intellectual property rights for some material may be so restrictive that there is no real possibility of access to data being made available in the future. In this case, it is probably pointless to expend resources on curating the data.

There are other drivers for keeping data. Some data are required for a project to continue, such as data about the administration of a research project and about agreements made with its funding body. Some employers may require data created by their employees in the course of their employment to be deposited in an institutional repository. Some drivers, such as the potential reuse value of the data to people other than those who initially created and used them, may not become clear until long after the data have been created. Understanding these drivers and meeting their requirements is part of appraisal.

The benefits and risks of keeping or not keeping data are increasingly driving digital curation. Questions that are asked, taking a risk management approach, include: What are the consequences of not keeping the data? How much would it cost to re-create them in the future? Is it even possible to re-create them in the future? Risk management principles and processes applied to digital curation can be considered as a form of appraisal in that they help answer the key questions posed when appraising data, such as what data are of value and how long should they be kept.

Risk management seeks to reduce risk by first identifying compromising events and then applying actions to reduce the likelihood of these events occurring (see Chapters 9 and 10 for some examples) or to limit their effect if they do occur. Organizations need to define the level of risk they are prepared to accept, as risk cannot be completely eliminated. The steps that are typically carried out using a risk management approach are, first, to decide which materials are at risk and then to prioritize them according to the level of risk. (Figure 11.1 shows a matrix of risks.) Next, the actions required to address these risks are determined, and this allows the resources required to be identified. It provides the basis for comparing alternative preservation strategies. It can also provide the

Figure 11.1. Risks Matrix

Probability	Risk Level				
Almost certain	Significant	Major	High	Severe	Severe
High	Moderate	Significant	Major	High	Severe
Moderate	Low	Moderate	Significant	Major	High
Unlikely	Insignificant	Low	Moderate	Significant	Major
Rare	Insignificant	Insignificant	Low	Moderate	Significant
Consequence	*Insignificant*	*Minor*	*Moderate*	*Major*	*Catastrophic*

Source: Clifton, 2005.

basis for developing indicators to signal when risks are approaching a critical point at which they need to be addressed (e.g., the approaching obsolescence of a file format). These indicators may be the trigger for reappraisal of a data set.

The British Library (McLeod, 2008) has developed and applied a risk assessment methodology to prioritize handheld digital information (i.e., data stored on media that are small and portable, such as CD-ROM, DVD, and tape). Their methodology asks questions about these digital materials, such as where they were located and their extent (e.g., "How big [MB] are the digital assets?"), and about technical details such as operating system and software ("What media formats do you have? . . . What software environment [operating system, applications] is required to use the assets in question?"). This initial survey resulted in the identification of 23 groups of risks based on the main categories: physical deterioration of the medium; physical damage to the medium; environmental damage to the medium; technological obsolescence of the medium (e.g., DVD-R, LTO3 magnetic tape); technical obsolescence of the file system (e.g., FAT, NTFS); technical obsolescence of the file format (e.g., JPEG, TIFF, Word.doc); technical obsolescence of the hardware environment (e.g., PC, Sun, Amiga); technical obsolescence of the software environment (e.g., Mac OS X, Atari TOS, Linux); acquisition (e.g., risks could be "No standardized verification of acquired media"); ingest (e.g., "No standardized analysis of acquired media"); metadata (e.g., "Insufficient creation of metadata"); access (e.g., "DOM not ready to use"); storage (e.g., lack of digital curators); and preservation (e.g., lack of developed digital preservation tools). This identification has allowed the British Library to develop policy and strategy for addressing risks, focusing on the most critical and urgent risks (McLeod, 2008).

Why We Can't Keep Everything

The question of what data we want to keep is based on the assumption that it is not feasible to keep all of it. Some of the reasons most commonly referred to for taking a selective approach are the expense of keeping large amounts of data, the lack of organizational capacity, and the shortage of skilled personnel. This assumption is sometimes questioned.

The argument for appraising data and making a selection of them to curate is based on the reality of exponential growth in data, resulting in too much data to curate effectively. The resources available for curation are limited. Responsive solutions (solutions that are applied at the point of request, as opposed to predictive solutions, which attempt to determine future use), such as digital archaeology and reliance on information retrieval, are too expensive and limited in their effectiveness. Therefore, the argument goes, high-quality curation requires appraisal and selection to limit the quantity of data to an amount that can be handled appropriately.

The arguments against making a selection of data to curate have a technological and social base. Everything can be kept, the argument goes, as the costs of data storage are falling and our ability to retrieve information from large quantities of data is improving. It is argued that there are too many problems inherent in appraisal and selection. One of these is that it is impossible to predict who the future users of the data will be and how they might use data, so it is pointless to attempt to do this; another is that bias cannot be avoided in appraisal, as all appraisal and selection is value-laden. More about these arguments is presented by Neumayer and Rauber (2007), together with some responses to it, on the web.

How Long Do We Want to Keep Those Data?

Another question is: how long do we want to keep the data? Answers to this question help determine the resourcing needed to effectively carry out digital curation. The answer is often phrased in different ways:

- in terms of changes of technology (e.g., through several generations of hardware);
- in terms of the mission of the organization curating it (e.g., to meet specific business requirements); and
- in terms of user requirements (e.g., as evidence to verify conclusions derived from research).

Whatever is decided, it is important to reflect on the length of time the data may be required to be curated. When considering this question, it should also be kept firmly in mind that the answer is not necessarily forever, for as long as possible, or for posterity. Each of these may well be the appropriate answer for some archives whose mission is to preserve specific kinds of materials for as long as possible, but for many other organizations the periods for which data are to be retained could be shorter. One way of looking at this question is to use the concept of long-term, medium-term, and short-term preservation, as articulated by Jones and Beagrie in *The Preservation Management of Digital Materials* (Digital Preservation Coalition, 2008). *Long-term preservation* aims to provide indefinite access to data. *Medium-term preservation* attempts to ensure continued access to data for a defined time, perhaps long enough to encompass changes in technology. *Short-term preservation* aims to ensure that access to data is maintained until technological changes make it inaccessible or for the length of time (relatively short) during which those data are likely to be in use. Careful determination of the length of time that data need to be kept assists planning, for example, for allocating resources.

The Curation Lifecycle Model contains the Occasional Action *Reappraise*. It may not be possible at the initial appraisal stage to determine with certainty how long data should be kept, but after time has passed it may be clearer. This is where reappraisal might be applied: the data are assessed again against the appraisal criteria to see if they are still to be curated. If the decision is made not to continue to curate those data, the action is then to dispose of them, either by destroying them or passing them to another archive.

Appraisal and Selection Policies

Appraisal and selection policies are developed to assist in answering the key questions of appraisal and selection (Do we want to keep the data? Do we need to keep the data? How long do we keep the data?) and to ensure that the right data are kept for valid reasons. Policies are important because they allow informed consistent decisions to be made that can be defended if challenged. An appraisal and selection policy for digital objects or data typically addresses five themes:

1. Future users (the designated community)
2. The feasibility of preservation (both economic and technical feasibility)
3. Legal and intellectual property rights
4. Whether data is mission-critical, vital to the success of a project or organization
5. Associated data (metadata or description and representation information)

The Data Audit Framework, developed in the United Kingdom by HATII at the University of Glasgow and the DCC, articulates these themes in its five principal classification questions (Jones, 2008). These help auditors decide whether data sets can be classed as vital, important, or minor:

- Are these data central to your research?
- Will the data be useful in the future?
- Are you the intellectual owner?
- Are they documented and in a sustainable form?
- Are they already being preserved elsewhere?

More specifically, an appraisal and selection policy for digital objects or data assists data curators to answer questions such as these:

- Does the digital object or data fit into the archive's selection policy?
- Who will or might use the digital object or data in the future? Is there a defined designated community?
- Is it economically feasible to keep the digital object or data?
- Can acceptable legal and intellectual property rights, to keep and reuse the digital object or data, be negotiated?
- Is there a legal requirement to keep the digital object or data for a certain period of time? Is there a requirement to make them accessible during this period?
- Does the digital object or data constitute the "vital records" of a project or organization and therefore need to be retained indefinitely?
- Is it both technically feasible and worthwhile in cost/benefit terms to preserve the digital object or data?

- Does sufficient documentation and metadata exist to explain the character and enable the discovery of the digital object or data?

Examination of appraisal and selection schemes provides further guidance. One example is the Data Preservation Alliance for the Social Sciences (2005) appraisal guidelines. These guidelines provide a consistent framework for appraisal decision-making for social science data. Eight questions are posed:

1. How significant are the data for research?
2. How significant is the source and context of the data, particularly in regard to scientific progress and society?
3. Is the information unique?
4. How usable are the data?
5. What is the timeframe covered by the information?
6. Are the data related to other data in the archives?
7. What are the cost considerations for long-term maintenance of the data?
8. What is the volume of data?

Although these criteria are intended for data archives, specifically social science archives, they are more widely applicable. Questions 5 (What is the timeframe covered by the information?) and 6 (Are the data related to other data in the archives?) address the relationship that the data set being appraised has with other data, as this may enhance its value: for example, the data set may be a continuation of a longitudinal study and valuable for this reason. Question 8 (What is the volume of data?) relates to the feasibility of preservation, as an archive may not be equipped to store and curate large quantities.

The DISC-UK DataShare project's *Policy-making for Research Data in Repositories* (Green, Macdonald, and Rice, 2009) provides valuable assistance for developing appraisal criteria. For example, its "Content Coverage" section asks about scope (subject areas excluded and included, language considerations such as whether all documentation needs to be in English) and about which versions of data or digital objects will be retained—master copies, drafts, earlier versions? Will the archive accept material only in specific file formats, and, if so, what are they? Other sections cover metadata (what metadata must be supplied with the data or digital object for them to be accepted by the archive?); eligibility to deposit (who is eligible to deposit material into the archive, and will data or digital objects from ineligible organizations or individuals be considered?); data quality (what happens if the deposited material does not meet the archive's requirements for data quality?); and retention periods (indefinitely, for a minimum number of years, for the lifetime of the archive?), among other relevant topics.

Who Decides?

Who develops appraisal and selection criteria, and who applies them? Ideally, both the information professionals who curate data and the creators of that data should be involved. Information professionals who curate data have the responsibility of developing selection policies and guidelines for appraisal. They liaise with creators and depositors to ensure data sets are in the best shape to ensure preservability (see Chapter 9 and 10). They also have the role of locating sufficient resources (funding, staff, technical infrastructure) to ensure that effective appraisal is possible.

Data creators should, ideally, ensure that data sets they create have sufficient metadata and documentation and that their data are in curation-ready (usually open) formats. They should have a clear understanding of which data are vital, which are important, and which are minor. As noted in other chapters, data stand the best chance of being successfully curated if planning for curation begins when their creation is being planned.

Appraisal and selection policies and specific criteria should be developed, ideally, with input from stakeholders. This is where the concept of the designated community is important. The designated community is "an identified group of potential consumers who should be able to understand a particular set of information" (Consultative Committee for Space Data Systems, 2002: 1–10). What will (or might) the designated community consider sufficient in the future? For instance, will it be sufficient to keep just the information content of a database but not its functionality (such as the ability to search and manipulate its contents)? A precise definition of the designated community for the data or digital objects being appraised and a clear understanding of what that community requires when it uses data or digital objects in the future are important factors in effective appraisal.

Appraisal Tools

Few tools for appraisal are available yet. Tools—that is, software, templates, or models, usually available online and open source—play a significant role in digital curation. (This role is described in detail in Chapter 13.)

The *Decision Tree for Selection of Digital Materials for Long-Term Retention* (Digital Preservation Coalition, 2006), part of the Digital Preservation Coalition's handbook, is an online interactive tool that helps in making appraisal and selection decisions. This decision tree first poses questions relating to selection policy: Does the material fit into the institutional selection policy? Is the material of long-term value? A second group of questions is about rights and responsibilities: Have acceptable rights been negotiated? Can they be? Technical questions form a third group of questions: Can you handle the file format, now and in the future? Can the material be transferred to a more manageable format? The existence of documentation and metadata form a fourth group: Has sufficient metadata been supplied?

Another appraisal tool is the Data Audit Framework (Humanities Advanced Technology & Information Institute, 2008), already noted in this chapter. This methodology and online tool is based on risk management. Its methodology allows an organization to determine more precisely what data assets are held and how they are being managed. It has four stages: planning the audit, identifying and classifying data assets, assessing the management of data assets, and reporting results and making recommendations. The outputs of the process are twofold. First there is an inventory of data assets, classified according to how significant they are and containing information useful to their curation, such as rights and restrictions on the data set, the frequency of use, any backup and archiving policy relating to the data set, and its management to date. Second, the process results in a report that makes recommendations about how data management could be improved (Jones, Ross, and Ruusalepp, 2008).

The U.S. Geological Survey's Center for Earth Resources Observation and Science provides the EROS *Records Appraisal Tool* online (eros.usgs.gov/government/ratool). This tool assists the Geological Survey with appraising collections of records that they are offered or seek. The rationale for appraising these collections is stated by Faundeen and Oleson (2007: 5):

> We should be expending our resources on the data we most value. Determining that value requires us to make judgments, but utilizing a repeatable and comprehensive scheme can allow us to judge data responsibly. Documenting those judgments is essential, because future generations will depend on the current scientists and records managers to preserve the data that will "advance knowledge."

Although the EROS tool is not specifically for records in digital form, much of it can be applied to appraising data sets. It asks questions in seven categories. The first category is *Mission Alignment Characteristics*, where the questions seek to determine how well the data set fits into the collection policy and mission and the relevance of the data to the designated community. The second category, *Access and Distribution Characteristics*, asks about the data set's authenticity, reliability, integrity, and usability and about any rights that may be associated with those data. *Additional Characteristics*, the third category, requests information about spatial and temporal coverage of the data set, its creation, volume, and other features. *Physical Characteristics* are requested in the fourth category, such as the media types, their physical condition, file naming conventions, and compression techniques used. The fifth category, *Metadata Characteristics*, seeks to ascertain the amount, quality, level, and availability of metadata and associated information describing the data set. *Economic Characteristics*, the sixth category, asks about funding sources to cover the costs of acquiring, preserving, and making the records accessible; requests an estimate of the costs of reproducing the data set; asks about scientific, operational, or secondary value; and requests an estimate of the approximate costs of identifying, appraising, accessioning, and processing the collection to make it accessible. Also requested is an estimate of the costs of deaccessioning or disposing of the data set. Responses to these questions are entered into an online form and a response is computed. The full list of appraisal questions asked by the EROS Records Appraisal Tool is well worth investigating by anyone developing appraisal criteria.

Two Examples

Two examples illustrate some of the concerns and procedures of appraisal and selection: selection and archiving of websites and appraisal of scientific data sets.

Selection and Archiving of Websites

Selection of websites for archiving is described in *PoWR: The Preservation of Web Resources Handbook* (JISC-PoWR, 2008, especially Chapter 5). Three approaches are noted: bulk or domain harvesting, criteria-based selection, and event-based selection. These approaches have been developed by national libraries, which are among the key players in developing web archiving techniques and procedures. They can, however, be readily scaled down to meet the requirements of smaller organizations.

Bulk or domain harvesting is basically collecting everything possible. An example is a domain harvest carried out by a national library that would attempt to collect all websites hosted in that country or with significant content relevant to that country. The National Library of Sweden's Kulturaw3 project (www.kb.se/english/find/internet/websites) is an example. This selection process (or, rather, avoidance of selection) is considered to be more comprehensive, more objective, less time-consuming, and require less staff time than more selective approaches. Arguments against it refer to the accumulation of very large quantities of data, much of which are potentially not relevant, with attendant storage requirements and difficulty of accessing these data.

In *criteria-based selection*, websites are selected according to criteria that have been closely defined. Examples are all websites produced by a specific department, all the blogs produced by one organization, or all websites about a specific subject. The Arthur and Elizabeth Schlesinger Library on the History of Women in America at Radcliffe Institute, Harvard University, provides an example. From 2007 the library has collected the blogs of women in its "Blogs: Capturing Women's Voices" project (nrs.harvard.edu/urn-3:RAD.SCHL.WAX:2222628). This selective approach is usually considered to be a good way of piloting a web archiving program, and it results in a collection of websites that is a close fit with an organization's collection development policy. The main disadvantage of this approach is the highly labor-intensive nature of the decisions about whether or not to include specific websites.

Event-based selection focuses on a specific important event, such as an election or a disaster. Websites created during such events are often updated very frequently and may be taken down from the web after a short period of time. The Library of Congress had collected websites relating to the 2006 Crisis in Darfur, Sudan, the 2003 Iraq War, the 2005 Papal Transition, September 11, 2001, and United States Elections in 2000, 2002, and 2004, among other events (lcweb2.loc.gov/diglib/lcwa/html/lcwa-home.html).

An important question to address is: What *aspects* of web resources must we capture? Do we want to preserve the full experience if it is possible to do so? This involves capturing the content of the website, its appearance, metadata about the site (about its creation, original location, authorship, access rights, and so on), and its behavior, including links. Or are we interested primarily in capturing the information content on the website? This is less demanding: a sample might be sufficient to indicate appearance and content. If the website is being captured for evidential purposes, for example, to provide evidence for legal purposes, it may be necessary to keep much more: an audit trail of changes, a change history, contextual information about who wrote it, used it, added to it, when it was written and changed, when the site was published and taken down—all this in addition to capturing the content, appearance, and behavior of the site.

The U.S. National Library of Medicine has developed a methodology for appraising its web documents (Byrne, 2005). Its four "permanence levels" are based on three characteristics of web documents: identifier validity, resource availability, and content invariance. They are:

- **Permanent: Unchanging Content**—will be kept available permanently, with a persistent identifier, and without change to its contents (for example, minutes of board meetings)
- **Permanent: Stable Content**—will be kept available permanently, with a persistent identifier, and with only minor corrections or additions to its contents (for example, fact sheets)
- **Permanent: Dynamic Content**—will be kept available permanently, with a persistent identifier; its content could be revised or replaced (for example, a homepage)
- **Permanence Not Guaranteed**—could become unavailable at any time; content and identifier could change (for example, a FAQ [Frequently Asked Questions] page) (Byrne, 2005)

Appraisal of Scientific Data Sets

A useful framework for identifying scientific data sets is Witt and Carlson's (2007) "Conducting a Data Interview." This presents ten questions to be asked of a data creator by an information professional. It is described as "a practical tool to draw out information" rather than a comprehensive strategy.

Question 1, *What is the story of the data?*, provides the context for the data set: how and why it was created and how it was processed and analyzed. Question 2, *What form and format are the data in?*, asks questions such as what computing environments are required to use the data, and is there any existing metadata? Question 3, *What is the expected lifespan of the data set?*, investigates whether there are any specific requirements for keeping those data, such as the requirements of funding agencies, or what its value is likely to be in the future. Question 4, *How could the data be used, reused, and repurposed?*, is a primary selection criterion that is closely related to how those data are accessed and to any policies about their use that may exist. Question 5, *How large is the data set, and what is its rate of growth?*, asks about the size of the data set. Question 6, *Who are the potential audiences for the data?*, is another primary selection criterion. This question also raises the issue of any embargos or restrictions on their use and if so for what period. Question 7, *Who owns the data?*, establishes who owns intellectual property represented by the data. Question 8, *Does the data set include any sensitive information?*, seeks information about the contents of the data set, for example, whether it includes data that can identify individuals. Question 9, *What publications or discoveries have resulted from the data?*, establishes an objective way of determining the value of the data. Finally, Question 10, *How should the data be made accessible?*, asks about such things as using a conventional web-based user interface or a machine-to-machine interface.

The process used by the EROS group at the U.S. Geological Survey is described by Faundeen and Oleson (2007). (The EROS Records Appraisal Tool is described earlier in this chapter.) It is applied both to data sets generated by the U.S. Geological Survey and to data sets that are offered to it. Its application has resulted in data sets being retained with scientific justification for the commitment of ongoing resources to their curation, although this does not preclude reappraisal in the future. The process has nine steps:

1. Identification of data set to be appraised
2. Appraisal team assembled
3. Data set facts collected
4. Science review
5. Facts and science review documented using online tool
6. Briefing to archivist and project lead conducted
7. Written recommendation sent to senior management
8. Senior management question and answer session
9. Senior management formal response provided (Faundeen and Oleson, 2007: 2)

Some aspects are worth further comment. For step 2, assembling the appraisal team, and step 4, science review, the input of scientists or others who know the data is essential. They assess the data, addressing specific questions about the value of those data, such as, "Is there another organization within the science community that might benefit from or have an interest in these records? What were the original scientific uses for these records? What may be future scientific uses of these records?" (Faundeen and Oleson, 2007: 3). At the U.S. Geological Survey, the appraisal process stops at this point if input by scientists is not available. The facts collected and the reviewers' opinions are documented using the online EROS Records Appraisal Tool (step 5).

Reappraisal

Reappraise is an Occasional Action in the Curation Lifecycle Model. It is an outcome of decisions made at the *Preservation Action* stage (see Chapter 13). The activities associated with Reappraise are stated in the Curation Lifecycle as "returning data which fails validation procedures for further appraisal and reselection" (Digital Curation Centre, 2008). The key tasks of reappraisal are, first, specifying the conditions that trigger reappraisal and then testing data sets that meet these conditions against the appraisal criteria.

Reappraisal, "the process of identifying materials that no longer merit preservation and that are candidates for deaccessioning" (Pearce-Moses, 2005), is undertaken in specified circumstances—for example, when there is a major change in an archive's operating conditions (such as a significant change in resources), when there is a change in the mandate of the archives, or when there is an unanticipated serious event (Craig, 2004). Reappraisal is resource intensive and has traditionally been carried out years, or even decades, after the records have been created. Examples of the circumstances that could trigger reappraisal of digital objects include Technology Watch (e.g., obsolescence of format, media, or rendering application; migration and/or normalization becomes impossible or too expensive), change in designated community (e.g., a university drops a course), and legislative change (e.g., revision of legal deposit regulations for some materials).

An appraisal decision about data is not a decision that is made once and for all time. As requirements and needs change, so too do appraisal outcomes. Revisiting appraisal decisions (i.e., reappraising) may occur as circumstances require. The appraisal policy should include a statement of reappraisal principles and a reappraisal schedule. As an example, initial appraisal of research data sets could result in the retention of most data sets; criteria for reappraisal are developed, and reappraisal is undertaken at defined intervals to test the data set against these agreed criteria to determine whether it still meets the conditions for applying resources to its long-term retention. Appraisal and reappraisal processes might result in a decision not to commit further resources to curation of some data. If such a decision were to be made, these data could be offered to another repository or disposed of.

Disposal of Data

Dispose is an Occasional Action in the Curation Lifecycle Model. It is a possible outcome of decisions made at the *Appraise and Select* and *Reappraise* stages. The activities associated with Dispose are stated in the Curation Lifecycle as "Dispose (by transfer elsewhere, or destruction) of data which has not been selected for longterm curation and preservation in accordance with documented policies, guidance or legal requirements" (Digital Curation Centre, 2008). The options in Dispose are transferring the data or digital objects to another archive or destroying them in a secure manner.

The decision to dispose of data or digital objects is made by assessing them against appraisal criteria developed by archives, repositories, and data centers and used to determine whether they are relevant to their aims and, therefore, worthy of committing resources to their long-term maintenance. If the decision is made not to commit resources to the long-term curation of a data set or digital object, it can either be transferred to another archive, repository, data center, or custodian, or it can be destroyed. The decision to dispose of data or digital objects may also arise from reappraisal (testing them against agreed on criteria to decide whether they still meet the conditions for applying resources to their long-term retention).

All archives should have a policy about disposal, with an indication of the archive's practice in three areas: the conditions for disposal of data or digital objects, what happens to the data or digital objects that are disposed of, and what happens to metadata associated with data or digital objects that are disposed of. As well as decisions arising from a reappraisal exercise (which might, for example, deem a digital object as no longer significant to its designated community), disposal decisions might result from such concerns as violation of copyright or other legal requirements, national security, the confirmation that research has been falsified, or concerns about confidentiality of the data. If data or digital objects are disposed of, what happens to them? Decisions are required about a range of possibilities. Are they deleted entirely from the database, or are they only removed from public access? Are the identifiers or URLs for them retained, and, if so, for how long? Similar decisions are needed about the metadata associated with data or digital objects that are disposed of. Will it be retained as a record, or will all of it be deleted too? (Green, Macdonald, and Rice, 2009: 33).

Transfer of Data

If data or digital objects are determined not to be relevant to one archive, repository, or data center, they may be transferred to another that is interested in them. For example, a data set may be transferred at the end of a research project from its creator to a data archive whose mission is to maintain data sets for long-term use. Appropriate and adequate metadata and documentation about the data set also need to be transferred, as they are essential to ensure that the data set can be curated by the receiving organization.

Consideration should also be given to what happens if an archive closes down. Will the data be transferred to another archive, or will they be offered back to their creators or donors? (Green, Macdonald, and Rice, 2009: 33).

Destruction of Data

Some data or digital objects may need to be disposed of by destroying them completely. For some data or digital objects, there may be legal requirements that they must be destroyed in a secure manner. Many countries have legislation to protect the rights of individuals with regard to their personal data—for example, the Data Protection Act 1998 in the United Kingdom. If data sets contain personal data that have not been anonymized to ensure that individuals cannot be identified, it is likely that they will need to be destroyed in a secure manner. Some data legislation requires documentation of decisions about what was destroyed.

Any data that are to be destroyed should be disposed of securely so that they cannot be reused or reconstructed. Simply erasing or deleting files does not achieve this. Software tools that remove all data so that they cannot be reconstructed are widely available. For example, a "wiping" program deletes data and also overwrites them several times with random data. Standards that define approved methods of data destruction include the DoD 5520.22-M Standard: Chapter 8 and the National Industrial Security Program Operating Manual (NISPOM). Guidance about how to ensure that data are fully deleted includes the Gutmann Method (Gutmann, 1996), which is relevant for the destruction of extremely sensitive data.

Summary: The Necessity for Appraisal and Selection

Appraisal and selection are desirable because they improve management of resource limitations by reducing the quantity of data and digital objects maintained and, thus, increase the economic viability of long-term retention of data by reducing the cost of maintaining very large quantities of data. This leads to better digital curation.

Although appraisal policies and practices have been developed by archivists and are most commonly encountered in the archives context, their value has increasingly been recognized by all digital curation communities, as the examples in this chapter indicate. As noted by O'Brien (2009), they are highly relevant to personal digital resources.

The next chapter notes *Ingest*, the next Sequential Action in the Curation Lifecycle. It covers the preparation of data and digital objects for their addition to a digital archive and the process of adding them to the archive.

References

Byrne, Margaret M. 2005. "Permanence Levels and the Archives for NLM's Permanent Web Documents." *NLM Technical Bulletin* no. 343 (March–April). Available: www.nlm.nih.gov/pubs/techbull/ma05/ma05_ archive.html (accessed April 26, 2010).

Clifton, Gerald. 2005. "Risk and the Preservation Management of Digital Collections." *International Preservation News* no. 36: 21–23. Available: www.ifla.org/VI/4/news/ipnn36.pdf (accessed April 26, 2010).

Consultative Committee for Space Data Systems. 2002. *Reference Model for an Open Archival Information System (OAIS): Recommendation for Space Data System Standards.* Washington, DC: CCSDS Secretariat. Available: public.ccsds.org/publications/archive/650x0b1.pdf (accessed April 26, 2010).

Cox, Richard J. 2007. "Appraising the Digital Past and Future." Paper presented at DigCCurr 2007, Chapel Hill, NC, April 18–20. Available: ils.unc.edu/digccurr2007/papers/cox_paper_4-5.pdf (accessed April 26, 2010). Used by permission of Richard Cox.

Craig, Barbara. 2004. *Archival Appraisal.* München: K.G. Saur.

APPRAISE AND SELECT: REVIEW

Key points: *Appraise and Select* is the process of evaluating data to determine whether to keep them for the long term.

Key activities:
- Develop, document, and apply policies about appraisal and selection, including:
  - Define the designated community
  - Identify properties of the data to preserve
  - Decide how long the data needs to be maintained
- Develop appraisal criteria
- Evaluate data against the appraisal criteria

REAPPRAISE: REVIEW

Key points: *Reappraise* is the process of submitting data that fails validation procedures for further appraisal.

Key activities:
- Develop criteria for reappraisal
- Test data that meet these criteria against the appraisal criteria

---

DISPOSE: REVIEW

Key points: *Dispose* is the process of disposing of data that has not been selected for long-term curation and preservation.

Key activities:
- Assess the data against appraisal criteria
- Transfer the data to another relevant archive, or
- Destroy data in a secure manner

Data Preservation Alliance for the Social Sciences. 2005. "Appraisal." Ann Arbor, MI: Data Preservation Alliance for the Social Sciences (February 9, 2005). Available: www.icpsr.umich.edu/DATAPASS/pdf/appraisal.pdf (accessed April 26, 2010).

Digital Curation Centre. 2008. *The DCC Curation Lifecycle Model.* Edinburgh: Digital Curation Centre. Available: www.dcc.ac.uk/docs/publications/ DCCLifecycle.pdf (accessed April 26, 2010).

Digital Preservation Coalition. 2006. *Decision Tree for Selection of Digital Materials for Long-Term Retention.* York: Digital Preservation Coalition (March 8, 2006). Available: www.dpconline.org/decision-tree.html (accessed April 26, 2010).

———. 2008. *Preservation Management of Digital Materials: The Handbook.* York: Digital Preservation Coalition (November 2008). Available: www.dpconline.org/advice/digital-preservation-handbook.html (accessed April 26, 2010).

Ellis, J. 1993. *Keeping Archives,* 2nd ed. Melbourne: Australian Society of Archivists.

Esanu, J., J. Davidson, S. Ross, and W. Anderson. 2004. "Selection, Appraisal, and Retention of Digital Scientific Data: Highlights of an ERPANET/ CODATA Workshop." *Data Science Journal* 3: 227–232. Available: www .jstage.jst.go.jp/article/dsj/3/0/3_227/_article (accessed April 26, 2010).

Faundeen, J.L., and L.R. Oleson. 2007. "Scientific Data Appraisals: The Value Driver for Preservation Efforts." Paper presented at the Ensuring the Long-Term Preservation and Adding Value to the Scientific and Technical Data Symposium (PV-2007), Oberpfaffenhofen/Munich, Germany, October 9–11. Available: www.pv2007.dlr.de/Papers/Faundeen_AppraisalsValue_ for_Preservation.pdf (accessed April 26, 2010). Used by permission of John Faundeen.

Green, Ann, Stuart Macdonald, and Robin Rice. 2009. *Policy-Making for Research Data in Repositories: A Guide.* Version 1.2. Edinburgh: EDINA and University Data Library. Available: www.disc-uk.org/docs/guide.pdf (accessed April 26, 2010).

Gutmann, Peter. 1996. "Secure Deletion of Data from Magnetic and Solid State Memory." Paper presented at the Sixth USENIX Security Symposium, July 22–25, San Jose, California. Available: www.usenix.org/publications/ library/proceedings/sec96/full_papers/gutmann (accessed April 26, 2010).

Humanities Advanced Technology & Information Institute. 2008. "Data Audit Framework: Four Steps to Effective Data Management." Glasgow: HATII (October 1, 2008). Available: www.data-audit.eu (accessed April 26, 2010).

JISC-PoWR. 2008. *PoWR: The Preservation of Web Resources Handbook: Digital Preservation for the UK HE/FE Web Management Community.* London: University of London Computer Centre. Available: www.scribd.com/doc/ 7760433/JISC-PoWR-The-Preservation-of-Web-Resources-Handbook (accessed April 26, 2010).

Jones, Sarah. 2008. "Data Audit Framework." Presented at Digital Curation 101, October 6–10, Natural e-Science Centre, Edinburgh.

Jones, Sarah, Seamus Ross, and Raivo Ruusalepp. 2008. "The Data Audit Framework: A Toolkit to Identify Research Assets and Improve Data Management in Research Led Institutions." In *Proceedings of The Fifth International Conference on Preservation of Digital Objects: Joined Up and Working: Tools and Methods for Digital Preservation, British Library, London, 29–30 September* (pp. 213–219). London: British Library. Available: www.bl.uk/ ipres2008/ipres2008-proceedings.pdf (accessed April 26, 2010).

McLeod, Rory. 2008. "Risk Assessment: Using a Risk Based Approach to Prioritise Handheld Digital Information." Paper presented at iPres 2008, British Library, London, September 29. Available: www.bl.uk/ipres2008/presentations_day1/20_McLeod.pdf (accessed April 26, 2010).

Neumayer, Robert, and Andreas Rauber. 2007. "Why Appraisal Is Not 'Utterly' Useless and Why It's Not the Way to Go Either." Glasgow: Digital Preservation Europe (November 12, 2007). Available: www.digitalpreservationeurope.eu/publications/position/appraisal_final.pdf (accessed April 26, 2010).

O'Brien, Chris. 2009. "Time to Clean Up Your Digital Closet." MercuryNews.com (July 30, 2009). Available: www.physorg.com/news168717176.html (accessed April 26, 2010).

Oliver, G., S. Ross, M. Guercio, and C. Pala. 2008. *Report on Automated Re-Appraisal: Managing Archives in Digital Libraries.* Pisa: DELOS NoE.

Pearce-Moses, Richard. 2005. "A Glossary of Archival and Records Terminology." Chicago: Society of American Archivists (2005). Available: www.archivists.org/glossary (accessed April 26, 2010).

Research Information Network and British Library. 2009. *Patterns of Information Use and Exchange: Case Studies of Researchers in the Life Sciences.* London. Available: www.rin.ac.uk/system/files/attachments/Sarah/Patterns_information_use-REPORT_Nov09.pdf (accessed April 26, 2010).

Witt, Michael, and Jake R. Carlson. 2007. "Conducting a Data Interview." Poster presented at the 3rd International Digital Curation Conference, Washington DC, November 11–13. Available: docs.lib.purdue.edu/lib_research/81 (accessed April 26, 2010).

Ingesting Data

The previous chapter outlined the decisions that need to be made about what data and digital objects are archived. This chapter notes *Ingest*, the fourth Sequential Action in the Digital Curation Centre (DCC) Curation Lifecycle Model. Two sets of activities are noted for Ingest: "Transfer data to an archive, repository, data centre or other custodian" and "Adhere to documented guidance, policies or legal requirements" (Digital Curation Centre, 2008).

The term *Ingest* refers to the processes of preparing data and digital objects for adding to a digital archive and of adding them to the digital archive. Ingesting materials into a managed repository environment is a prerequisite for effective curation. It is assumed that the data or digital objects to be ingested have already been appraised and selected as appropriate for long-term curation (see Chapter 11) and the terms under which they are to be transferred to the archive (such as security, confidentiality, and intellectual property rights: see Chapter 14) have been agreed.

The processes undertaken during ingest can be more fully described as:

- developing and maintaining policies about ingest,
- developing procedures for the ingest process,
- identifying tools that can be used for ingest,
- receiving appraised data and digital objects, and
- preparing appraised data and digital objects for placing in long-term storage.

The fifth process, preparing for long-term storage, involves actions such as assigning a persistent identifier; checking that there are no viruses or other malicious spyware or malware; extracting, creating, and adding relevant description and representation information; creating fixity values (e.g., checksum, hash value) to assist with checking integrity; identifying and confirming technical details (e.g., file format, MIME type); uncompressing or unencrypting the data or digital object, if necessary; and combining the data or digital object and their associated description and representation information into an AIP (Archival Information Package).

OAIS and Ingest

Ingest is one of the seven key functions in the OAIS Reference Model (see Chapter 3). Relevant to the Ingest action from this Model is the concept of Information Package. An information package consists of the digital object to be preserved, the metadata (description and representation information) required at that point in the system, and the Packaging Information linking the digital object and the metadata. For the Ingest action two kinds of Information Package, the SIP (Submission) and the AIP (Archival), are important.

As described in more detail in Chapter 3, a SIP comprises the digital object and its accompanying metadata as presented at the start of the Ingest action; and an AIP is based on a SIP, to which additional information needed to manage preservation, the PDI (Preservation Description Information), is added. PDI has four components: Reference Information: a unique and persistent identifier (see Chapter 6); Provenance Information: the history of the archived object; Context Information: relationship to other objects, for example, the hierarchical structure of a digital archive; and Fixity Information: a demonstration of authenticity, such as a hash value.

The OAIS Reference Model (Consultative Committee for Space Data Systems, 2002: 4-5–4-6) notes the Ingest procedure as:

- Receive and accept Submission Information Package (either through FTP or physical media).
- Prepare the SIP for storage and management.
- Perform quality assurance on the SIP through Cyclic Redundancy Checks (CRCs), generating checksums, or using system log files to determine presence of errors.
- Initiate file format conversion to create the Archival Information Package (AIP).
- Generate AIP.
- Extract descriptive information from AIP (generate metadata for search and retrieval).
- Coordinate updates—send AIPs to storage and the descriptive information to the data management database.
- Send confirmation that AIP has been added to permanent storage.

In other words, ingest is the process of moving data and digital objects out of the hands of the creator and into the hands of the curator. In the terms used in the OAIS Reference Model, it is the process of turning SIPs into AIPs.

Ingest Processes in More Detail

The Ingest action consists of the following processes. Not all of these processes may be needed; for example, a digital object may not be encrypted, so unencryption will not be required. (This section is based in part on material developed by the Complex Archive Ingest for Repository Objects project; cairo.paradigm.ac.uk.)

Submitting SIPs

The first set of processes relate to submitting SIPs to the archive. Chapter 10 notes the requirements for submission policies to govern the submission process. These policies cover eligibility to deposit data and digital objects in the archive; data quality requirements; the metadata that is required; confidentiality and disclosure; whether the data and digital objects are embargoed; rights and ownership; preferred or required file formats; and any volume and size limitations on the data and digital objects received by the archive. The submission policy and its associated procedures will indicate how the data are to be transferred. As examples, they could be transferred using FTP, by e-mail, or on physical media such as CDs or USB drives.

Receiving SIPs

The second set of processes relate to receiving SIPs in the archive. Chapter 10 notes the specific tasks that are carried out when data and digital objects are received by an archive: sort, identify, and list the data or digital objects to be transferred; ensure that a depositor agreement has been completed; transfer the data or digital objects; review them for their relevance to the archive; recheck their integrity; check whether the metadata records supplied are accurate; add persistent identifiers; and assess the quality of the data.

The data or digital objects received are often maintained in a quarantine space for a period of time. A quarantine or staging server (one not connected either physically or via a network to any other server) stores the submitted material for a specified period, typically four weeks, during which time checks for the presence of malware, viruses, and completeness are carried out. The material is rechecked for viruses and malware at the end of the period, before it moves on to the next stage.

The steps are described below in more detail. (Note that some of these tasks may have been completed as part of the submission process.) They can be grouped into four categories of actions: validation, health check, annotation, and transformation.

Validation actions are intended to ensure that the material received is complete and to identify characteristics of the material that are needed for curation. Specific actions in this category could include the following:

- Sort and identify the data or digital objects: check for completeness, to ensure that what is expected is present, and identify duplicates.

- Acknowledge receipt of the data or digital objects transferred to the archive.

- List the data or digital objects: information should be available about the file formats; present, media, operating system and version, programs and versions used to create the material, who created them (and for what reason and when), the quantity of material, and the metadata present.

- Confirm that all files can be opened.
- Uncompress or unencrypt digital objects received in compressed or encrypted formats.
- Make a copy of all material received.
- Ensure that a depositor agreement has been completed.
- Review the data received for their relevance to the scope of the archive, whether file formats are acceptable to the archive, and whether spam has been excluded.
- Confirm technical characteristics: for example, file format, using JHOVE ID, DROID ID, or other tools.

Health check actions are aimed at ensuring the quality of the data or digital objects. Specific actions in this category could include the following:

- Assess the data quality: for example, the required metadata has been provided by the data creator or depositor, and variable names in a data set match up with the variable names in a codebook.
- Check the data or digital objects to ensure that they are not corrupted and are free of viruses and malware.
- Recheck integrity of the data or digital objects to determine whether it has been maintained during the submission process.
- Add fixity information that guarantees that files have not been changed during storage, for example, by generating a checksum during the ingest process which is then verified in later processes.

Annotation actions are related to the description and representation information associated with the data or digital objects. Specific actions in this category could include the following:

- Check whether the metadata records supplied are accurate.
- Provide additional metadata, both technical and descriptive (see Chapter 6).
- Add representation information or link to it in another repository (see Chapter 6).

Transformation activities may also be applied. Depending on the archive's policy on normalizing file formats, it may also be necessary to migrate an object to a different file format as part of the ingest process.

One further point needs to be noted. It is important to make a copy of the bit stream as early as possible in the ingest process in order to protect the original data and to check that the medium on which they were transferred is accessible.

Generating AIPs

As the final step in the ingest process, the AIP is generated. The tasks carried out in this process are listed next. Note that there could be overlap with the submission and receiving processes, so some of these tasks may have been completed earlier:

- Assign identifiers to the digital object: unique identifier and persistent identifiers (see Chapter 6).
- Add additional metadata, both technical and descriptive, if required (see Chapter 6).
- Add representation information or link to it in another repository (see Chapter 6).
- Recheck integrity of the digital object to determine whether it has been maintained during the submission process.
- Confirm technical characteristics if required.
- Rerun antivirus and anti-malware checks.
- Create a wrapper or container: for example, create a METS AIP file containing PREMIS metadata.

Normalizing may be required as a part of the ingest process. It is not noted in this chapter but is covered in Chapter 13.

An AIP could contain all of the following kinds of information, although some may not be relevant to a particular digital object:

- descriptive metadata for the object(s) in the package and/or pointers to external descriptive information;
- business information regarding the producer's desired or contracted-for treatment of the object;
- general and format-specific technical metadata pertaining to the files comprising the object;
- the perceived significant properties of the object;
- rights information governing the access and use of the object;
- information about the creation and derivation of the object and its component files;
- documentation of any actions taken by the repository involving the object, including read-only actions such as virus checking;
- structural metadata describing the internal organization of the object;
- information about the relationships between this object and other objects both internal to and external to the source repository;
- information about agents (people, organizations, software) that have a relation to the object. (Caplan, 2008)

Two examples illustrate the steps in the ingest process. The first is for a small archive using readily available applications. Four minimum steps are required:

1. Create a disk inventory using a spreadsheet such as Excel, noting disk type, file size, description on disk, and any additional notes.
2. Copy the files and folders onto the hard drive of a computer running the Windows operating system.

3. Create a catalog of the files using software such as WinCatalog Light, which harvests metadata and exports it in a format readable by spreadsheet software.

4. Check for viruses using Norton AntiVirus or similar antivirus software.

The second example is for a larger archive. These are the steps:

1. Create an AIP, consisting of an XML file using METS.

2. Calculate a new checksum.

3. Validate the AIP's compliance to format specifications.

4. Check the rights agreement to ensure that appropriate permissions are available.

5. Check format.

6. Ascertain the preservation level for that format: such as, Fully supported—will be migrated; Supported with reasonable efforts; or Byte-level preservation—no migration.

7. Verify structure and relationships within source files.

8. Perform manual quality assurance.

9. Verify presence of all files.

10. Verify that checksums match.

11. Update metadata to include ingest date and time.

12. Deposit AIP into archive.

Ingest Tools

The costs associated with acquisition and ingest are high. As noted in Chapter 7, one estimate is that the highest percentage of overall costs occur at the acquisition and ingest stages rather than the storage and preservations stages—42 percent and 23 percent, respectively (Alliance for Permanent Access, 2008: 3). This is in large part because many of the procedures required for the Ingest action are labor intensive. The automation of more of these procedures will be essential for handling larger quantities of data than are handled at present.

Automating the ingest process is currently limited by the lack of tools to assist in the ingest workflow. Stand-alone tools exist for some ingest processes, for example, generating technical metadata and creating checksums. (See Chapter 13 for further discussion of tools relevant to ingest.) Examples of ingest tools in common use include:

- DROID (Digital Record Object Identification), which performs automated batch identification of file formats (sourceforge .net/projects/droid);

- Jacksum, a tool for calculating and verifying checksums, hash algorithms, and Cyclical Redundancy Checks (sourceforge.net/ projects/jacksum);

- JHOVE (JSTOR/Harvard Object Validation Environment), which performs format identification, validation, and characterization of digital objects (hul.harvard.edu/jhove);

- NLNZ (National Library of New Zealand) Preservation Metadata Extraction Tool, which automatically extracts preservation-related metadata from the headers of a range of file formats and outputs that metadata in XML (meta-extractor.sourceforge .net); and

- the prototype ingest tool developed by Tufts University and Yale University's *Fedora and the Preservation of University Records* Project (dca.lib.tufts.edu/features/nhprc/reports).

A fuller listing of ingest tools is provided in the CAIRO Project's *Cairo Tools Survey: A Survey of Tools Applicable to the Preparation of Digital Archives for Ingest into a Preservation Repository* (cairo.paradigm.ac.uk/ projectdocs/index.html).

Research into tools development continues (see Chapter 13). The processes of receiving data into an archive and of ingest are increasingly automated. This research has resulted in the release of software such as BagIt, PreScan, and the Audit Control Environment (ACE).

The BagIt specification and software tools associated with it were released by the Library of Congress as part of its Transfer Tools project. BagIt is based on the concept of packaging data in "bags" for the purposes of transferring them to a repository. The bags consist of the digital objects being transferred plus a machine-readable manifest listing the contents. Checksums are applied to verify that the data have been transferred successfully. The Library of Congress has also developed open-source software tools that automate part of the process of sending and receiving these bags. They enable the Library of Congress to transfer data over networks to its repository rather than the data being uploaded to the Library, with the advantages that the data transfer is faster than transferring them on portable media (such as a hard drive) and that the data are accessible from where they are stored (Library of Congress, accessed 2010; Ashenfelder, 2009).

The PreScan software tool automates processes relating to the creation of metadata and their curation. It automatically extracts metadata embedded in the digital objects, offers the possibility of combining this with metadata created manually, and assists in managing that metadata. It is available as open-source software and is one of the tools developed as part of the CASPAR Project (Marketakis, Tzanakis, and Tzitzikas, 2009).

ACE automates the process of checking the integrity of collections of digital objects. Developed by the University of Maryland, ACE continuously monitors cryptographic representations (strings of characters representing bit streams) of digital objects. It has two components: the Audit Manager software, which is installed at an archive to monitor collections; and the Integrity Management Service, which is installed at a different site and compares and validates details about digital objects. This software audits collections, provides reports of missing or damaged files to the archive manager, and logs any changes to a collection. ACE is being used by the Chronopolis Project (chronopolis.sdsc.edu) to monitor the integrity of its holdings, currently auditing over a million files per day. The software is available from the web (adapt.umiacs.umd.edu/ace; Library of Congress, 2009).

Policies for Ingest

As is the case with all actions in the Curation Lifecycle, Ingest is most effectively implemented where policy statements and guidance are well developed. These policies need to be documented and kept up-to-date, for example, with respect to changes in legal requirements. Documented policies are useful for ingest procedures, as they are for all other aspects of digital curation, because they clarify responsibilities and lines of communication, promote standardization, allow risks to be managed, and address compliance issues. Chapter 7 notes these and other points about policies in more detail.

An ingest policy specifies a repository's policy about submission and file formats, addressing questions such as:

- Does the repository have a policy on submission file formats?
- Are there any restrictions on file formats ingested?
- Does the repository transform submitted formats in any way?

Summary: Automation Is the Key

The requirements for ingest are well understood, and ingest procedures are well developed. What are not yet mature, however, are automated ways of ingesting digital material to an archive. Although many software tools that automate parts of the ingest action are available and more are being developed, there are not yet enough.

The next chapter notes the next sequential action in the DCC Curation Lifecycle, *Preservation Action*, and the related Occasional Action *Migrate*. *Preservation Action* is the process of ensuring long-term preservation and retention of data and aims (as does *Migrate*) to ensure that data and digital objects remain authentic, reliable, and usable while at the same time maintaining their integrity over time.

References

Alliance for Permanent Access. 2008. *Keeping the Records of Science Accessible: Can We Afford It?* The Hague: Alliance for Permanent Access. Available: www.alliancepermanentaccess.eu/index.php?id=3 (accessed April 26, 2010).

Ashenfelder, Michael. 2009. "21st Century Shipping: Network Data Transfer to the Library of Congress." *D-Lib Magazine* 15, no. 7/8 (July/August). Available: www.dlib.org/dlib/july09/ashenfelder/07ashenfelder.html (accessed April 26, 2010).

INGEST: REVIEW

Key points: *Ingest* is the process of preparing data for adding to a digital archive, and of adding data to the digital archive.

Key activities:
- Develop, maintain, and apply policies about ingest
- Develop guidelines for the ingest process
- Identify tools that can be used for ingest
- Prepare appraised data, including:
  - Assign a persistent identifier
  - Check for and remove viruses
  - Add relevant description information and representation information
  - Create a checksum or hash value for the data
  - Identify and confirm technical details
  - Uncompress and unencrypt the data, if necessary
  - Combine the data and their associated description and representation information into an AIP (Archival Information Package)

Caplan, Priscilla. 2008. "Repository to Repository Transfer of Enriched Archival Information Packages." *D-Lib Magazine* 14, no. 11/12 (November/December). Available: www.dlib.org/dlib/november08/caplan/11caplan .html (accessed April 26, 2010).

Consultative Committee for Space Data Systems. 2002. *Reference Model for an Open Archival Information System (OAIS): Recommendation for Space Data System Standards.* Washington, DC: CCSDS Secretariat. Available: public.ccsds.org/publications/archive/650x0b1.pdf (accessed April 26, 2010).

Digital Curation Centre. 2008. *The DCC Curation Lifecycle Model.* Edinburgh: Digital Curation Centre. Available: www.dcc.ac.uk/docs/publications/ DCCLifecycle.pdf (accessed April 26, 2010).

Library of Congress. "Digital Content Transfer Tools." Washington, DC: Library of Congress. Available:www.digitalpreservation.gov/library/challenge/ data-transfer.html (accessed April 26, 2010).

———. 2009. "ACE Trumps Digital Integrity Threats." Washington, DC: Library of Congress (February 26, 2009). Available: www.digitalpreservation .gov/news/2009/20090226news_article_ace.html (accessed April 26, 2010).

Marketakis, Yannis, Makis Tzanakis, and Yannis Tzitzikas. 2009. "PreScan: Towards Automating the Preservation of Digital Objects." Paper presented at the International ACM Conference on Management of Emergent Digital EcoSystems (MEDES), Lyon, October 27–30. Available: www.casparpreserves .eu/Members/metaware/Papers/prescan-towards-automating-the-preservation -of-digital-objects/at_download/file (accessed April 26, 2010).

Preserving Data

This chapter investigates the fifth of the Sequential Actions of the Digital Curation Centre (DCC) Curation Lifecycle Model, *Preservation Action*, and one of the Occasional Actions, *Migrate*. Preservation Action is the process of ensuring long-term preservation and retention of data. The activities that comprise Preservation Action are stated in the DCC Curation Lifecycle Model as "Undertak[ing] actions to ensure long-term preservation and retention of the authoritative nature of data." The aim of these actions is to "ensure that data remain authentic, reliable and usable while maintaining its integrity" and this is done by activities such as "data cleaning, validation, assigning preservation metadata, assigning representation information and ensuring acceptable data structures or file formats" (Digital Curation Centre, 2008).

Migrate is included in this chapter because migration is one of the most commonly applied preservation actions in digital curation. The Occasional Action Migrate is usually triggered by decisions made during the Preservation Action stage. Its activities are described in the DCC Curation Lifecycle as "Migrate data to a different format. This may be done to accord with the storage environment or to ensure the data's immunity from hardware or software obsolescence" (Digital Curation Centre, 2008).

The aim of these preservation actions (and also of migration) is to ensure that data and digital objects remain authentic, reliable, and usable while at the same time maintaining their integrity over time. Chapter 5 describes authenticity, integrity, longevity, and accessibility in more detail and notes how these aims are achieved in practice.

It is important to note the relationships of Preservation Action with other actions in the DCC Curation Lifecycle Model. It depends heavily on the rest of the curation process. Preservation Action has direct relationships with *Ingest*, which immediately precedes it, and *Store*, which follows it. There are also strong links to two other Sequential Actions, *Appraise and Select* (through the Occasional Action *Reappraise*) and *Transform* (through the Occasional Action *Migrate*). In addition, there are links to the Full Lifecycle Actions *Description and Representation*

IN THIS CHAPTER:

✔ Digital Preservation Methods

✔ Migration in Practice

✔ Automating Preservation Actions

✔ Tools

✔ Summary: Methods and Tools

✔ References

Authenticity: The data have not been manipulated, forged, or substituted.

Integrity: The data are authentic.

Longevity: The data are available for as long as their current and future users require them.

Accessibility: The data can be located and used in the future in ways acceptable to their users.

Information, *Preservation Planning*, and *Community Watch*. These relationships illustrate the difficulty of developing a model that fully represents practice. The DCC Curation Lifecycle Model breaks the curation process into discrete parts, but this is not necessarily what happens in practice.

We can see some of the dependent relationships if we examine a list of preservation actions commonly agreed on as necessary to ensure that data and digital objects are in the best possible shape to be stored in an archive or repository (this list is based on Lord and Macdonald, 2003: 31):

- Keep the original bit stream as well as any "preservation version" in the likelihood that preservation methods are developed in the future.

- Clean and validate data to ensure they can be managed and reused over time (strong links with *Create or Receive*: see Chapter 10).

- Add high-quality preservation metadata and representation information to increase potential for discovery, reuse, and preservation (strong links with *Description and Representation Information*: see Chapter 6).

- Ensure acceptable data structures or file formats, for example, by using nonproprietary, well-documented data format standards (such as ASCII/UNICODE and XML) to increase the chance of future recoverability (strong links with *Create or Receive*: see Chapter 10).

- Apply good data management practices (strong links with *Store*: see Chapter 14).

- Implement secure storage and institutional or organizational continuity (strong links with *Store*: see Chapter 14).

These preservation actions are prerequisites for implementing preservation methods such as migration and emulation.

Digital Preservation Methods

Digital preservation strategies fall into three main families: technology preservation, technology emulation, and information migration. Also available is digital archaeology, a reactive strategy for recovering at-risk or damaged data. The range of methods applied to preserving data within these strategies is relatively stable. The summary in Lord and Macdonald's 2003 *E-science Curation Report* (2003: 30–31) is still valid.

Lord and Macdonald report the main preservation methods as migration, emulation, "formal descriptions" (the Universal Virtual Computer), digital archaeology, and "computer museums" (technology preservation). Migration focuses on preserving the *data*, transforming it from one format to another. Emulation focuses on the *technology*, developing computer programs that emulate obsolete computer systems and thereby enabling the original applications and data to be processed on current computers. The Universal Virtual Computer (Lord and

Macdonald's "formal descriptions") also focuses on the *technology*, providing the software specifications for a virtual computer that can be run on computers to be built in the future; it is similar to emulation in some respects. Digital archaeology attempts to recover data from obsolete media and systems. Technology preservation (Lord and Macdonald's "computer museums"), also focusing on the *technology*, maintains obsolete computers and software in working condition. In practice migration and emulation are the primary preservation methods, but no single method can be applied by itself (e.g., they all depend on migration to a greater or lesser degree).

The selection of methods to apply is determined by factors such as the nature of the data and digital objects to be preserved, technical issues, costs, and organizational requirements (Lord and Macdonald, 2003: 31). Preservation strategies should not be seen as competing with each other but are best viewed as different strategies working together (perhaps migration for some data sets and emulation for others). The key criteria to be considered when choosing an appropriate digital preservation method or combination of methods are the following:

- The nature of the data and digital objects to be preserved (e.g., Although it is standard practice to keep the original bit stream when migrating data, for some materials, such as very large databases, the costs of doing this are prohibitive; the designated community's requirements will determine what characteristics of data are preserved; see the discussion of significant properties in Chapter 10.)

- The technical infrastructure required (e.g., Getting data off obsolete media in order to migrate it requires aspects of technology preservation.)

- Costs (Can the organization afford to implement a particular strategy? Can it afford the cost of maintaining the data set over time when applying that method? Committing to data migration means ongoing expenditure on future migrations.)

- Organizational factors (e.g., Some disciplines have well-established preservation strategies in place.)

- Rights management (e.g., Does the organization own the rights to re-engineer software? This could be relevant if emulation software is developed.)

The procedures described by the Digital Curator of the Wellcome Library (library.wellcome.ac.uk/node288.html) illustrate some of these criteria in practice. The overriding factor at the Wellcome Library is its fundamental commitment to keep permanently the materials it acquires and make them available for reuse. The preservation approach selected for born-digital material is based on available resources. "If we can't afford, or can't find the resources to bring material to the point where it can be retained permanently AND made available then we may decline it." After material is accepted, the preservation method applied is format migration. For material created on obsolete media by obsolete hardware and operating systems, the decision to accept is again made on the basis of the availability of staff resources: is the staff time and expertise available? The cost of acquiring the obsolete hardware required to access material that may turn out not to be very significant to the collection is also a factor in accepting material (Thompson, 2009).

The choice of the best preservation methods, or combination of methods, can be assisted by using software tools. An example is the Plato preservation planning tool, developed by PLANETS. Plato is described in more detail later in this chapter.

The main characteristics of each of the digital preservation methods discussed in this chapter are summarized in Figure 13.1, using a six-part framework: definition, relationship to other digital preservation methods, where applied, points to note, pros, and cons; for some methods, specific

Figure 13.1. Comparison of the Main Digital Preservation Methods

	Migration[a]	Emulation	Universal Virtual Computer (UVC)[b]
Definition	Transferring digital objects from one technology (one generation of hardware or software) to another, preserving their intellectual content and retaining the ability for users to retrieve, display, and otherwise use them. By contrast with refreshing, which is a simpler process of maintaining the bit stream by copying to a new medium, migration changes or transforms the digital object so that it can be used with new hardware or software. There are different approaches of migration, which are noted in the "Migration in Practice" section of this chapter.	Emulation is the process of developing software that mimics obsolete systems on current and future generations of computers by emulating applications, operating systems, and/or (most commonly) hardware architecture.	A UVC is software in simple machine language, completely independent of any existing hardware or software, to emulate the basic architecture of a computer. The software allows for that basic architecture to be reimplemented at any time in the future on any platform. Because of the simplicity of the software, it will be relatively easy in the future to emulate the software of the original computer on any real computer.
Relationship to other digital preservation methods	Migration and refreshing are the basis of, or are required for, many other methods (e.g., emulation).	Emulators themselves need to be migrated. Emulation could be a useful backup mechanism for providing access to the "digital original" form and may be the only viable approach to preserving digital materials whose interactive behavior needs to be maintained. They are closely associated with the UVC method.	A UVC combines emulation (of a computer that has never actually existed as hardware) and migration of the bit stream of the UVC.

(Columns continue on facing page.)

sources for further information are also noted. More detailed descriptions and analyses of these methods are available in many sources. Excellent starting points are the Preservation Strategies section (4.3.2) of the Digital Preservation Coalition's (2008) *Preservation Management of Digital Materials* and the pages on migration in the National Library of Australia's (2009) "PADI—Migration."

Migration in Practice

The DCC Curation Lifecycle Model's Occasional Action *Migrate* is included in this chapter because migration is one of the most commonly applied preservation actions in digital curation. The Migrate action is

(continued p. 168)

Figure 13.1. *(Columns Continued)*			
Digital Archaeology[c]	**Technology Preservation**	**Standardizing Data Formats (Normalization)**	**Encapsulation**
Digital archaeology refers to the application of data recovery techniques to recover digital objects or data from storage media that have become inaccessible or damaged.	Technology preservation refers to maintaining obsolete hardware and software in working condition so that digital materials that require this software and hardware can be accessed.	Standardizing data formats refers both to the conversion of digital materials into a limited number of file formats that are likely to be viable for longer periods, are typically open, are widely available, and are well supported and to an undertaking to support these formats over time.	Encapsulation refers to packaging together a digital object and the means of providing access to it, such as metadata and software viewers, usually in a wrapper that describes the contents so it is readily understood (e.g., an XML document).
Digital archaeology is related to technology preservation, because it requires access to obsolete equipment.	Technology preservation is usually considered as an interim strategy that is applied while long-term strategies are being developed. It plays a role in supporting data recovery, such as in digital archaeology.	Limiting the number of formats makes all other digital preservation strategies more feasible. Standardizing data formats is not a long-term digital preservation strategy, as it only slows down the effects of obsolescence of file formats rather than addresses problems of their future obsolescence.	This method is best considered as either a part of, or a prerequisite for, other digital preservation approaches. It is a key part of some emulation techniques.

(Table continues on following page.)

Figure 13.1. Comparison of the Main Digital Preservation Methods *(Continued)*

	Migration[a]	Emulation	Universal Virtual Computer (UVC)[b]
Where applied	Migration has a long history and is the principal preservation technique applied to date. There is considerable expertise in migration for some kinds of digital objects and formats, particularly documents and data sets. It is best applied to less complex digital objects and to collections of materials that are in uniform formats.	Emulation is in recent years closely associated with the Koninklijke Bibliotheek (National Library of the Netherlands) and the Nationaal Archief of the Netherlands, which in 2007 released Dioscuri, an emulator designed for digital preservation. Dioscuri has been incorporated into the PLANETS Project, which has also developed other emulators.	The UVC method has been developed by the Koninklijke Bibliotheek in conjunction with IBM as a prototype for archiving PDF documents and as a UVC tool for images in JPEG and GIF formats.
Points to note	Migration procedures need to be fully documented in metadata. The original bit stream is usually also retained. Strict quality-check procedures should be implemented.	Emulation aims to overcome technological obsolescence. It has a well-developed history in the computing industry, for example, emulators that run Mac OS under Windows and emulators used in computer gaming. Emulation requires high levels of expertise to develop and, ideally, needs thorough and accurate documentation to be available for the systems that are emulated.	A UVC uses a combination of emulation and migration to reconstruct digital objects in their original appearance at any time in the future. It is based on the concept of a virtual machine, which emulates a computer that has never actually existed as hardware. A UVC allows for digital objects to be read without the original hardware or software.
Pros	Migration is widely used, with well-established procedures; relatively simple technology is needed. It is a reliable way to preserve the intellectual content of simple digital objects (e.g., page-based documents). Conversion software for some formats is readily available.	Emulation re-creates the look and feel and the functionality of the original digital object, providing the user with the original experience of using dynamic content such as applications or games. It reduces the need to understand a wide range of arbitrary formats. It may be more cost-effective for preserving large collections, despite the high start-up costs associated with developing emulators, as it avoids the repeated costs and problems associated with migration. Emulation may offer the best prospects for preserving complex digital objects, for example, objects that depend on executable code.	The UVC method provides a single platform and thereby potentially minimizes the effort needed to handle many combinations of hardware and software. It minimizes the need to migrate digital objects (including emulation software).

(Columns continue on facing page.)

Figure 13.1. *(Columns Continued)*

Digital Archaeology[c]	Technology Preservation	Standardizing Data Formats (Normalization)	Encapsulation
Digital archaeology is usually considered as an emergency recovery or last-resort solution because of its expense. Because it is an emergency recovery strategy and is expensive, it is likely to be used only when data are of sufficient significance to warrant the high costs involved.	Technology preservation plays an important role as an interim strategy, but, given the large number of formats, hardware, and software that become obsolete, it is only viable for the short term.	Standardizing data formats works best for materials where retaining content is essential but retention of other characteristics is less important, because the process of converting from a nonpreferred file format to a preferred format may mean that some aspects of digital objects, such as functionality, are lost. It has a long history in data archives and is currently applied in some significant archive contexts, such as the National Archives of Australia (in its Xena digital preservation software; xena.sourceforge.net), and in institutional repositories where file formats for submission of theses and other materials are specified as a requirement for receipt of data.	Encapsulation is widely used. An example is the National Archives of Australia's Xena digital preservation software (xena.sourceforge.net).
Trained specialists in data recovery, using specialist software and hardware and highly specialized skills, are required. Commercial data recovery services are available.	Technology preservation requires that documentation of hardware and software is also retained.	Standardizing data formats requires clear policies and guidelines about which formats are acceptable to an archive, effective data conversion processes, and high standards of quality control.	The encapsulation concept is commonly used in digital preservation environments; an example is the information package concept in the OAIS Reference Model. Encapsulation requires a secure wrapper to ensure that data, metadata, and representation information are kept together.
It is technically possible to recover a wide range of data from damaged or obsolete media. Specialist third-party services offer this service.	Technology preservation retains the functionality, look, and feel of the digital materials and the technology and software platforms that render them for as long as that hardware and software still function. It buys time by delaying the need for long-term preservation methods.	Standardizing data formats has the potential to use digital preservation resources in the most efficient way, because, for example, it simplifies migration and achieves economies of scale. It may slow the rate at which file formats become obsolete because relevant software is likely to be available for longer periods. It is not tied to specific hardware and software platforms.	Encapsulation ensures that all information required for access (representation information) is maintained with the data as one unit.

(Table continues on following page.)

	Migration[a]	**Emulation**	**Universal Virtual Computer (UVC)**[b]
Cons	Migration needs to occur on a regular basis throughout the life of the digital objects to which it is applied. It incurs significant ongoing costs. It does not, at present, handle complex digital objects well, because functionality is lost and integrity compromised. Repeated migrations, each of which may make small changes to data, may accumulate into major alteration of the digital objects.	Emulation is not yet sufficiently tested in practice. Emulators are expensive to develop and require high levels of expertise and access to documentation of hardware and software. Migration of the emulators is required. Software copyright issues may impede the development of emulators.	The UVC method is still experimental. It has not yet been tested beyond a small number of applications. It requires high investment in expertise to develop.

(Columns continue on facing page.)

Figure 13.1. Comparison of the Main Digital Preservation Methods

usually triggered in response to hardware or software obsolescence, as an outcome of decisions made at the *Preservation Action* stage, particularly in relation to the requirement to "ensure acceptable data structures or file formats to increase the chance of future recoverability," and in applying good data management practices. The activities that comprise Migrate are:

- develop policies about what data and digital objects are migrated, including deciding the formats that they are migrated to, and how often migration should occur;
- document migration processes in metadata; and
- apply checking procedures to maintain accuracy and authenticity of the data and digital objects.

Migration refers to transferring digital materials from one technology (one generation of hardware or software) to another, or from one format to another, preserving their intellectual content and retaining the ability for users to retrieve, display, and otherwise use them. Migration is different from refreshing, which is a simpler process of maintaining the bit stream by copying it to a new, usually more durable, medium. Migration is one of two primary preservation methods (emulation is the other). It focuses on the content or properties of digital objects, and it attempts to maintain these over time by making them usable on new software and hardware rather than focusing on the technology by attempting to keep obsolete technology working or creating emulators. Other preservation methods depend on migration to some extent. It is a process that is well understood, applied in response to changes in file

Figure 13.1. *(Columns Continued)*

Digital Archaeology[c]	Technology Preservation	Standardizing Data Formats (Normalization)	Encapsulation
Specialist facilities, equipment, and expertise are required. The process recovers data but does not necessarily recover the ability to understand those data, especially if no metadata or documentation is available. It is expensive and is not, therefore, cost-effective, except for high-value data. There is no guarantee that data will be recovered.	Technology preservation is very resource-intensive. It is useful only as an interim approach. Replacement parts for hardware and the expertise to maintain these become scarce rapidly. It requires access to documentation, such as software and hardware manuals, that may not be readily available.	Standardizing data formats is not suitable for materials where important characteristics will be lost when converting to a standard file format, especially those characteristics that ensure that the material can be understood.	Encapsulation does not address the issue of obsolescence; for example, encapsulated software still becomes obsolete. Encapsulation can result in very large files.

a. See also the section "Migration in Practice" in this chapter.
b. The UVC concept and details of an application are available on the website of the Koninklijke Bibliotheek (accessed 2010).
c. A 1999 study, *Digital Archaeology: Rescuing Neglected and Damaged Data Resources* (Ross and Gow, 1999), remains the best introduction to this method.

formats (such as impending obsolescence), or to changes in the storage environment or the technology platform, and to counteract hardware or software obsolescence.

There are several different approaches to migration:

- Simple version migration (such as within one software product, e.g., new versions of Microsoft Word work with earlier versions of Word, although the number of versions for which such backwards compatibility exists is typically limited by the software manufacturers)

- Migration to newer or standard file formats when obsolescence has occurred or is imminent

- Migration on request: migration occurs at the time that access to digital material is requested

There are variations of these approaches. One is to keep the original bit stream and migrate the software tools that allow users to access that bit stream.

A commonly encountered example of migration on request occurs when access is sought to documents that have been created in earlier versions of a software package. Some software allows for documents that have been created in its earlier versions to be opened in later versions. For example, the open-source software suite OpenOffice (www.openoffice.org) supports files created in the word processing software Microsoft Word 6.0/95/97/2000/XP (.doc and .dot file extensions), Microsoft Word 2003 XML (.xml), Microsoft WinWord 5 (.doc),

StarWriter formats (.sdw, .sgl, and .vor), AportisDoc (Palm) (.pdb), Pocket Word (.psw), WordPerfect Document (.wpd), WPS 2000/ Office 1.0 (.wps), DocBook (.xml), and others. It also provides similar capabilities for other suites of office software.

Implementing Migration

Migration is acknowledged to be most suitable for dealing with large collections of digital objects of similar types that are simple in structure (e.g., bitmap page images, ASCII files, well-defined XML formats). It is often applied in conjunction with standardizing data formats when digital materials are ingested into an archive. When data formats are standardized, there are fewer formats to handle and economies to be made by such actions as automating as many of the tasks involved as possible.

When data are migrated, the following procedures should be followed. It is essential to select acceptable data structures or file formats as the target format (the format that files are to be migrated to); for example, use nonproprietary, well-documented data format standards to increase the chance of data being recovered in the future (see Chapter 10). It is also essential to document migration procedures fully in the metadata. Standard advice is to retain the original bit stream whenever it is possible to do so. (An exception to this arises when the quantities of data are so large that the expense of retaining the bit stream makes this not feasible; this is noted earlier in this chapter.) Strict quality-checking procedures must be developed and enforced rigorously. Migration tools are available to assist the process (see the "Tools" section later in this chapter).

Although migration is a method that is commonly applied, it is by no means perfect. One limitation is the nature of the digital objects for which migration is the best option. It is most suitable for simple digital objects and collections of materials that are in uniform formats; it does not yet handle complex materials well. Another significant limitation of migration is that it needs to occur on a regular basis throughout the life of the materials. For example, data may need to be migrated to new media every three to five years; they may also need to be migrated to new formats every five to ten years, before the software applications that are needed to access them become obsolete. Because it needs to occur on a regular basis, migration incurs significant ongoing costs. It is a labor-intensive method, for example, in the effort needed to carefully document the process, essential for ensuring the integrity and authenticity of migrated data.

Perhaps the most significant limitation associated with migration is that many problems may arise in ensuring the integrity and authenticity of data that have been migrated. Repeated migrations, each of which may make small changes to data, may accumulate over time into major alterations of the original data.

Migration Changes Data

Every migration changes data, and these changes are compounded after repeated migrations. It is very rare that there will be a one-to-one conversion of data in any migration process. The result is likely to be information loss and/or changes in system behavior. Chris Rusbridge (2008) describes a common experience, migrating from earlier versions of PowerPoint to

> today's PowerPoint, and then from today's to tomorrow's Power-Point, and then from tomorrow's to the next great thing, I will introduce cumulative errors whose impact I will only be able to assess at some horribly cringe-making moment, like in the middle of a presentation using a host's machine.

Because functionality is likely to be lost and integrity compromised as a result of migration, care must be taken to establish and implement strict quality-checking procedures, for example, to compare the original bit stream and the migrated bit stream by comparing checksums.

Automating Preservation Actions

Current digital preservation methods are labor-intensive and are often referred to as "artisan" or "hand-crafted." This imposes limitations on the quantities of data that can be curated. To handle the quantities of data we need to curate, ways of automating curation workflows and preservation actions are essential.

Automated curation procedures need software tools. Many software tools for digital curation are being developed in projects such as the digital preservation projects CASPAR and PLANETS, both funded by the European Union, by the DCC in the United Kingdom, and by NDIIPP (National Digital Information Infrastructure and Preservation Program) in the United States. What tools will be developed and implemented as standard curation practice? The "theoretical ideal" situation in ten years time, as described in 2007 by the Preservation and Curation Working Group of the Office for Science and Innovation in the United Kingdom, is that there will be tools and services for:

> automatically monitoring digital files, identifying risks, and addressing digital preservation challenges [and] well-developed certification and audit processes for these services and tools. . . . [W]e will have seen an increase in the level of automation possible, based on more R&D in knowledge and preservation technologies. (Beagrie, 2007: 12)

Tools

Useful and usable tools that can be applied to many preservation actions are needed for identifying data and digital objects (e.g., where they are located, what formats they are in); describing data and digital objects (e.g., automated metadata creation); manipulating data and digital objects (e.g., data management, data storage, repositories); preserving data and digital objects (e.g., migration, emulation); data registration;

documentation of commonly used terms and concepts; and rights management and access control. Recent research and development projects have as key objectives the development and dissemination of usable tools. A notable characteristic of these tools is that they are open source. Some projects for the development of tools are described in this chapter; these and other projects should be monitored on an ongoing basis (see Chapter 8) to see if the tools developed are applicable to local digital curation activities.

Lists of data curation tools are available on the web. Among those that are updated on a regular basis include the PADI list "Digital Preservation Tools" (www.nla.gov.au/padi/topics/535.html), the DCC's

---

SOME DIGITAL CURATION TOOLS AND PROJECTS

Metadata Tools
- Metadata Extraction Tool (meta-extractor.sourceforge.net)
- Ecological Metadata Language (EML) editor (knb.ecoinformatics.org/software)

Format Validation, Format Registry, and Obsolescence Notification Tools
- Format validation: DROID (droid.sourceforge.net)
- Format validation: JHOVE (hul.harvard.edu/jhove)
- Format registry: PRONOM Technical Registry (www.nationalarchives.gov.uk/pronom)
- Format registry: Unified Digital Formats Registry (www.udfr.org)
- Obsolescence notification tool: Automatic Obsolescence Notification System II (sourceforge.net/projects/aons)

Normalizing and Encapsulation Tools
- XML Electronic Normalizing for Archives (Xena; xena.sourceforge.net)
- kopal Library for Retrieval and Ingest (koLibRI; kopal.langzeitarchivierung.de/index_koLibRI.php.en)

Migration Tools
- ImageMagick (www.imagemagick.org)
- SoX (sox.sourceforge.net)

Emulation Tools
- Dioscuri (dioscuri.sourceforge.net)
- Amiga Forever (www.amigaforever.com)

Web Archiving Tools
- Heritrix web crawler (crawler.archive.org)
- Web Curator Tool (webcurator.sourceforge.net)
- NetarchiveSuite (netarchive.dk/suite)
- International Internet Preservation Consortium (IIPC) Web Archiving Toolset (netpreserve.org/software/downloads.php)

Other Curation Tools
- Library of Congress Transfer Tools project (sourceforge.net/projects/loc-xferutils)
- Australian Research Enabling Environment (ARCHER; www.archer.edu.au/products)
- File Information Tool Set (FITS; code.google.com/p/fits)
- Home and Office Painless Persistent Long-Term Archiving (HOPPLA; www.ifs.tuwien.ac.at/dp/hoppla)

Tool Development Projects
- Cultural, Artistic and Scientific Knowledge for Preservation, Access and Retrieval (CASPAR; www.casparpreserves.eu)
- Preservation and Long-Term Access through Networked Services (PLANETS; www.planets-project.eu)
- Keeping Emulation Environments Portable (KEEP; www.keepproject.eu)
- Sustaining Heritage Access through Multivalent ArchiviNg (SHAMAN; shaman-ip.eu/shaman)

"Digital Curation Tools" (www.dcc.ac.uk/tools/digital-curation-tools), and the NDIIPP "Partner Tools and Services Inventory" (www.digital-preservation.gov/partners/resources/tools/index.html). An indicative sample of existing tools follows.

Metadata Tools

Metadata tools include software for extracting technical metadata from digital objects and tools for converting this extracted metadata into XML schema elements. One example is the National Library of New Zealand's Metadata Extraction Tool, which automatically extracts preservation metadata from a number of common file formats, such as MS Word (various versions), WordPerfect, OpenOffice, MS Works, MS Excel, MS PowerPoint, TIFF, JPEG, WAV, MP3, HTML, PDF, GIF, and BMP, and outputs it in XML format. It can then be loaded into a preservation metadata repository. It is available as open-source software from Sourceforge (meta-extractor.sourceforge.net). Another example is the Ecological Metadata Language (EML) editor, a set of tools designed to work with the metadata standard EML, a modular and extensible XML-based standard metadata standard for the field of ecology. EML accommodates information on methods, geographic coverage, temporal coverage and detailed descriptions of tabular data. A data management application, Morpho, combines an interface to EML with a number of tools to assist ecologists to document their data. It is available from the Knowledge Network for Biocomplexity (knb.ecoinformatics.org/software).

More tools for preservation metadata implementation are listed on the PREMIS metadata schema website (Library of Congress, 2007) and on the METS website (Library of Congress, accessed 2010).

Format Validation, Format Registry, and Obsolescence Notification Tools

Tools for identifying file formats and validating them (verifying that they are correctly formed according to the format's specification) are essential to the preservation of digital materials. Two of the best known of these are DROID and JHOVE. DROID (droid.sourceforge.net) is a software tool developed by The National Archives (United Kingdom) to perform automated batch identification of file formats. DROID identifies and reports the specific file format versions of digital files, and the results are stored in an XML signature file that is generated from information recorded in the PRONOM Technical Registry (noted later). JHOVE (hul.harvard.edu/jhove) was developed by JSTOR and Harvard University Library to allow the automatic identification, validation, and characterization of a range of digital object types. JHOVE2 (confluence.ucop.edu/display/JHOVE2Info/Home) is under development and is expected to be available in 2010.

Closely associated with format validation tools are online format registries. Format validation tools link to these format registries, which provide updated technical information about file formats and are available as online services. The PRONOM Technical Registry (www.national archives.gov.uk/pronom), developed by The National Archives, is a knowledge base of technical information about file formats and software tools. It is usually used in conjunction with the DROID file format identification tool and has been made available through The National Archives' website. In 2009 plans were released for the Unified Digital Formats Registry (www.udfr.org), which will combine PRONOM's formats and software database with Harvard University's Global Digital Format Registry.

Another tool related to file formats is an obsolescence notification tool. An example is the Automatic Obsolescence Notification System II (AONS) (sourceforge.net/projects/aons), designed to monitor the risk of file format obsolescence in repositories and notify managers when file formats in their repositories are obsolete or at risk of becoming obsolete. Developed by the National Library of Australia and the Australian Partnership for Sustainable Repositories (APSR), this tool links to file format registries such as PRONOM.

Normalizing and Encapsulation Tools

Tools to normalize (convert data to stable standard formats) and encapsulate (package data in these stable file formats with related metadata and other data relevant to their preservation) include XML Electronic Normalizing for Archives (Xena) and kopal Library for Retrieval and Ingest (koLibRI). Xena (xena.sourceforge.net), developed by the National Archives of Australia, determines file formats and converts files into standards-based, open formats for preservation. koLibRI (kopal .langzeitarchivierung.de/index_koLibRI.php.en), developed as part of the German kopal project, supports the compilation and preparation of data for the archive as a data package (an OAIS AIP).

Migration Tools

Because migration, the most commonly applied preservation method, is a standard technique used in many areas of data management, migration tools abound. As examples, tools used for format migration in one institution include the open-source program suite ImageMagick (www.imagemagick.org) for image format migration and another open-source software program, SoX (sox.sourceforge.net), for sound file migration. Another institution uses the commercial software tools Acrobat Professional, Solid PDF, and Amber Lotus 1-2-3 Converter. Projects such as Conversion and Recommendation of Digital Object Formats (CRiB) (crib.dsi.uminho.pt) aim to provide tools to assist in implementing migration procedures. Open-source software that is readily available can be used for migration; open-source tools used to migrate social science and scientific data from legacy media (CD-ROM, DVD, floppy disks) in one experiment include OpenOffice to convert Microsoft Word, Power-Point, and Corel WordPerfect files to PDF (Woods and Brown, 2008).

Emulation Tools

Although many emulators are available, few are specifically for digital curation. One emulator developed for this purpose was released in 2007. Dioscuri (dioscuri.sourceforge.net) emulates an Intel 8086-based computer platform and runs 16-bit operating systems, such as MS-DOS, and applications, such as WordPerfect 5.1, DrawPerfect 1.1, and Norton Commander. It is being developed further to emulate newer computers (286, 386, 486, and Pentium) and will then run operating systems such as MS Windows 95/98/2000/XP and Linux Ubuntu. Many other emulators are available, although these are not specifically developed for digital curation purposes. One example of the many emulators available for obsolete hardware and software platforms is the Amiga Forever emulation software (www.amigaforever.com).

Web Archiving Tools

Many tools to assist with web archiving have been developed and are widely used. Some are available as integrated toolkits; others can be used in conjunction with other tools or as stand-alone tools. Examples include the Heritrix web crawler (crawler.archive.org), developed by the Internet Archive in conjunction with the Nordic National Libraries to harvest websites for archiving; the web Curator Tool (webcurator .sourceforge.net), developed by the National Library of New Zealand and the British Library to support selective and thematic web harvesting; and the NetarchiveSuite (netarchive.dk/suite), web archiving open-source software developed through the Danish Netarchive project. Built around the Heritrix web crawler, it is used to plan, schedule, and run web harvests. The International Internet Preservation Consortium (IIPC) Web Archiving Toolset (netpreserve.org/software/downloads .php) consists of tools for all processes involved with web archiving: for acquisition, Heritrix, the curator tools Web Curator Tool and NetarchiveSuite; BAT (BnFArcTools) for collection storage and mainte-nance; and the access and finding aids NutchWAX, WERA, and Xinq.

Other Curation Tools

The preceding list of curation tools is not comprehensive. Many others are available or under development. One trend is for the development of tool sets, suites of programs that are integrated and work together to address a set of curation actions. Four examples (again, this is no more than an indicative list) are noted next to illustrate this trend.

Tool sets that package data with associated description and represen-tation information for ease and accuracy of transfer of data are important in digital curation because they facilitate archiving and reuse of data. The Library of Congress Transfer Tools project (sourceforge.net/projects/ loc-xferutils) provides open-source tools developed by the Library of Congress and the California Digital Library for validating and transferring data conforming to the BagIT specification (a specification for packaging digital content for transfer in which a digital collection is packed into a directory [the bag] with a manifest file [the tag] listing the contents). The tools validate a bag (checking for missing, extra, and duplicate files), verify checksums, and speed up file transfer.

Tool sets that assist researchers to collaborate and to carry out digital curation tasks are being developed by many groups. One of these is the ARCHER (Australian Research Enabling Environment) Project, a collaboration of Australian universities. Their tool set (described at www.archer.edu.au/products) includes open-source software to help researchers collect, capture, and retain large data sets from a range of different sources, deposit data files and data sets to storage repositories, add metadata, allow annotation of data sets, facilitate online collaboration, and support publication, dissemination, and access.

Tool sets that identify, validate, and extract technical metadata from files are significant for reducing the costs of providing the metadata that are essential for effective curation. An example is the File Information Tool Set (FITS) (code.google.com/p/fits), developed by the Harvard University Library. FITS combines several open-source tools that identify, validate, and extract technical metadata, normalize their output to a common format, and provide a report of any errors in an XML file. The tools included are JHOVE, the National Library of New Zealand Metadata Extractor, DROID (already noted in this chapter), and other tools that identify and validate metadata such as Exiftool and FFIdent. The significance of FITS lies in the way that it wraps together a number of file format identification tools that, in combination, work with a broader range of formats than each of the tools handles on its own.

Home and Office Painless Persistent Long-Term Archiving (HOPPLA) (www.ifs.tuwien.ac.at/dp/hoppla) is a system being developed for private users and small organizations that know they need a digital preservation system but do not have the skills and knowledge to develop one. HOPPLA aims to provide a fully automated archiving system that requires no technical knowledge. It is described as supporting multiple migration paths, documenting preservation actions applied in metadata, and using multiple backups on different storage media.

Tool Development

Recent digital curation and preservation research and development projects have as their key objectives the development and dissemination of usable tools. The trend of developing tool sets, suites of software that are integrated and work together to address a set of curation actions, is evident in recent projects, particularly in the work of the CASPAR and PLANETS projects.

The outputs of the CASPAR project (www.casparpreserves.eu) are "a suite of flexible, sustainable, and interchangeable digital preservation services" (Lamb, Prandoni, and Davidson, 2009). As suggested by the project's acronym, three domains—scientific, cultural heritage, and creative arts—are represented. CASPAR's work is based on the principles of compliance with the OAIS Reference Model, portability, independence from specific domains, and the preservation of authenticity and digital rights. Among the components of the suite are a registry and repository of representation information that allows it to be shared and reused; a representation information toolbox to assist with creating, maintaining, and reusing this information; a preservation data store; a digital rights manager; and an authenticity management tool.

PLANETS (www.planets-project.eu) is developing a set of tools that will assist curators at each stage of the digital preservation process. Among the tools it has developed so far are the Planets Core Registry, which lists details of file formats and the preservation tools that can be used with them, and emulation tools (Dioscuri plus two others, available by remote access using PLANETS' GRATE [Global Remote Access to Emulation Services] tool). The Planets Testbed is a central component of the PLANETS tools. It provides "a controlled, measured, part-automated and reproducible environment for the testing and evaluation of third-party preservation tools" (Donnelly, 2008) and a forum for sharing the results of experiments run on the Testbed. Another key component of the PLANETS software is Plato, a decision-support tool that helps in preservation workflow planning. It allows preservation strategies to be tested and evaluated by comparing samples of data and digital objects against specific criteria. From this a preservation plan can be built. All of the PLANETS tools will be integrated so that they work together seamlessly. PLANETS tools are being integrated into digital curation activities at the British Library, the Swiss Federal Archives, the Koninklijke Bibliotheek and Nationaal Archief in the Netherlands, Det Kongelige Bibliotek (National Library of Denmark), and the Öster-reichische Nationalbibliothek (Austrian National Library) ("Integrating Planets into Libraries and Archives," 2009).

CASPAR and PLANETS are by no means the only examples of digital curation research and development projects. Other projects funded by the European Union include Keeping Emulation Environments Portable (KEEP) and SHAMAN. KEEP (www.keepproject.eu) will develop emulation tools and also aims to improve understanding about how emulation strategies can be integrated into digital archives. It is aimed principally at cultural heritage institutions. SHAMAN (shaman-ip .eu/shaman) is building a digital preservation framework, using new technologies such as grid computing and virtualization and distribution technologies with associated tools, focusing on three prototype areas: scientific publishing and parliamentary archives; industrial design and engineering; and scientific applications.

In the United Kingdom, JISC funds tool-development projects. In the United States, tool development is being funded by NDIIPP. Among a number of other projects in the United States is PeDALS (Persistent Digital Archives and Library System; www.pedalspreservation .org), which aims to develop "an automated, integrated workflow to process collections of digital publications and records" and to "implement 'digital stacks' using an inexpensive, storage network that can preserve the authenticity and integrity of the collections."

Summary: Methods and Tools

This chapter describes *Preservation Action*, a Sequential Action of the DCC Curation Lifecycle, and a related Occasional Action, *Migrate*. It notes the most common strategies and activities that are used in digital preservation to ensure that data remain authentic, reliable, and usable while maintaining their integrity. The actions required by these strategies and activities are increasingly automated, so we will soon have a range of software tools and integrated sets of tools available to us to assist in many curation activities.

As with other actions in the DCC Curation Lifecycle, the activities carried out in *Preservation Action* are applicable in most digital curation contexts. Libraries and archives that operate digital archives will need to be intimately acquainted with these activities and will in the near future be able to select easy-to-implement tools to automate many digital curation procedures. Activities such as emulation and migration, and the software tools associated with them noted in this chapter, are also of relevance to individuals interested in curating personal data.

The next chapter notes *Store*, the sixth Sequential Action in the Curation Lifecycle. It covers the process of storing data, together with their associated description and representation information, in a secure manner.

References

Beagrie, Neil. 2007. *E-infrastructure Strategy for Research: Final Report from the OSI Preservation and Curation Working Group.* London: Office for Science and Innovation. Available: www.nesc.ac.uk/documents/OSI/preservation .pdf (accessed April 26, 2010). Used by permission of OSI Preservation and Curation Working Group (Beagrie, 2007).

Digital Curation Centre. 2008. *The DCC Curation Lifecycle Model.* Edinburgh: Digital Curation Centre. Available: www.dcc.ac.uk/docs/publications/ DCCLifecycle.pdf (accessed April 26, 2010).

Digital Preservation Coalition. 2008. *Preservation Management of Digital Materials: The Handbook.* York: Digital Preservation Coalition (November 2008). Available: www.dpconline.org/advice/digital-preservation-handbook .html (accessed April 26, 2010).

Donnelly, Martin. 2008. "Planets Testbed." Edinburgh: Digital Curation Centre (September 4, 2008). Available: www.dcc.ac.uk/resources/briefing- papers/technology-watch-papers/planets-testbed (accessed April 26, 2010).

"Integrating Planets into Libraries and Archives." 2009. *Planetarium* 7 (July): 4–5. Available: www.planets-project.eu/docs/newsletters/Planetarium7_ July09.pdf (accessed April 26, 2010).

Koninklijke Bibliotheek. "The UVC for Images." Den Haag: Koninklijke Bib- liotheek. Available: www.kb.nl/hrd/dd/dd_onderzoek/uvc_voor_images-en .html (accessed April 26, 2010).

Lamb, David, Claudio Prandoni, and Joy Davidson. 2009. "CASPAR." Edin- burgh: Digital Curation Centre (May 29, 2009). Available: www.dcc.ac.uk/ resources/briefing-papers/technology-watch-papers/caspar (accessed April 26, 2010).

Library of Congress. "METS Tools and Utilities." Washington, DC: Library of Congress. Available: www.loc.gov/standards/mets/mets-tools.html (accessed April 26, 2010).

———. 2007. "Tools for Preservation Metadata Implementation." Washington, DC: Library of Congress. Available: www.loc.gov/standards/premis/tools .html (accessed April 26, 2010).

Lord, Philip, and Alison Macdonald. 2003. *E-science Curation Report: Data Curation for E-science in the UK: An Audit to Establish Requirements for Future Curation and Provision.* Twickenham: Digital Archiving Consultancy. Available: www.jisc.ac.uk/uploaded_documents/e-sciencereportfinal.pdf (accessed April 26, 2010).

National Library of Australia. 2009. "PADI—Migration." Canberra, ACT: National Library of Australia. Available: www.nla.gov.au/padi/topics/ 21.html (accessed April 26, 2010).

Ross, Seamus, and Ann Gow. 1999. *Digital Archaeology: Rescuing Neglected and Damaged Data Resources. A JISC/NPO Study within the Electronic Libraries (eLib) Programme on the Preservation of Electronic Materials.* Glasgow: Humanities Advanced Technology and Information Institute (HATII). Available: prints.erpanet.org/47 (accessed April 26, 2010).

Rusbridge, Chris. 2008. "Migration on Request: OpenOffice as a Platform?" Digital Curation Blog, comment posted March 20, 2008. Available: digital curation.blogspot.com/2008/03/migration-on-request-openoffice-as.html (accessed April 26, 2010).

Thompson, Dave. 2009. "Most Popular Method of Digital Preservation in the UK?" DCC Forum, comments posted April 14 and 24, 2009. Available: forum.dcc.ac.uk/viewtopic.php?f=18&t=263 (accessed April 26, 2010).

Woods, Kam, and Geoffrey Brown. 2008. "Migration Performance for Legacy Data Access." *International Journal of Digital Curation* 3, no. 2: 74–87. Available: www.ijdc.net/index.php/ijdc/article/viewFile/88/59 (accessed April 26, 2010).

Storing Data

This chapter notes *Store*, the sixth of the Sequential Actions of the DCC Curation Lifecycle Model. The activities that comprise Store are stated in the DCC Curation Lifecycle Model as "storing the data in a secure manner adhering to relevant standards" (Digital Curation Centre, 2008).

After data have been appraised (evaluated to determine whether they are worth keeping, why, and for how long—see Chapter 11) and ingested (transferred to an archive, repository, data center, or other custodian—see Chapter 12), and appropriate preservation actions have been determined and applied (see Chapter 13), they need to be stored securely. For this a storage facility is required in which data are stored in a way that does not compromise their integrity over time. The storage facility, which must adhere to relevant standards, needs to be reliable so that data are not lost, and it needs to allow access to data in storage so they can be gotten out of storage for use and reuse.

The key activities involved in *Store* are:

- develop, maintain, and apply policies relating to secure data storage;
- ensure that sufficient description and representation information is stored with data;
- use a reliable storage medium, preferably on more than one carrier and with geographically distributed backup systems;
- monitor events that might trigger other preservation actions (e.g., file format migration, file corruption);
- regularly check to ensure the integrity of the stored data and their description and representation information;
- ensure system and physical security;
- maintain and replace the technical infrastructure as necessary; and
- develop, and administer as necessary, data recovery procedures.

IN THIS CHAPTER:

✔ Storage Requirements

✔ Ensuring Quality of Storage

✔ Backing Up Data

✔ Data Security

✔ Repository Software and Storage Solutions

✔ New Models for Collaboration

✔ Summary: Storing Data Securely

✔ References

Storage Requirements

Storage activities in digital curation are based on two key understandings. The first is that digital storage media are inherently unreliable, which means there will be loss of data for reasons such as manufacturing defects and media deterioration. The second is that the storage media will eventually become obsolete. There are no such things as long-lived digital storage media. As noted in Chapter 1, all digital storage media deteriorate, and, even if they do not, or if a truly stable media type is developed, there remains the near certainty that the data stored on them will become inaccessible because of the obsolescence of the reading device needed to access the media or of the software to access that data and allow them to be understood or because of the loss of our ability to understand the file format.

What is required of a long-term data store? What should it be capable of doing? This question was addressed by participants at a 2007 meeting. They determined the ten basic characteristics of digital preservation repositories to be the following:

1. The repository commits to continuing maintenance of digital objects for identified community/communities.
2. Demonstrates organizational fitness (including financial, staffing structure, and processes) to fulfill its commitment.
3. Acquires and maintains requisite contractual and legal rights and fulfills responsibilities.
4. Has an effective and efficient policy framework.
5. Acquires and ingests digital objects based upon stated criteria that correspond to its commitments and capabilities.
6. Maintains/ensures the integrity, authenticity, and usability of digital objects it holds over time.
7. Creates and maintains requisite metadata about actions taken on digital objects during preservation as well as about the relevant production, access support, and usage process contexts before preservation.
8. Fulfills requisite dissemination requirements.
9. Has a strategic program for preservation planning and action.
10. Has technical infrastructure adequate to continuing maintenance and security of its digital objects. (Center for Research Libraries, 2007)

Some of these characteristics are noted in other chapters of this book. Requirement 4 concerns policy and is noted in Chapter 10; requirement 5 is noted in Chapter 11; Chapters 12 and 13 cover the ground indicated by requirement 6; requirement 7 equates with Chapter 6; requirement 8 with Chapter 15; and requirement 9 with Chapter 7.

Another constructive list of characteristics is the DCC's "Data Management Plan Content Checklist," available at the time of writing as a "Draft Template for Consultation" (Donnelly and Jones, 2009). Section 6 notes the considerations about short-term storage and data management to be kept in mind when developing a data management plan. What are the likely volumes of data that the store will need to accommodate? (6.1). The quantity of data has significant implications for how storage is handled; for instance, if the quantities are very large, the costs of keeping the original bit stream may be too great. On what kind of storage media, and where, will the data be stored? Who will take responsibility for it? In what form will it be transmitted (moved to other storage or to another computer system), and is the data sensitive or confidential so that encryption is necessary when it is transmitted? (6.2). How will access arrangements be managed? How will data security be managed? (6.3). How frequently will data be backed up? Who takes responsibility for this? How will it be backed up? (6.4). Section 7 provides a checklist for deposit and long-term preservation. Where will data be archived? How will it be transmitted to that archive, and is encryption appropriate? (7.4). In addition to the data set, what other information will need to be deposited (such as reports, research papers, original bid proposal, documentation about software and data sets)? (7.5). What procedures does the archive have in place for preservation and backup? Who takes responsibility for this? What methods are applied (e.g., format normalization, migration)? (7.7).

The key message to take out of these requirements is that, to be suitable for long-term curation purposes, a data storage facility must be more than just an installation of repository software such as DSpace or Fedora. It must be *sustainable* both in its organizational structure and continuity and in its technical infrastructure and practices.

Organizational Structure and Continuity

To be sustainable, a long-term data storage facility should:

- be committed to continuing maintenance of digital objects for an identified community (*Designated Community* in the OAIS Reference Model terminology) or communities;

- ensure adequate and appropriate funding and staffing to fulfill the commitment to continuing maintenance;

- negotiate the requisite contractual and legal rights and fulfill the legal responsibilities that these require;

- develop an effective and efficient policy framework; and

- develop a strategic program for preservation planning and action.

It is easier to list these requirements than it is to meet them, as the section on trusted digital repositories elsewhere in this chapter indicates.

There is, as yet, no standard model or range of models for a long-term data storage facility. Although the requirements for sustainability have been articulated in detail for the establishment of the trusted digital repository, how this will look is not yet fully understood. Rusbridge suggests a classification of "curation players": individuals; departments or groups; institutions; communities of institutions, "either formal (as consortia) or informal (as in the case of the LOCKSS system)"; disciplines; publishers; national services, such as national libraries, archives, or data services; and third parties. (Rusbridge, C., 2008: 210–211) For example, institutions may have in place a repository based on DSpace. Communities may develop around a system such as LOCKSS (e.g., the USDocs Private LOCKSS Network (www.lockss.org/lockss/Government_Documents _PLN), which preserves U.S. government documents). The discipline of astronomy operates virtual observatories, such as the U.S. National Virtual Observatory (www.us-vo.org). Other third-party services include Portico for scholarly material in digital form (www.portico.org), OCLC's Digital Archive (www.oclc.org/digitalarchive), and Iron Mountain's data backup services (www.ironmountain.com/solutions). There is no doubt that new models will develop, such as the combination of the institutional and discipline models, or cloud computing, as Chris Rusbridge (2008) has suggested.

Technical Infrastructure and Practices

As well as a sustainable organizational structure, a second requirement for the sustainability of a long-term data storage facility is a technical infrastructure that provides continuing maintenance and security for the digital objects stored within it—that is, an infrastructure that can maintain over time the integrity, authenticity, and usability of the digital objects stored in the facility.

A sustainable facility bases its operations on appropriate practices. It should first acquire and ingest data and digital objects according to stated criteria that correspond to its commitments and capabilities. Next, to store these sustainably, the facility should follow five practices:

1. It should store the data and digital objects in formats that do not manipulate them in any way that causes data loss or compromises their authenticity. These formats must be widely implemented and supported, be preferably open, and have the potential for longevity. (Chapter 10 provides more detailed information about file formats.)

2. It must store enough metadata and representation information to support identification, access, and preservation processes.

3. It should store data, in reliable storage formats, on at least two types of media.

4. It should make multiple copies of bit streams, which are checked and verified regularly.

5. It should replace carriers and software as the market demands, with plans to migrate the content to the next type of reliable carrier. (based on Bradley, Lei, and Blackall [2007] and on the Center for Research Libraries' "Core Requirements" [2007])

Best Practice in Data Storage

There is plenty of experience of long-term storage of data from which we can develop a description of current best practice. A particularly useful statement comes from the UK Data Archive (2009) in its *Managing and Sharing Data: A Best Practice Guide for Researchers*. It begins with the observation that "digital storage media are inherently unreliable unless they are stored appropriately" (p. 13). David Rosenthal (2008: 2) provides confirmation of this by examining the evidence about storage media failure from which he draws three conclusions:

1. The more copies the safer
2. The more independent the copies the safer
3. The more frequently the copies are audited the safer

These are in fact the basis of best practice in data storage. *Managing and Sharing Data* next notes that "all file formats and physical storage media will ultimately become obsolete" (UK Data Archive, 2009: 13). Best practice in data storage also includes the following:

- Use "preservation-friendly" formats to store data in (usually nonproprietary or open standard formats: see Chapter 10).
- Copy paper documentation into digital format (e.g., PDF-A format).
- Copy or migrate data to new media at regular intervals (every two to five years is proposed).
- Check the integrity of all stored data at regular intervals.
- Ensure that all data are stored on a minimum of two different forms of storage.
- Ensure that stored data are organized so they can be readily located.
- Make sure that data storage areas are appropriate for this function, for example, they are protected from fire or flood and are structurally sound. (based on UK Data Archive, 2009: 13)

The UK Data Archive's best practice for data backup is noted elsewhere in this chapter.

These recommended practices, which come from one organization, albeit an authoritative one, are corroborated by examination of practices at a range of other organizations. For example, the practice of storing data in preservation-friendly formats is stated by the Georgia Archives in terms of maintaining both a preservation copy in an open file format and a "presentation" copy. Checking data integrity regularly is noted by the JISC Digital Repositories Programme in terms of performing periodic validation, as bit-level integrity checking by The National Archives (which contracts this activity to the UK Data Archive at the University of Essex) and as testing and sampling records to ensure continued accessibility at the Georgia Archives, which also notes checking for viruses and corrupt media or disks/drives. (Integrity checking is one area where there is keen interest in the development of automated processes, especially for large quantities of data. An example is the University of Maryland's ACE, which can continuously monitor large quantities of files per day; wiki.umiacs.umd.edu/adapt/index.php/Ace; see Chapter 13.) The practice of using different forms of storage is implemented by The National Archives (at the University of Essex), which duplicates data on two separate tapes in the library, and by the UK Data Archive (at the University of Essex), which makes up to six copies of the data file on four different preservation servers and also create a CD-ROM offline copy.

Another statement about best practice comes from the Technical Committee of the Association for Recorded Sound Collections. It notes five basic storage principles: make backup copies of all files as soon as possible; store backups separately from the original, making at least two copies of the original data and storing them in different locations; verify the integrity of data by using checksums or other methods; monitor the media for degradation; and monitor the file formats and migrate to new ones when required (Association of Recorded Sound Collections, 2009: 7).

Despite the lessons that have been learned about the inherent unreliability of digital storage media and about declining ability over time to access data stored because of obsolescence (of the media, associated hardware, file formats, and so on), there is still interest in and research into long-lived storage media. Solutions to the "apocalypse scenario" for data storage are based on passive media that do not require electric power to maintain the data recorded on them. Examples include digital microfilm (see Hofmann and Giel, 2008) and the Millennial Disc (www.millenniata.com/index.html).

Ensuring Quality of Storage

Two relevant sets of guidelines that define criteria for ensuring the quality of long-term data storage facilities are the OAIS Reference Model and the Trusted Digital Repository.

OAIS Reference Model

The key set of guidelines is the OAIS Reference Model (International Organization for Standardization, 2003). (More information about OAIS is provided in Chapter 3.) Three of the five functions defined by OAIS are especially relevant to the *Store* action:

- The *Archival Storage* function: this is responsible for storing, maintaining, and retrieving the Archival Information Packages (AIPs) in the archive.

- The *Data Management* function: this manages the Descriptive Information about the archive's AIPs and also manages system information.

- The *Administration* function: this manages the archive's day-to-day operation.

Archival Storage defines requirements for the effective storage of AIPs, routine integrity checking, and disaster recovery. Indicative components include:

- for effective storage of AIPs: moving AIPs from Ingest into permanent storage, refreshing the storage media, and providing the information needed to allow objects to be disseminated from the repository;

- for routine integrity checking: checking the stored bit stream regularly to assess whether it is identical to the original bit stream; and

- for data recovery (such as recovering from media breakdown or obsolescence, or data damage or loss caused by a disaster): ongoing media refreshment, ongoing monitoring of media for deterioration, and geographically distributed backup systems.

Data Management defines all aspects of the OAIS repository's management. Indicative components include:

- providing effective access controls;
- ensuring authentication of users of the repository;
- providing statistical information to improve operation; and
- developing and implementing policies for, and monitoring of, the allocation of unique identifiers.

Archive Administration defines the services needed for day-to-day maintenance of the repository. Indicative components include:

- negotiating submissions agreements with content producers and providers;
- reviewing procedures;
- maintaining systems configurations for hardware and software;
- developing and maintaining repository policies and standards; and
- negotiating user access agreements with service providers or others.

These functions of the OAIS Reference Model have been influential in developing digital archives, for example, through the central role that the OAIS Reference Model plays in defining the trusted digital repository.

Trusted Digital Repositories

A trusted digital repository is defined as "one whose mission is to provide reliable, long-term access to managed digital resources to its designated community, now and in the future" (RLG-OCLC, 2002). To be trusted, a digital repository must meet certain requirements, one of which is that it should be compliant with the OAIS Reference Model. Other requirements are to:

- accept responsibility for the long-term maintenance of digital resources on behalf of its depositors and for the benefit of current and future users;
- have an organizational system that supports not only long-term viability of the repository but also the digital information for which it has responsibility;
- demonstrate fiscal responsibility and sustainability;

- design its system(s) in line with commonly accepted conventions and standards to ensure the ongoing management, access, and security of materials deposited within it;
- establish methodologies for system evaluation that meet community expectations of trustworthiness;
- be trusted to carry out its long-term responsibilities to depositors and users openly and explicitly; and
- have policies, practices, and performance that can be audited and measured. (based on RLG-OCLC, 2002).

Audit and Certification

How does one know if a digital repository can be trusted? What assurance is there that a digital repository can maintain its contents over time? Audit and certification of digital repositories is one way of establishing their trustworthiness.

Current audit and certification of digital repositories are based on self-assessment. Tools have been developed to assist repositories that wish to carry out an assessment. The most commonly encountered example is the *Trustworthy Repositories Audit and Certification (TRAC) Criteria and Checklist* (RLG-NARA Task Force on Digital Repository Certification, 2007). This lists characteristics that trusted repositories should demonstrate—for example, "Repository has procedures and policies in place." The TRAC checklist does not indicate how these characteristics can be assessed. Another checklist-based tool is nestor's *Catalogue of Criteria for Trusted Digital Repositories* (nestor Working Group, 2006).

More formalized auditing methodologies have been developed. The Digital Repository Audit Method Based on Risk Assessment (DRAMB-ORA) toolkit (www.repositoryaudit.eu), developed by the DCC and Digital Preservation Europe, provides a more formal auditing methodology based on risk assessment, resulting in a structured registry of risks. The Planning Tool for Trusted Electronic Repositories (PLATTER) (www.digitalpreservationeurope.eu/publications/reports/Repository_Planning_Checklist_and_Guidance.pdf) has been developed to complement DRAMBORA and other repository audit and certification tools by assisting with planning of repository goals, objectives, and performance targets to establish trusted repository status.

Backing Up Data

An essential practice in managing data is to back them up at regular intervals, following a well-defined schedule. Backing up refers to making copies of files so that if data are lost, the original data can be restored from the copies. Regular backups protect against accidental data loss caused by hardware, software, or media failure; failure of the power supply; human error; and fires, floods, earthquakes, and other natural disasters. A regular backup regime also protects against malicious data loss, such as from computer viruses or hacking.

Best practice for backing up data is indicated by the UK Data Archive (2009) in its *Managing and Sharing Data: A Best Practice Guide for Researchers*. Factors for which decisions must be made and policy planned and implemented include the following:

- Which files are to be backed up (Should the entire system be backed up, or only specific files?)

- How frequently backups should be made (Should backups be made every time data are changed, or at regular intervals, perhaps daily for frequently used files and critical data?)

- Whether there is an institutional backup policy that carries out regular backups automatically. (Identify any institutional backup policy that is supposed to back up your institution's data regularly, and check that it is actually implemented and that data can be recovered from it.)

- Whether to carry out incremental or differential backups (For incremental backup an initial copy is made of all relevant files, and then only files that have changed since the last backup are copied. In differential backups an initial backup of all relevant files is also made, and then any files changed or created since the first full backup are made.)

- Procedures for regularly verifying backup files (Best practice is to fully restore the backup files to another location and check them against the originals.)

- Procedures for checking backup files for completeness (It is common practice to compare the checksum values, file size, and date with the original file.)

- What media to store backup files on (Recordable CD/DVD, networked hard drive, removable hard drive, magnetic tape? Factors such as how much data need to be backed up and how backups are carried out will affect this decision.)

- Formats selected for storing backup files (Ideally the data should be in preservation-friendly formats; see Chapter 10.)

- Where the backup files are located (Will they be online or off-line, stored on removable media or transportable hard drives? This raises another critical point about security of backups—data stored off-line on transportable media can be stored in a different location. Off-site storage may mean in another building in the same city, or in another city, or in another country.)

- Procedures for organizing and labeling backup files (based on UK Data Archive, 2009: 12)

In practice the issues are less clear-cut and the advice about backing up less rigorously followed. Backup, "or rather the lack of it," Chris Rusbridge calls "preservation's dirty little secret." He gives examples: a research group has desktop and laptop computers with Microsoft Windows (several versions), Mac OS X (again, several versions), and Linux (also several versions) operating systems. While the desktop computers were protected institutionally through organized backups of networked drives, the laptops, some of which were the primary computers used by the researchers, were not backed up in this way. Rusbridge (2009) suggests "a service I can subscribe to on behalf of everyone in my project [which has] agreed backup policies,...clients for all the major OS [operating system] variants,...[the ability for] individuals to specify whether it should be a bootable or partial backup, which parts of the system are included or excluded, and for management to specify the overall backup regime (full and incremental backups, cycles, and any 'archiving' of deleted files, etc)," and which works externally as well as in the office.

Not enough attention is currently given in digital curation to the recovery of data after mishaps. Business continuity support services are available as a standard commercial offering. They provide services such as data recovery on demand, including the operating system, applications, and data. Private sector companies that offer disaster recovery services are typically certified as meeting the requirements of the information security management system standard ISO 27001. The ISO 27001 certification process involves conducting risk analysis, developing an information security management system (ISMS) that handles the risks, and continuously reviewing the risks. Typically, however, central computer services in institutions such as universities, large libraries, and archives are not adequately equipped to respond to disasters.

Data Security

Data security refers to protecting data from unauthorized access, use, change, disclosure, and destruction and also includes preventing unwanted changes to data. We need to be concerned about data security for a range of reasons. For some data, an assurance of their security is required by legislation—for example, to ensure that personal data (data that allow the identification of individuals) are only available to people authorized to use them. Such assurance is required by legislation such as the United Kingdom's Data Protection Act and by the legislation applicable to specific sectors in the United States, such as the State of California's California Online Privacy Protection Act 2003. It is common practice to store personal data separately from related anonymized data (data from which all information that allows the identification of individuals has been removed). Data containing personal information should be treated with higher levels of security than data that do not contain personal information. (This section is based on *Managing and Sharing Data* [UK Data Archive, 2009: 14].)

Another kind of data that need special attention to ensure their security are mission-critical data whose loss would seriously impede the operation of the project or organization. More information about the kinds of data that might be assessed as important, and about determining the risks to such data, is provided in Chapter 11. Arrangements aimed at ensuring data security need to take account of the kind of data and the risks involved. Three aspects of data security should be addressed: physical security; network security; and file security.

Physical Security

Physical security refers to keeping secure the physical sites where data are stored and computers housed and limiting access to those sites only to people who are authorized to enter them. It requires actions such as restricting access to buildings and areas where data, information storage media, and computers are located; monitoring who removes and accesses media; ensuring that data are destroyed appropriately so that they are unusable (see Chapter 11 for more about the disposal and destruction of data); and ensuring the safe destruction of files on a computer when it is disposed of, for example, by removing and disposing securely of hard drives (UK Data Archive, 2009: 14).

Network and File Security

Network security refers to keeping secure the data housed on computers or servers that are connected to an external network, such as the Internet. An example is confidential data containing personal information that should not be available to unauthorized users. Security of computer networks and systems is ensured by actions such as requiring use of passwords to authorize access to a computer system; installing and maintaining firewalls to minimize unauthorized access; using virus detection software that is kept up-to-date; password-protecting files; and requiring confidentiality agreements for users of confidential data (UK Data Archive, 2009: 15).

File security ensures that files are rendered unavailable to unauthorized users through encryption (converting them into a version that can be accessed only by authorized people). Encryption of data, for example, during its transmission to an archive, is managed using encryption software, which is readily available. A widely used example is Pretty Good Privacy (PGP), an industry-standard encryption technology.

Managing and Sharing Data provides two informative examples. The first is of data held by the British Library. Digital audio files in .wav format recorded the English spoken in Wales from 1969 to 1995. The British Library's Digital Library has four mirror sites (two at the primary British Library sites in Boston Spa and London, one in Wales, and one a "dark" archive hosted by a third party), and the data stored on the servers at these sites is routinely checked for integrity. Copies are available to users as .mp3 files at the British Library and on a British Library website (UK Data Archive, 2009: 14). The second is of data generated in a research project. Field data are collected on handheld PDAs and are transmitted each day to a network drive. These files are password protected and are identified by an individual version number and creation date. The version information is stored in a spreadsheet on the networked drive. The networked drive is fully backed up onto Ultrium LTO2 data tapes, with incremental backups each day from Monday to Thursday and with a full server backup over the weekend. The data tapes are stored in a separate building in secure conditions. When the research is completed the data set is deposited in a digital repository (UK Data Archive, 2009: 13).

Repository Software and Storage Solutions

What, currently, are digital repositories aiming to do? From the digital curation perspective, the answers to this question are important. A repository may not necessarily aim at long-term storage but may be primarily interested in shorter term goals; this has an effect on the kinds of software and infrastructure that it requires. It may, for example, be interested mainly in access to and usability of the data it holds only in the short term (perhaps three years), or for the medium term (perhaps ten years), or for the long term (more than ten years—requiring OAIS compliance). It is, therefore, important to recognize this when investigating and adopting repository software that is to be used to meet long-term storage requirements.

Not all of the repository software that is in wide use is focused on or best suited for long-term data storage. To function effectively as a long-term storage facility, a digital repository needs to meet requirements such as ensuring persistent access to the data it stores. Most repository software, however, is aimed at shorter term goals such as allowing more efficient management of institutional assets and providing fast, easy access to its contents from remote locations.

Fedora, DSpace, EPrints, and Other Repository Software

Fedora and DSpace are probably the two repository software applications most commonly encountered in the United States; another, EPrints, is also in common use in the United Kingdom.

Fedora (Flexible Extensible Digital Object and Repository Architecture) is open-source software for a digital object repository management system. It is in widespread use. Fedora is based on principles of flexibility, interoperability, and extensibility. It is written in Java and can therefore be run on different operating systems. A core set of software tools that can integrate with other applications, such as search and display software, is provided. Fedora's key features include, according to the FedoraCommons website (www.fedora-commons.org/about/features), the ability to store and manage all types of content and associated metadata, scalability up to "millions of objects," provision of web access and search facilities, a wide range of storage options, and a "Rebuilder Utility" for disaster recovery and data migration. Software, documentation, and support from the FedoraCommons user community are available from the FedoraCommons website.

The potential for Fedora to be operated as the basis of a digital archive was explored in research by Tufts University and Yale University

("Fedora and the Preservation of University Records," 2006). The Tufts/Yale study determined that Fedora has value as "a preservation application, in conjunction with "the appropriate people, infrastructure, policies, and procedures." The overall conclusion was that:

> The Fedora core provides a promising basis for a preservation system. Its agnostic view towards file formats and object types enables it to manage essentially any type of file. It has the ability to manage objects with complex—including hierarchical—relationships with its use of RDF or METS metadata. It can manage multiple bitstreams for a single object, which can enable archivists to track and store the original bitstream of an ingested record and the bitstreams of subsequent transformations. It has versioning and persistent identifier capabilities for all content objects, metadata, and disseminators.... Fedora objects are articulated in XML... making it feasible to migrate records out of Fedora. ("Fedora and the Preservation of University Records," 2006: Section 4.1)

Fedora supports preservation in many ways. It uses open standards such as METS and XML. The way the system is structured, separating data from other parts of the system and from applications, means that migrating the data objects is more easily carried out. The system architecture can readily accommodate the OAIS Reference Model. Its extensibility and flexibility mean that it can handle metadata from a range of sources (Pennock, 2006c).

DSpace is the other main repository software in common use. Like Fedora, it is open-source software that offers a repository system that can handle a wide range of digital objects, is written in Java so can be run on different operating systems, and has a wide user base. Submitting data to the repository and accessing them can be carried out via the web. Software, documentation, and support are available from the DSpace website (www.dspace.org).

DSpace was developed from its inception to support long-term preservation. It "is committed to going beyond reliable file preservation to offer functional preservation where files are kept accessible as technology formats, media, and paradigms evolve over time for as many types of files as possible" ("DSpace Diagram," accessed 2010). Features that support preservation include the automatic calculating and verification of a checksum for each file uploaded into the repository and regular checking of these checksums to ensure integrity of the files; automatic identification of the file formats of objects added to the repository; use of standards such as METS to maintain the links between files and the Handle system to provide unique identifiers for items; and maintaining the bit stream of items added to the repository. This last feature allows systems administrators to keep a list of what level of preservation is applied to each format type. For example, the Massachusetts Institute of Technology implementation categorizes its holdings as "supported" formats such as TIFF, PDF, and HTML, "known/unsupported formats" such as Microsoft Word and Lotus 1-2-3, and "unknown/unsupported" formats (Pennock, 2006a).

The EPrints website makes the claim that it was "the first professional software platform for building high-quality OAI-compliant repositories" (www.eprints.org/software). It is available as open-source software, is widely used (with a strong user base in the United Kingdom), has a web-accessible interface for searching, and can handle a wide range of types of digital content. It is available for several operating systems (Pennock, 2006b). Although preservation was not originally intended as an aim of EPrints, the EPrints team has recently started participating in digital preservation activities such as the KeepIt project (preservation .eprints.org/keepit) and the Preserv and Preserv2 projects (www.preserv .org.uk). The EPrints Preservation Team is developing tools and services for preservation actions such as identifying file and format types, risk analysis, and migration and is integrating these into the EPrints software (EPrints Services, accessed 2010).

More recently, repository software is being designed from the ground up with long-term data storage as a primary objective. An example is Repositório de Objectos Digitais Autênticos (RODA; roda.di.uminho.pt), developed for the Portuguese Archives with the aim of meeting trusted digital repository standards. It is open source, based on key curation standards such as the OAIS Reference Model, METS, Encoded Archival Description (EAD), and PREMIS, is compliant with the TRAC audit and certification requirements, has high levels of security built in, is scalable, and is accessed from the web.

Storage Solutions

Digital archives based on repository software such as Fedora, DSpace, and EPrints are not the only way in which data and digital objects are stored for long-term preservation. Here LOCKSS (Lots of Copies Keep Stuff Safe), cloud storage developments, and one example of a vendor's services are noted.

The principle of redundancy is well understood in the context of preservation of library and archival materials. It refers to the location of multiple copies at multiple locations, the duplication of data meaning that if one instance of those data is corrupted, lost, or otherwise becomes unusable, another intact copy is available. This principle has been applied to data storage in the LOCKSS technology. LOCKSS established the feasibility of replication and peer-to-peer polling using standard personal computers for preserving digital objects. Initially developed to enable low-cost archiving of web-published electronic journals by libraries, it has expanded to be applicable to any web-published content. The open-source software allows content to be collected by a web crawler and stored in a LOCKSS box (a low-end computer). This content is continually checked against the same content stored in other LOCKSS boxes using a polling audit algorithm. If changes to the data are detected, it is automatically repaired from a copy held elsewhere in the LOCKSS network (Rusbridge, A., 2008). LOCKSS is being used as the basis of PLNs (Private LOCKSS Networks), which have been established by libraries and archives collaborating to preserve digital objects, usually on a thematic basis. Examples are PeDALS for state archives from Arizona, Florida, New York, and Wisconsin (rpm.lib.az.us/pedals) and the Alabama Digital Preservation Network (www.adpn.org) for locally created digital content (Reich and Rosenthal, 2009). The LOCKSS software is available from the web (www.lockss.org/lockss).

Cloud storage is being investigated for long-term storage. This refers to storing data on the web (probably using the services of a data storage vendor) and accessing that data on demand. Many cloud storage services are available, such as Amazon S3 (Simple Storage Service), Microsoft Azure Storage, EMC Atmos Storage, and Sun Cloud Storage. EPrints is working with Sun to enable its software to use the Sun Cloud storage service in combination with local storage and already has a software plug-in available for Amazon S3 (aws.amazon.com/s3). While there is currently some skepticism about the ability or willingness of cloud storage vendors to provide true long-term storage and meet trusted digital repository requirements, there seems little doubt that cloud storage will develop to offer reliable and affordable archival storage. Fedorazon, a research project to investigate the combination of Amazon cloud storage and Fedora repository software, reported late in 2009 (www.jisc.ac.uk/whatwedo/programmes/reppres/sue/fedorazon.aspx).

In May 2009 Fedora and DSpace announced plans to merge to form a new organization, DuraSpace (duraspace.org). Both DSpace and Fedora will continue to be supported and will develop new services. One of these is DuraCloud (duraspace.org/duracloud.php), a storage service that will use cloud storage and cloud computing for online backup of data and will preserve data through duplicating and housing them in multiple locations. As one of its initiatives is aimed at enhancing its preservation capability, EPrints is investigating linking with DuraSpace's DuraCloud service.

OCLC's Digital Archive is an example of a data storage service provided by a vendor. Its practices relating to data preservation include providing secure physical facilities for its data storage systems; monitoring disk storage devices and replacing them regularly; checking file integrity of data copied to the new devices; and disaster recovery procedures. Data verification is carried out as data are received when all files are checked against the shipping manifest and checked for the presence of viruses, a "fixity key" (such as a checksum) is generated, and the file format is verified. The virus, fixity, and format verification checks are automatically carried out periodically, and monthly "health reports" are supplied (OCLC, accessed 2010).

New Models for Collaboration

Collaboration is at the heart of HathiTrust (www.hathitrust.org/preservation), a collaboration of universities that are members of the Committee on Institutional Cooperation (CIC) and the University of California system. HathiTrust originated in an initiative by a cooperative of libraries to make publicly available the backup of books they owned that had been digitized by Google. Its aim is to archive and share the digitized collections of its members by preserving the intellectual content and, where possible, the materials' exact appearance and layout.

Preservation actions implemented to date include format validation, migration, and error checking. All content that is ingested has its format validated, and error checking is applied. Its storage system automatically runs error checking and checking of media. To ensure persistence of the data it stores, HathiTrust uses a LOCKSS-like system by creating at least two versions of data, stored in different physically secure locations in different states. These two versions are automatically checked and synchronized. The secure locations also employ techniques that ensure high levels of data redundancy. Files ingested are required to be in well-documented preservation formats, allowing effective migration of the archived data over time. In the longer term, HathiTrust is aiming at compliance with the TRAC criteria and is using DRAMBORA methodology to assess its activities. It is developing its services in compliance with the OAIS Reference Model.

Another collaborative based on storage is MetaArchive. It is a network of cultural memory organizations that collaborate in order to preserve their digital collections. It is based on a decentralized model and operates a Private LOCKSS Network (PLN), being the first to set one of these up. It is therefore a distributed digital preservation network that enables its members to securely cache and preserve content in geographically dispersed sites. It is a cooperative venture, so its members invest in the preservation infrastructure rather than paying for services. This cooperative model is one way by which storage and other activities are made available to institutions for curation purposes (Halbert and Skinner, 2008).

Summary: Storing Data Securely

This chapter describes the *Store* action of the DCC Curation Lifecycle. A comment very relevant to this chapter was made in a posting about long-term personal data storage on the Ask Slashdot forum: "An archive is not a backup that you keep for a long time. It's much, much more than that. Once you start thinking about all of the issues that come up, you'll see that the media is the least of your problems" ("An Archive Is Not a Long-Term Backup," 2008). Most of the key themes of this chapter have been summarized in a "Provisional List of Do's and Don'ts" aimed at libraries considering a digital curation program. It directs us to:

- Never store important digital information on floppy disks, CD-ROMs or local computers, but store it on more robust hardware.
- Make a back-up of your information regularly and make a deal with a colleague that you will take care of each other's back-ups.
- Make an inventory of the digital information you have in your custody and keep it up to date.
- Find a trustworthy custodian for your digital data. . . . If there is no official way to gauge an archive's trustworthiness, look at the organization as a whole and ask yourself: is this organisation itself likely to be around fifty or a hundred years from now?
- Concentrate all your efforts on *access*, because in the end *access* is what matters. All else is but a means to make access possible. (Angevaare, 2009: 9)

STORE: REVIEW

Key points: *Store* is the process of storing data, plus their associated description and representation information, in a secure manner.

Key activities:
- Develop, maintain, and apply policies about secure data storage
- Ensure that sufficient description and representation information is stored with data
- Use a reliable storage medium
- Monitor triggers for preservation action
- Regularly check to ensure the integrity of the stored data and description and representation information
- Ensure system and physical security
- Maintain and replace the technical infrastructure as necessary
- Develop, and administer as necessary, data recovery procedures

The next chapter notes *Access, Use, and Reuse*, the seventh Sequential Action in the Curation Lifecycle, concerned with ensuring that data are accessible and that appropriate access controls and authentication procedures are applied. It also includes *Transform*, the eighth and final of the Curation Lifecycle's Sequential Actions, covering the creation of new data from existing data.

References

"An Archive Is Not a Long-Term Backup." Ask Slashdot Blog, comment posted December 13, 2008. Available: ask.slashdot.org/askslashdot/08/12/13/1434216.shtml (accessed April 26, 2010).

Angevaare, Inge. 2009. "Taking Care of Digital Collections and Data: 'Curation' and Organisational Choices for Research Libraries." *LIBER Quarterly* 19, no. 1 (April): 1–12. Available: liber.library.uu.nl/publish/articles/000278/article.pdf (accessed April 26, 2010).

Association of Recorded Sound Collections. 2009. *Preservation of Archival Sound Recordings*. Annapolis, MD: ASRC Technical Committee. Available: www.arsc-audio.org/pdf/ARSCTC_preservation.pdf (accessed April 26, 2010).

Bradley, Kevin, Junran Lei, and Chris Blackall. 2007. *Towards an Open Source Repository and Preservation System*. Paris: UNESCO. Available: portal.unesco.org/ci/en/ev.php-URL_ID=24700&URL_DO=DO_PRINTPAGE&URL_SECTION=201.html (accessed April 26, 2010).

Center for Research Libraries. 2007. "Core Requirements." Chicago: Center for Research Libraries (January 2007). Available: www.crl.edu/archiving-preservation/digital-archives/metrics-assessing-and-certifying/core-re (accessed April 26, 2010). Used by permission of Center for Research Libraries.

Digital Curation Centre. 2008. *The DCC Curation Lifecycle Model*. Edinburgh: Digital Curation Centre. Available: www.dcc.ac.uk/docs/publications/DCCLifecycle.pdf (accessed April 26, 2010).

Donnelly, Martin, and Sarah Jones. 2009. "Data Management Plan Content Checklist: Draft Template for Consultation." Edinburgh: Digital Curation Centre (June 17, 2009). Available: www.dcc.ac.uk/docs/templates/DMP_checklist.pdf (accessed April 26, 2010).

"DSpace Diagram." DSpace. Available: www.dspace.org/images/stories/dspace-diagram.pdf (accessed April 26, 2010).

EPrints Services. "EPrints Digital Preservation." Southampton: EPrints Services. Available: preservation.eprints.org (accessed April 26, 2010).

"Fedora and the Preservation of University Records." 2006. Medford, MA: Tufts University; New Haven, CT: Yale University (September 2006). Available: dca.lib.tufts.edu/features/nhprc/reports (accessed April 26, 2010). Used by permission of Digital Collections and Archives, Tufts University, and Manuscripts & Archives, Yale University.

Halbert, Martin, and Katherine Skinner. 2008. "The MetaArchive Cooperative: A New Collaborative Service Organization Providing a Distributed Digital Preservation Infrastructure." *CLIR Issues* no. 66. Available: www.clir.org/pubs/issues/issues66.html (accessed April 26, 2010).

Hofmann, A., and D.M. Giel. 2008. "DANOK: Long Term Migration Free Storage of Digital Audio Data on Microfilm." In *Archiving 2008: Final Program and Proceedings, June 24–27, 2008, Bern Switzerland* (pp. 184–187).

Springfield, VA: Society for Imaging Science and Technology. Available: publica.fraunhofer.de/documents/N-94186.html (accessed April 26, 2010).

International Organization for Standardization. 2003. *Space Data and Information Transfer Systems—Open Archival Information System—Reference Model.* Standard 14721:2003. Geneva: International Organization for Standardization.

nestor Working Group. 2006. *Catalogue of Criteria for Trusted Digital Repositories.* Frankfurt am Main: nestor Working Group Trusted Repositories—Certification. Available: edoc.hu-berlin.de/series/nestor-materialien/8en/PDF/8en.pdf (accessed April 26, 2010).

OCLC. "Digital Archive: Overview." Dublin, OH: OCLC. Available: www.oclc.org/digitalarchive/overview (accessed April 26, 2010).

Pennock, Maureen. 2006a. "DSpace Digital Repository Software." Edinburgh: Digital Curation Centre (June 23, 2006). Available: www.dcc.ac.uk/resources/briefing-papers/technology-watch-papers/dspace (accessed April 26, 2010).

———. 2006b. "EPrints Digital Repository Software." Edinburgh: Digital Curation Centre (August 25, 2006). Available: www.dcc.ac.uk/resources/briefing-papers/technology-watch-papers/eprints (accessed April 26, 2010).

———. 2006c. "Fedora Digital Repository Software." Edinburgh: Digital Curation Centre (November 24, 2006). Available: www.dcc.ac.uk/resources/briefing-papers/technology-watch-papers/fedora (accessed April 26, 2010).

Reich, Victoria, and David Rosenthal. 2009. "Distributed Digital Preservation: Private LOCKSS Networks as Business, Social, and Technical Frameworks." *Library Trends* 57, no. 3 (Winter): 461–475.

RLG-NARA Task Force on Digital Repository Certification. 2007. *Trustworthy Repositories Audit & Certification: Criteria and Checklist.* Chicago: Center for Research Libraries. Available: www.crl.edu/sites/default/files/attachments/pages/trac_0.pdf (accessed April 26, 2010).

RLG-OCLC. 2002. *Trusted Digital Repositories: Attributes and Responsibilities.* Mountain View, CA: Research Libraries Group. Available: www.oclc.org/programs/ourwork/past/trustedrep/repositories.pdf (accessed April 26, 2010).

Rosenthal, David S.H. 2008. "Bit Preservation: A Solved Problem?" Paper presented at iPres (September 30, 2008). Available: www.bl.uk/ipres2008/presentations_day2/43_Rosenthal.pdf (accessed April 26, 2010).

Rusbridge, Adam. 2008. "The LOCKSS Approach to Electronic Journal Archiving." Edinburgh: Digital Curation Centre (April 18, 2008). Available: www.dcc.ac.uk/resource/technology-watch/lockss (accessed April 26, 2010).

Rusbridge, Chris. 2008. "Tomorrow, Tomorrow, and Tomorrow: Poor Players on the Digital Curation Stage." In *Digital Convergence: Libraries of the Future* (pp. 207–217), edited by Rae Earnshaw and John Vince. London: Springer. Used by permission of Chris Rusbridge, Digital Curation Centre.

———. 2009. "My Backup Rant." Digital Curation Blog, comment posted July 28, 2009. Available: digitalcuration.blogspot.com/2009/07/my-backup-rant.html (accessed April 26, 2010). Used by permission of Chris Rusbridge, Digital Curation Centre.

UK Data Archive. 2009. *Managing and Sharing Data: A Best Practice Guide for Researchers.* Colchester: UK Data Archive. Available: www.data-archive.ac.uk/news/publications/managingsharing.pdf (accessed April 26, 2010). Used by permission of the UK Data Archive, University of Essex.

Using and Reusing Data

This chapter notes the seventh of the Sequential Actions of the DCC Curation Lifecycle Model, *Access, Use, and Reuse*, and the eighth and final Sequential Action, *Transform*. Access, Use, and Reuse is the process of ensuring that data are accessible to authorized users for use and also later reuse. The activities that comprise Access, Use, and Reuse are indicated in the DCC Curation Lifecycle Model as ensuring that data are accessible to designated users and to reusers, on a day-to-day basis, usually (but not necessarily) in the form of publicly available published information; and applying robust access controls and authentication procedures where applicable. The key activities encompassed by Access, Use, and Reuse are:

- applying standards that ensure appropriate metadata are present so data can be located;
- ensuring that the required legal permissions are available so data can be used and reused;
- providing tools that allow collaboration in the use and reuse of data; and
- applying access controls and authentication procedures to ensure that data are accessible only by authorized users.

Transform is included in this chapter because it is most frequently the outcome of the Access, Use, and Reuse action, which precedes it. It refers to the process of creating new data from the original data by "creating a subset, by selection or query, to create newly derived results, perhaps for publication" (Digital Curation Centre, 2008).

Access, Use, and Reuse

The point of curating data and digital objects is that they remain available for use and reuse. The aim of the specific actions included in *Access, Use, and Reuse* is to ensure that data and digital objects can be located, used, and used again by legitimate users. Science and scholarship are built, brick by brick, upon the course of bricks laid by the previous generation so that they "stand on the shoulders of giants" (in the words of Isaac Newton). New tools and techniques are enabling researchers to use and reuse data to investigate new questions in ways that are completely different from those used in the past.

As noted in Chapters 1 and 2, the ways in which research and scholarship, indeed nearly all work and play, are being carried out are changing significantly. In science and engineering research, for example, immense quantities of data are being produced, accessed, analyzed, integrated, and stored daily. Not only are new ways of generating and managing data being developed and implemented, but different ways of using data are also developing; the large data sets that have already been assembled are being revisited and analyzed anew. The National Science Foundation (2007: 12) notes that "the dynamic integration of data generated through observation and simulation is enabling the development of new scientific methods" and the development of new tools for data mining, analysis, and visualizing of data, such as DNA sequencing data, sky surveys, and "monitoring socioeconomic dynamics over space and time." New kinds of digital objects are resulting from contemporary experimental methods, such as microarrays, combinatorial chemistry, and sensor networks. Some of these new kinds of digital objects are workflows, provenance, ontologies, and lab books. New players are participating in scientific research as a result of the decreasing costs of participating through web-connected computers so that citizen science—research projects in which untrained individuals often participate, for example, in gathering data through observation—is increasingly common. A good example is eBird (ebird.org), developed by the Cornell Lab of Ornithology and National Audubon Society, which uses reports on bird sightings by amateur and professional bird watchers to gather data about the distribution and abundance of birds. "In time," the eBird website promises, "these data will become the foundation for a better understanding of bird distribution across the western hemisphere and beyond."

Such changes in the way we work are not limited to science. The rapid development and use of social networking tools, such as wikis, blogs, Facebook, instant messaging, and Twitter, are influencing activities as diverse as individuals' purchasing decisions and government policy making. Collective intelligence is becoming a reality through increasing participation in online tagging, reviewing, and discussion activities. (These and other ideas in this section are based on Rusbridge [2008a].)

Sharing Data

It is worth revisiting the benefits of sharing data, an essential prerequisite to their use and reuse, as has already been noted in Chapter 1. Data are a resource into which time and money have been put, giving them value, including value that extends beyond the immediate reason for their creation. Sharing data, therefore, makes economic sense. Their availability means that research and scholarship are improved; outcomes based on data can be scrutinized and research methods validated; they can be built on through further research; their duplication can be avoided, together with associated additional costs; and their availability can enhance the reputations of researchers (UK Data Archive, 2009: 4).

It is important to note, though, that there are barriers to data sharing, and these are often determined by the norms in a discipline or domain. An excellent summary of these is available in *Scholarly Information Practices in the Online Environment* (Palmer, Teffeau and Pirmann, 2009: 32–33). The "my data" issue—who has the sole right to use data and for how long—is considered to be the greatest barrier to data sharing (Lyon, 2007: 20). For example, in neuroscience, as reported in the CARMEN Project, researchers may be reluctant to share data because of the cost and difficulty of generating them and have "tended to horde data and trickle out a series of publications, following a kind of subsistence model" (Pryor, 2008: 26). Disciplines and domains differ in the data they generate and how they manage those data; the size and quantity of digital objects, the complexity of these objects, the extent to which these objects are manipulated or processed, and ethical and legal implications of data all result in differences in policies, practices, and incentives (Rusbridge, 2008b: 209).

Research data can be shared in a variety of ways, ranging from the informal to the highly structured. Informal data sharing takes place on a peer-to-peer basis, with a researcher e-mailing data or mailing them on a CD or other information storage media. Data may be shared by making them available through a project website. They may be formally deposited in an institutional repository or in a specialist data center or archive. Because data types and their characteristics vary significantly among disciplines, there is considerable variance in data-sharing methods.

Sharing and reusing data require new ways of thinking about, valuing, and managing data, each of which has its associated challenges. There are, for instance, major challenges to the centuries-old primacy of the scientific article as the primary mechanism for disseminating results and as the basis of the reward system that provides incentives for doing good research. A meeting in 2009 on this topic posed these questions:

- Is the traditional research paper still the optimal format for the dissemination of the outputs of scientific research? If not, what are the alternatives?

- More and more scientific findings are "born digital." The traditional format of the research article is being transformed into a multimedia digital object with linked content, video, audio, data sets, and reader annotation. This raises new possibilities and challenges. How should these newer types of content be peer reviewed? Are researchers really able to make the most of them? Does a link to a data set or image always provide sufficient context to enable informed reuse or validation?

- Outside of the peer-reviewed article, what mechanisms are available for ensuring standards of quality in both contexts?

- What social, legal, economical, and technological challenges remain to enable global access to the outputs of scientific research? (drawn from "Scientific Findings in a Digital World," 2009)

The emphasis on sharing and reusing data is noteworthy and arguably represents one of the new contributions of data curation. There is an increasing realization that data created as a result of research are valuable resources that can be reused in the future. This places new emphasis on ensuring that data are preserved and remain usable over time. How, more specifically, is this done? What needs to be in place to share data so they can be reused?

Building Blocks for Sharing and Reusing Data

The list of requirements is long. It begins with strategies and techniques to ensure the sustainability of data: keeping data in secure storage; maintaining data quality; perhaps normalizing data by converting them to a standard data format; ensuring regular backups are made and tested; migrating data when changing formats demand; and many more. These are noted in earlier chapters. To this list we can add actions more specifically related to data discovery, use, and reuse. They start with making sure that data are able to be located through online catalogs, that rights to use them have been negotiated, and that standards are in place for citing data and indicating their provenance. When data are used, access may need to be controlled, for example, access to confidential or sensitive data, and mechanisms for doing this are required. The availability of data needs to be promoted to users, and the means of disseminating data easily to users has to be put in place (UK Data Archive, 2009: 5).

Open data is one building block that needs to be in place. The term "open data" is used here to mean the free availability of data without intellectual property or other restrictions, a concept that is part of a more encompassing set of "open" philosophies, such as open source for software. The ideal situation, for digital curation purposes, is that not only are the data publicly available but also the services and tools needed to use and reuse those data. We are seeing in science, for example, initiatives such as the Science Commons (sciencecommons.org), which is designed to make research data and materials easier to find and use; the Public Library of Science (www.plos.org); and the proliferation of open-access journals.

Interoperability is another building block. Reuse of data requires that the data can be shared, which in turn requires implementation of common standards. Another example from science: increasingly, workflows (a set of tasks that comprise a specific procedure, especially a repetitive procedure that can be automated) are being shared, as are scripts (a small software program or set of instructions embedded in another program), statistical models, and many other tools and techniques. This allows research to be more easily repeatable, reproducible, and reusable. The myExperiment website (www.myexperiment.org), developed so that digital objects associated with research (especially scientific workflows) can be shared, is an example (Goble and de Roure, 2008).

Trust by users in the data is a third building block. Users require that data be authentic, that their provenance is known, that they are accessible and usable, and that they can be searched for and located (Snow et al., 2008: Section 5.3). (These concepts are noted in other chapters, particularly Chapter 5.)

Standards

Providing access to data depends heavily on agreement about and widespread implementation of standards. First, standards are needed so that the data are discoverable: their existence and location can be identified, for example, through listings in databases or catalogs. Second, standards are required so that the data are in a form that allows people to use them. As noted in Chapter 8, standards lie at the heart of interoperability, which is essential for effective digital curation. An example of a standard recently launched to promote interoperability is the InChI Trust's International Chemical Identifier standard (inchi.info). This allows chemical structures to be represented as machine-readable strings of information, enabling better searchability, handling, and linking of chemical structures on the web.

Standards particularly relevant to Access, Use, and Reuse include:

- standards for preservation repository functionality and information packages, such as the OAIS Reference Model (ISO 1472; see Chapter 3);

- standards for format representation, such as Dublin Core (ISO 15836), the Metadata for Images in XML Schema Z39.87, Open Document Format (ODF) for representing Office-type materials (i.e., documents, spreadsheets, presentations);

- standards that enable interoperability (communication among different systems), such as ISO 23950 Information Retrieval Standard (equivalent to ANSI Z39.50) and the CIMI Z39.50 Application Profile for Cultural Heritage Information; and

- standards for citing data, which vary from discipline to discipline.

Standards for Repository Functionality

The OAIS Reference Model is widely used as a standard to describe repository functionality. One of its functions is the *Access* function. When a user requests a digital object from storage, a Dissemination Information Package (DIP) is prepared, consisting of a copy of the digital object together with relevant metadata in METS files, and software to retrieve and use the digital object as necessary. This DIP is then delivered to the user. If the DIP is to be shared with other archives and/or users, it must be structured according to agreed-on standards that enable interoperability.

Standards for Interoperability

Interoperability is a prerequisite for viable access, use, and reuse of data and digital objects. Standards permit the construction of networks whose users add value to data and digital objects. For example, the use of standards such as Z39.50 protocols enable multiple web-accessible databases to be searched with one command, promoting access by making the discovery of data and digital objects relevant to a user's inquiry more straightforward.

Standards that enable interoperability should ideally be open standards with these characteristics:

- They are developed and maintained by a vendor-neutral body.
- They are publicly available for anyone to implement.
- They have no economic barriers to implementation; for example, they are royalty free.
- There are no technical barriers; for example, they are free of intellectual property restrictions.
- They can be implemented on competing platforms.

If closed or proprietary standards are used, interoperability becomes more difficult to achieve. Users are locked into products based on a standard, and their interests may not coincide with those of the owners of the standard. The community of users cannot develop the standard, and the value of the network used by that community of users is not enhanced and stagnates.

An illustration of how standards are necessary for data use and reuse can be seen in the increasing development of technologies to visualize and analyze data collaboratively. Web 2.0 technologies allow for the combination and visualization of data from many sources (mashups). Examples include Many Eyes (manyeyes.alphaworks.ibm.com/manyeyes), Swivel (www.swivel.com), and tools based on geographic data, such as Google Earth (earth.google.com) and Open Layers (openlayers.org). For these to function properly, adherence to standards both for structuring and processing data is necessary. Technologies such as these give researchers the ability to upload and analyze their own data using web-based tools (Green, Macdonald, and Rice, 2009: 24).

Structuring Data for Access

For data and digital objects to be used, shared, and reused, they need to be discoverable—that is, able to be identified and located. Discoverability is essential to keeping data and digital objects, processing them, making their ownership and allowable uses clear, and making them citable.

One requirement for discoverability is to provide appropriate and sufficient descriptive metadata. This is noted in Chapter 6. Discoverability requires a standardized method of identification that does not change, even if the locations of the data or digital objects change. This standardized method of identification is commonly referred to as a "persistent identifier" (noted in detail in Chapter 10).

Citing Data

Scientists are increasingly publishing their data in databases. For example, there are several hundred curated databases in the field of molecular biology. These databases typically contain source data, metadata, annotations, and relevant data extracted from other databases. Significant effort goes into the construction, development, and maintenance (in other words, the curation) of these databases.

Underlying the e-science and e-scholarship paradigms, with their emphasis on data and on the reuse of data to generate new knowledge, is the requirement to cite data precisely and accurately. Exchange and sharing of data requires that data in curated databases or deposited in repositories can be accurately referred to over time. There is no widely accepted standard for citing data, so it is difficult to identify and refer to data with precision.

Before a standard for citing data can be widely accepted, many issues need to be resolved:

- How do we deal with data set transience? (Many scientific data sets are subject to more or less continual revision as more data are collected—e.g., data covering a wider spatial or temporal domain—or data are revised as quality control is improved.)
- How do we cite something within a database or data set?
- If we want reputable data citation systems, how do we deal with refereeing?
- How do we deal with persistence of the digital objects that we cite? (based on a blog posting by Bryan Lawrence [2005])

Data curation is currently hampered by the lack of standards for citing data in databases. Citation of data should be a standardized and recognized activity. The ideal theoretical situation is described in this way:

> Citation of data will have become mainstream alongside citation of literature, leading to much more data-led research and new types of science. The academic reward system will provide appropriate credit and recognition for data contributions. A much improved understanding of the real requirements of different disciplines will lead to a cultural change in the attitude towards data sharing, licensing and automating access rights, which will lead to fruitful interactions within and between various disciplines and sub-disciplines. In addition, a developed and interoperable infrastructure will be in place, nationally and internationally, which focuses on access and re-use of data. Much larger scale interoperation of data resources will be available, easily discovered and seamlessly used—across data types—across the lifecycle of data—across silos of data—and in the context of the broader scholarly knowledge cycle. Automatic tools for semantic information import and export, autonomic curation (e.g., agents) and provenance capture will be deployed. All types of multimedia will be more easily indexed and searched than today. (Beagrie, 2007: Section 3.5)

Research is continuing into developing standards for citation of data. One project was Citation, Location, and Deposition in Discipline & Institutional Repositories (CLADDIER; claddier.badc.ac.uk), which identified user requirements for citing data. These included the key requirement that the citation refers precisely to a clearly defined unit that cannot be confused with another reference. The citation needs to be readable by people and not just by computers and needs to note, where relevant, the activity or tool that produced the data. It must also include the source of the data (e.g., a repository) if this is not the data producer. Citations to data also need to be recognized as equivalent to citations to academic papers and should facilitate searching for papers that cite data (Green, Macdonald, and Rice, 2009: 28). Another project, the Dataverse Network Project, provides standards and tools and claims that it "increases scholarly recognition and distributed control for authors, journals, archives, teachers, and others who produce or organize data" and "facilitates data access and analysis for researchers and students" (thedata.org). Its data citation standard (thedata.org/citation/standard) does this in part by using persistent identifiers in place of frequently changing URLs so that the location of data can always be known.

Legal Issues

Data access, use, and reuse should be carried out with full recognition of legal requirements. For example, there may be legal restrictions that mean data or digital objects cannot be shared: the owner may not allow reuse of that data or digital object, or intellectual property rights for some material may be so restrictive that access to it is not possible. Legal requirements fall into three categories:

1. Requirements of research funding bodies
2. Requirements specified in legislation about confidentiality and privacy
3. Intellectual property rights and digital rights management

Legislation relating to confidentiality and privacy, such as data protection acts and freedom of information acts, may restrict access, use, and reuse. Such legislation is noted in more detail in the section "Incentives for Digital Curation" in Chapter 1. Access to data so that it can be used, and reused in the future, by people other than their creators is increasingly a requirement of research funding bodies, whose requirements are also described in more detail in the section "Incentives for Digital Curation" in Chapter 1.

The legal constraints on our ability to curate data, and share and reuse them, are complex. A study of the impact of copyright and related laws in Australia, the Netherlands, the United Kingdom, and the United States on digital preservation notes that "there is no question that those laws present significant challenges" (NDIIPP et al., 2008: Section 6.1.1) and even where there are exceptions in the law for digital materials, applying them "is often an uncertain and frustrating exercise" (NDIIPP, 2008: Section 6.1.2).

These constraints and confusions pose many complexities for digital curators. The legal rights that curators may have to consider include the rights of the researchers, who own copyright of data they create, and also, in some cases, the rights of the database in which those data reside. If the data are in a database that is "the result of substantial intellectual investment in obtaining, verifying or presenting the content," the database structure acquires a database right. For data that are the result of collaborative research, the copyright is likely to be held jointly by many researchers or organizations. This is also the case for data derived from or based on other data. Copyright remains with the creator or database when the data enter an archive, so it is essential that full rights be negotiated by the archive (UK Data Archive, 2009: 22).

Against these constraints and confusions one must balance the open data movement's promotion of licenses that allow sharing of data and digital objects, such as the Creative Commons license (creativecommons .org), Science Commons (sciencecommons.org), and Open Data Commons (www.opendatacommons.org).

Confidential data raises specific legal issues for data curators. (Confidential data are those that can be connected to an individual or allow an individual to be identified or data that are provided in confidence.) Ethical guidelines are applied when gathering data from people, who usually have to provide their informed consent to the collection of those data and to the way they are used. This consent also applies to any long-term use of the data, such as their preservation, sharing, and reuse. Without the consent of the people from whom data have been gathered, they may not be able to be shared and reused. Researchers who generate confidential data need therefore to ensure that agreement for sharing data is one of the things that is sought as a component of informed consent from their research subjects. They may also need to anonymize data, that is, remove anything that may identify their research subjects (UK Data Archive, 2009: 16).

Collaboration Processes

Reuse of data and digital objects implies collaboration. Scientific data, for instance, are increasingly located in collaboratively curated databases that may contain source experimental data, annotations, metadata, and data extracted from other curated databases. Annotation of existing data now provides a new form of communication and collaboration among scholars. Knowing the provenance of data—where data have come from—is an important aspect of data quality management.

Annotation

At the general level, annotation refers to adding information to data to elaborate on them. Annotations can be applied to all kinds of digital data—to describe, correct, interpret, extend, or classify those data. Annotation is an essential part of scholarly practice in science and the humanities, enabling knowledge to be organized, shared, built on, and reused.

Annotation is often associated primarily with scientific data and databases, but it is also widely used in other fields of scholarship. In linguistics, annotations describe or analyze data about language in texts to form a linguistic corpus. Source code in computer programs is often annotated by programmers to explain what a particular piece of code does. Web resources can be annotated and the annotations used in some of the many social networking sites and Web 2.0 applications, such as wikis and blogs, which are providing new ways of organizing and retrieving and visualizing data and information. An annotation tool for British History Online (www.british-history.ac.uk) was launched in 2008. Using this tool, users can update, correct, and expand the information on that site, for example, by correcting factual errors or adding links to related information.

Annotation is used for many other purposes besides correcting errors or adding links to related data. Other purposes include information retrieval, where annotations of data are searched using keyword searching techniques. In some disciplines it can also provide a means of collaboration, allowing, for example, data gathering and input from anyone with a Web-enabled computer or other device so that amateur researchers—"citizen scientists"—can readily contribute. *The Birds of North America* (www.bna.birds.cornell.edu/bna) and *BugGuide* (www.bugguide.net/node/view/15740) are examples.

Over time, annotations can develop scholarly value in their own right and may even become more valuable than the data annotated. In the field of bioinformatics, a gene sequence could be annotated with information relating position to intron/extron boundaries, regulatory sequences, repeats, gene names, and protein products. Annotations are usually stored in predefined fields in biological databases, especially gene sequence databases. The quantities can be great; in the Ensembl project (www.ensembl.org/index.html), which produces and maintains automatic annotation on selected eukaryotic genomes, 80 percent of the data are annotations.

Annotation and provenance (noted in the following section) share some of the same issues as citation: for example, there are no widely accepted standards so that scholars and researchers have to learn different tools for different databases, and the annotations cannot be shared readily. The lack of usable annotation tools that are interoperable is noted by many commentators as a negative factor. Gazan (2008) suggests that "annotating digital collection items should be as easy as making marginal comments in a physical book. Forcing users to populate multiple fields or to use pull-down menus for controlled data entry risks the reaction that annotating is more effort than it's worth." Annotation tools are available in some disciplines, for example, GO Annotation Tools ("GO Annotation Tools," accessed 2010) and Annotation Tools ("Annotation Tools," accessed 2010). Research is also taking place into automating the annotation process, for example, in genome sequencing projects.

The Protein Data Bank (www.rcsb.org/pdb) is a curated database containing information about the structures of proteins, nucleic acids, and complex assemblies. The annotation process at the Protein Data Bank aims to "make each entry not only self-consistent but also consistent with the rest of the archive." Annotators do this by assisting authors to "represent their data in the best possible way"; they "routinely review the incoming data and perform many standard inspections." Where inconsistencies in the data are identified, annotators work with authors to correct these problems. Annotation of data in the Protein Data Bank consists of the following (derived from Burkhardt, Schneider, and Ory, 2006):

- Reviewing entry for self-consistency
- Matching given title to structure
- Correcting format errors in data and coordinates
- Checking sequence using BLAST
- Inserting sequence database reference
- Providing protein name and synonyms
- Checking scientific name of the source organism
- Confirming chemical consistency between ligand name and the three-dimensional coordinates
- Adding information describing the biological assembly
- Checking entry visually
- Generating validation reports
- Finding citation references with PubMed

Research into developing better annotation tools is ongoing. The Open Annotation Collaboration (www.openannotation.org) is focusing on making annotations interoperable by developing standards and tools that allow scholars working in different places to share annotations of data and digital objects.

Provenance

Provenance is closely linked to annotation. Curated databases typically contain data from a variety of sources, including other databases, and knowing where those data originated (the provenance of those data) is a major factor in assessing data quality. We also need to know the provenance of annotations, to allow us to assess the relative value of annotations from, say, a recognized expert as opposed to those of a newcomer to the field.

Many data sets result from complex analyses or simulations that require computation. Keeping a complete record of how the computation was performed is essential:

- to ensure repeatability;
- to catalog the result;
- to avoid duplication of effort; and
- to recover the source data from the output data.

Illustrations of the need to know provenance of data come from the Use Cases for Provenance in eScience workshop held in 2009 (wiki.esi.ac.uk/UseCasesForProvenanceWorkshop). Examples from a wide range of industries and research environments demonstrate why provenance information is necessary. In the aerospace industry, unpredicted behavior of products can result in major disasters. When such disasters happen, investigations attempt to establish the causes to prevent the recurrence of this unpredicted behavior. The provenance of design modifications—when they were made and by whom—is essential information for this process. In policy research, government departments in the United Kingdom require that research reports provide evidence to support what they conclude and recommend and also to provide the provenance of the evidence that lead to those conclusions and recommendations. Confidence in geological survey data is significantly reduced without information about provenance of those data and about how those data have been manipulated.

Access Controls and Authentication Procedures

Intrinsic to access, use, and reuse of data, digital objects, and databases are rights issues. Who has the right to access them? Who does not? Providing access to authorized users requires that:

- data, database, or digital object can be unambiguously identified (see the sections "Structuring Data for Access" and "Citing Data" in this chapter); and
- users can be authenticated (this should be standard good practice for computing facilities).

The mechanisms for providing access to research data should provide credit for and protect the rights of those who created or gathered the data and should also protect the interests of those who have intellectual property rights in the data (Research Information Network, 2008: 10).

First, the data or digital objects required need to be located, usually through searching online catalogs. They then need to be requested, possibly through the online catalog, which may initiate the creation of an access copy from the data archive. Next access conditions need to be established, and this can be complicated. There might be restrictions on reuse of the data even though access to them is allowed. There may be several sets of access conditions applying to a single data set, for example, in a data set that contains confidential information together with data with no access restrictions so that regulated access to confidential data is combined with user access to nonconfidential data. Confidential data may be placed under an embargo for a specified period, after which confidentiality is no longer an issue for those data, or they might be accessible only to approved researchers, who need to gain permission from the owner of the data (UK Data Archive, 2009: 21).

Controlling access is managed in a number of ways. One is the application of authentication procedures. These should ideally provide a single sign-on that offers seamless access to the full range of data resources the specified user is entitled to use, based on their status (such as faculty, student, general public, administrative staff). Another is by restricting access based on location (restricted to specific Internet protocol [IP] addresses or to a physical location).

Data can be delivered to authenticated users in a number of ways that range from very open to highly restrictive, depending on the access conditions for the data. Data without access restrictions could be made available online for users to search, browse, and analyze online or to download for analysis on local computers either as complete data sets or as subsets of data sets. It could also be made available on portable information storage media such as CD-R, DVD-R, flash drives, or portable hard drives. For data sets containing both confidential and unrestricted data, the confidential data might be excluded from the access copy made available to the requester. For confidential or otherwise restricted data, access might be available only through a non-networked secure server that is accessed using terminals in an archive's reading room. For highly confidential data, users may need to physically visit a data enclave where conditions are tightly controlled, such as the NORC Data Enclave at the University of Chicago (www.norc.org/DataEnclave).

The range of mechanisms for sharing data is illustrated in the Data Sharing Continuum developed by the DISC-UK DataShare Project (www.disc-uk.org/datashare.html; see Figure 15.1).

Transform

Transform, the eighth and final stage of the DCC Curation Lifecycle, is the process of creating new data from the original data. This happens in two principal ways: through migration and through generating a subset of the original data. Transformation of data can occur at two points in the Curation Lifecycle. One is the *Migrate* Occasional Action, where migration takes place as a planned action, for example, format migration for the purposes of preservation. The other is at the point at which data are reused, which may result in the creation of new data. These new data also have to be curated.

Migration

Migration refers to the process of transferring digital materials from one technology (hardware or software generation) to another or from one format to another. It is further differentiated as version migration, migration to newer or standard file formats, and migration on request. The process of migration changes data. These changes might transform the digital encoding so that it is suitable for preservation or transform the original into a form that can be processed with tools that are effective at the time of access. Repeated migrations, each making small changes,

Figure 15.1. DISC-UK DataShare: Data Sharing Continuum

Description	Level	Stage
Distributed high performance computing; analysis tools applied to data over secure international network; M2M interfaces	Data Grid	
Peer review of datasets; seamless link to publications; role-based layers of access; data overlay journals	Data publishing	Holy grail
Graphs, charts, maps configurable online	Data visualisation	
"Actionable" marked up dataset installed in a data browser tool subsetting capability	Data manipulation online	National Data Centres/Archives
Original format plus XML markup of data or XML database; open standards used appropriate to domain; metadata or setup files may be bundled with dataset for importing elsewhere	Data enhanced for reuse	
Quality assured metadata; guidance available for depositors; suitably anonymised/consent for sharing obtained from subjects; thorough documentation about data creation and methodology included; permanent IDs; formats validated and suitable for distribution; migration-based preservation commitment	Network of distributed repositories: subject and/or institutionally based	**DataShare exemplars aiming here**
Data files with minimal documentation (e.g. readme file describing each data file) downloadable from Internet	Zip and ship / Open access	
Metadata record of dataset on website or in repository; possibly with embargo and contact information to request access	Search and discovery enabled; restricted access	Institutional Repositories
Networked drive, available to research group, version control	Email dissemination by request	
Password protected, networked drive (backup procedures)	Privileged access	Typical status quo
Personal hard drives, un-networked	Simple data storage	

Source: Rice, R. 2007. Data Sharing Continuum. DISC-UK, September 2007, www.disc-uk.org/docs/data_sharing_continuum.pdf. Reproduced by permission of Robin Rice.

may cumulate into major alterations to the data—in other words, the data are transformed and become new data, with characteristics and behavior that differ from the original data. (Chapter 13 provides more information about migration.)

Creating New Data

New data are also produced from existing data by creating a subset of the existing data and transforming this subset to create newly derived results, perhaps for publication. The subset is created by making a selection of data or by querying a data set.

A hypothetical example is curated data used to verify results, as the basis of further experiments, and for cumulative analysis. These curated data, combined with other data from a wide variety of new and existing sources, and perhaps manipulated using software tools, are transformed and become new data, which themselves require curation. They become a new and reliable foundation for new research, science, knowledge, and discovery. A specific example comes from a Digital Curation Centre case study on integrative biology (IB). Users of the IB infrastructure are currently "predominantly data creators, running numerical codes to model physiology." In the future it is likely that "new numerical physiologists will become re-users, accessing the stored results of previous calculations for further analysis" (Donnelly, Boyd, and Spellman, 2008: 10–11).

Conclusion: The Lifecycle Continues

And so the Curation Lifecycle begins again. New data are created as an output of the *Transform* action and are fed into the *Create or Receive* action. But this happens only if data are created, appraised, ingested into an archive that applies preservation actions, and stores those data so that they can be accessed in usable form: in other words, if the data are curated.

The activities required for the curation of data and digital objects do not apply only to the data and digital objects that are managed in a digital archive. Many, perhaps most, of them can be applied with only minor adjustments to fit all contexts in which data or digital objects need to be kept over time and remain usable in the future. Careful reading of the chapters in this book will provide many examples that can either be adopted without change or altered to fit many contexts, including the curation of personal digital objects, the management of electronic records, and the stewardship of digital objects in libraries and archives of all kinds.

The PARSE.Insight Project (2009: 19) concludes from a large survey of digital preservation in research that "sharing and preserving research data seems desirable, but many hurdles prevent it from happening on a large scale . . . critical unsolved problems may be technical, but are also frequently social or organizational in nature." Many parts of the infrastructure, but not all, are in place to allow data to be accessed, used, and

ACCESS, USE, AND REUSE: REVIEW

Key points: *Access, Use, and Reuse* is the process of ensuring that data are accessible to authorized users for use and later reuse.

Key activities:
- Apply standards that ensure appropriate metadata are present
- Ensure that the required legal permissions are available
- Provide tools that allow collaboration in the use and reuse of data
- Apply access controls and authentication procedures

TRANSFORM: REVIEW

Key points: *Transform* is the process of creating new data from the original data.

Key activity:
- Generate a subset of data (by selection or query) to create newly derived results

reused and new data created. Different domains have radically different requirements for data access, use, and reuse, so it is difficult to make generalizations. The differences are illustrated for the United Kingdom in a 2008 survey of researchers' views on data preservation and access (Beagrie, Beagrie, and Rowlands, 2009).

We can say, though, that many of the standards are in place or in development and that the tools that allow data to be shared and reused are available, but new technologies and new ways of working (such as mashups, wikis, and other Web 2.0 tools) are making the situation very fluid. There are many positive signs, such as the policies of the journal *Nature* about availability of data (www.nature.com/authors/editorial _policies/availability.html) and the responsibilities of authors about sharing data (www.nature.com/authors/editorial_policies/authorship .html). The policy on availability of data and materials notes that "An inherent principle of publication is that others should be able to replicate and build upon the authors' published claims," and materials, data, and associated protocols must be made promptly available to readers "without preconditions" by authors who publish in a Nature Publishing Group journal. Any restrictions on availability of data or materials must be disclosed to the editors when the article is submitted. Senior team members on multiauthored submissions to Nature Publishing Group journals must take responsibility for "(1) ensuring that original data upon which the submission is based is preserved and retrievable for reanalysis; (2) approving data presentation as representative of the original data; and (3) foreseeing and minimizing obstacles to the sharing of data, materials, algorithms or reagents described in the work." As Chris Rusbridge (2009) notes, "This sort of policy from respected journals is seriously good for data curation!"

References

"Annotation Tools." Semantic Web Annotation & Authoring. Available: annotation .semanticweb.org/tools (accessed May 6, 2010).

Beagrie, Neil. 2007. *E-infrastructure Strategy for Research: Final Report from the OSI Preservation and Curation Working Group*. Edinburgh: National e-Science Centre. Available: www.nesc.ac.uk/documents/OSI/preservation .pdf (accessed April 26, 2010). Used by permission of OSI Preservation and Curation Working Group (Beagrie 2007).

Beagrie, Neil, Robert Beagrie, and Ian Rowlands. 2009. "Research Data Preservation and Access: The Views of Researchers." *Ariadne* 60 (July). Available: www.ariadne.ac.uk/issue60/beagrie-et-al (accessed April 26, 2010).

Burkhardt, K., B. Schneider, and J. Ory. 2006. "A Biocurator Perspective: Annotation at the Research Collaboratory for Structural Bioinformatics Protein Data Bank." *PLoS Computational Biology* 2, no. 10 e99 (October): 1186–1189. Available: www.ploscompbiol.org/article/info:doi/10.1371/ journal.pcbi.0020099 (accessed April 26, 2010).

Digital Curation Centre. 2008. *The DCC Curation Lifecycle Model*. Edinburgh: Digital Curation Centre. Available: www.dcc.ac.uk/docs/publications/ DCCLifecycle.pdf (accessed April 26, 2010).

Donnelly, Martin, Victoria Boyd, and Jill Spellman. 2008. "Digital Curation Centre Case Studies and Interviews: Integrative Biology." Edinburgh: Digital Curation Centre (April 2008). Available: www.dcc.ac.uk/resources/case-studies/integrative-biology (accessed April 26, 2010).

Gazan, Rich. 2008. "Social Annotations in Digital Library Collections." *D-Lib Magazine* 14, no. 11/12 (November/December). Available: www.dlib.org/dlib/november08/gazan/11gazan.html (accessed April 26, 2010).

"GO Annotation Tools." Gene Ontology Project. Available: www.geneontology.org/GO.tools.annotation.shtml (accessed April 26, 2010).

Goble, Carole, and David De Roure. 2008. "Curating Scientific Web Services and Workflows." *EDUCAUSE Review* 43, no. 5 (September/October): 10–11.

Green, Ann, Stuart Macdonald, and Robin Rice. 2009. *Policy-making for Research Data in Repositories: A Guide.* Version 1.2. Edinburgh: EDINA and University Data Library. Available: www.disc-uk.org/docs/guide.pdf (accessed April 26, 2010).

Lawrence, Bryan. 2005. "Data Citation." Bryan's Blog, comment posted December 22, 2005. Available: home.badc.rl.ac.uk/lawrence/blog/2005/12/22 (accessed April 26, 2010).

Lyon, Liz. 2007. *Dealing with Data: Roles, Rights, Responsibilities and Relationships Consultancy Report.* Bath: UKOLN. Available: www.ukoln.ac.uk/ukoln/staff/e.j.lyon/reports/dealing_with_data_report-final.doc (accessed April 26, 2010).

National Digital Information Infrastructure and Preservation Program (NDIIPP), et al. 2008. *International Study on the Impact of Copyright Law on Digital Preservation: A Joint Report.* Washington, DC: NDIIPP. Available: www.digitalpreservation.gov/library/resources/pubs/docs/digital_preservation_final_report2008.pdf (accessed April 26, 2010).

National Science Foundation. 2007. *Cyberinfrastructure Vision for 21st Century Discovery.* Arlington, VA. Available: www.nsf.gov/pubs/2007/nsf0728 (accessed April 26, 2010).

Palmer, Carole L., Lauren C. Teffeau, and Carrie M. Pirmann. 2009. *Scholarly Information Practices in the Online Environment: Themes from the Literature and Implications for Library Service Development.* Dublin, OH: OCLC. Available: www.oclc.org/programs/publications/reports/2009-02.pdf (accessed April 26, 2010).

PARSE.Insight. 2009. *First Insights into Preservation of Research Output in Europe: Interim Insight Report.* Didcot. Available: www.parse-insight.eu/downloads/PARSE-Insight_D3-5_InterimInsightReport_final.pdf (accessed April 26, 2010).

Pryor, Graham. 2008. *CARMEN: Code, Analysis, Repository & Modelling for E-neuroscience.* Edinburgh: Digital Curation Centre. Available: hdl.handle.net//1842/2611 (accessed April 26, 2010).

Research Information Network. 2008. *Stewardship of Digital Research Data: A Framework of Principles and Guidelines.* London Research Information Network. Available: www.rin.ac.uk/system/files/attachments/Stewardship-data-guidelines.pdf (accessed April 26, 2010).

Rusbridge, Chris. 2008a. "David de Roure on 'The New E-science.'" Digital Curation Blog, comment posted September 15, 2008. Available: digitalcuration.blogspot.com/2008/09/david-de-roure-on-new-e-science.html (accessed April 26, 2010). Used by permission of Chris Rusbridge, Digital Curation Centre.

———. 2008b. "Tomorrow, Tomorrow, and Tomorrow: Poor Players on the Digital Curation Stage." In *Digital Convergence: Libraries of the Future* (pp.

207–217), edited by Rae Earnshaw and John Vince. London: Springer. Used by permission of Chris Rusbridge, Digital Curation Centre.

———. 2009. "New *Nature* Corresponding Author Policy on Data." Digital Curation Blog, comment posted May 4, 2009. Available: digitalcuration .blogspot.com/2009/05/new-nature-corresponding-author-policy.html (accessed April 26, 2010).

"Scientific Findings in a Digital World: What Is the Genuine Article?" Nature Network (June 2009). Available: network.nature.com/groups/genuine_ article/forum/topics (accessed April 26, 2010).

Snow, Kellie, Bart Ballaux, Berthe Christensen-Dalsgaard, Hans Hofman, Jens Hofman Hansen, Perla Innocenti, Michael Poltorak Nielsen, Seamus Ross, and Jørn Thøgersen. 2008. "Considering the User Perspective: Research into Usage and Communication of Digital Information." *D-Lib Magazine* 14, no. 5/6 (May/June). Available: www.dlib.org/dlib/may08/ross/ 05ross.html (accessed April 26, 2010).

UK Data Archive. 2009. *Managing and Sharing Data: A Best Practice Guide for Researchers.* Colchester: UK Data Archive. Available: www.data-archive.ac.uk/news/publications/managingsharing.pdf (accessed April 26, 2010). Used by permission of the UK Data Archive, University of Essex.

Index

About the Author

Ross Harvey is Visiting Professor in the Graduate School of Library and Information Science, Simmons College, Boston, a position he has held since 2008. Before joining Simmons he was the inaugural Professor of Library and Information Studies at Charles Sturt University, Australia, from 1999 to 2008, and he has held positions at other universities in Australia, Singapore, and New Zealand. Visiting Professorships at the University of British Columbia (2008) and the University of Glasgow (2007–2008) allowed him to observe firsthand current digital preservation and digital curation practice and research.

Harvey's research and teaching interests focus on the stewardship of digital materials in libraries and archives, particularly on their preservation, and on the history of the book. He has extensive experience in research projects in Australia and the United Kingdom, most recently with the Humanities Advanced Technology and Information Institute at the University of Glasgow and the Digital Curation Centre. He has published widely in the fields of bibliographic organization, library education, the preservation of library and archival material, and newspaper history.